The Multihull Primer
– for the Past, Present and Future

By the same author

What were they Like to Fly?
Trimarans–an Introduction
The Lure of the Sea
East Coast Passage
Trimaran Development
An Evolution of Singlehanders

The Multihull Primer
– for the Past, Present and Future

D. H. Clarke

Adlard Coles Limited   London

Granada Publishing Limited
First published in Great Britain 1976 by Adlard Coles Limited
Frogmore St Albans Hertfordshire AL2 2NF and 3 Upper James Street
London W1R 4BP

Copyright © 1976 by D. H. Clarke

ISBN 0 229 11560 8
Set in Great Britain by Northumberland Press Ltd, Gateshead
Printed by Fletcher and Son of Norwich
and bound by Richard Clay (The Chaucer Press) Ltd, Bungay, Suffolk

Myself when young did eagerly frequent
Doctor and Saint, and heard great argument
About it and about: but evermore
Came out by the same door as in I went.

Fitzgerald: *Rubáiyát of Omar Khayyám*

For
Eileen Dean
who has been with me for some twelve years,
and must therefore have typed more words
about multihulls than anyone else in the world.

Contents

Acknowledgements

I am indebted to the following for supplying photographs: National Maritime Museum (1), John Walker of Planesail Ltd (2), Phil Patterson of P.T. Yachts Ltd (5), MacLear & Harris Inc. (10, and to Fritz Henle who took 24), Kenneth V. Cooper (11), Norman Cross (12 and 18), John Glennie (15 and 16), N.Z. Northern Advocate (14), Lord St David (17), Ruth Wharram of James Wharram Associates (19, 21 and 22), Roland Prout of G. Prout & Sons Ltd (23), John Cushing of Herbert Woods Ltd (25 and 25a).

The illustrations were obtained from many sources, and I am particularly grateful to the following for their permission to publish copyright material: *The Illustrated London News* (2), Dr E. C. B. Corlett of Burness, Corlett & Partners Ltd (3 and 9), The British Museum (4), Ken Roscoe, editor *Speed and Power* (10), the Amateur Yacht Research Society (11, 12, 13, 14, 16 and 17), Norman Cross (18, 21 and 23), Eugene A. Leeb (19), Paul Winch, by courtesy of *The Naval Architect* (20), John Walker of Planesail Ltd (38).

Information is more difficult to acknowledge individually, as I have so many correspondents all over the world: hundreds of amateurs and professionals have helped me, and I do not know how my books would be written without the kind help from every one of them. Sometimes it is a matter of just one word or one figure which they supply: the name of a boat, or a single dimension; sometimes it is a thick package of photographs, plans and literature, which gives me great joy at the time, but causes me many headaches when it comes to making a selection to illustrate a book. I am extremely grateful to you all, and I can only hope that now I have written about catamarans as well as tris I will be able to welcome a new batch of correspondents into the fold.

So for the writing of this book I can only say to all my 'spies' – whether I have used the material which you so kindly supplied, or not – thank you for making my task easier, and thank you again for your considerable interest.

I must add a separate personal appreciation to the many hard-pressed editors of yachting magazines who have been so helpful to me over many years (sometimes in spite of their own views about multihulls). In particular, in connection with this book, I thank the editors of the following magazines who published my letter requesting general information from designers and builders: *Rudder*, *Yachting* (USA); *Sea Spray* (NZ); *Seacraft* (Australia).

D. H. C.

List of Illustrations

Plates

x

Figures

Introduction

Seven years ago I wrote a book which I called 'Trimarans – an Introduction'. It contained a simple theme, which was adequately summed up by the title. The book did well – so well in fact that I believe it has proved more instrumental in converting monohullists to multihulls than all the hard work I put in during the years 1961–6 when I introduced the first commercially successful trimarans into Britain and Europe, and later into Africa.

Catamarans, on the other hand, I have mostly ignored – until recently, when I decided to write this primer* on the overall subject of multihulls. It is true that my tri builders – Contour Craft Ltd of Great Yarmouth, Norfolk, England – completed a Rudy Choy-designed cat at the end of our business venture, which had lasted for just over five years. She was launched as *Golden Cockerel*, but later became more famous as *Tahiti Bill*, named by her Australian owner Bill Howell; she came fifth in the 1968 Singlehanded Transatlantic Race and would have finished seventh in 1972 if a Russian trawler had not unfortunately been fishing in her path during a thick fog as she neared Nantucket Light Vessel towards the end of the race. With the port bow shattered, Howell had no alternative but to retire. It must have been a terrible disappointment.

Although considerable numbers of cruising multihulls have crossed oceans and circumnavigated over many years, interest in these craft has been more recently aroused by such famous races as the Singlehanded Transatlantic and the Round Britain – both inaugurated by the British Sunday newspaper, *The Observer*. I think it is true to say that the successes of multihulls in the 1972 Transatlantic and the 1974 Round Britain finally settled the argument which had been raging for years, i.e. that multihulls can/cannot work to windward as efficiently as first-class racing monohulls. Even those who have never heard of the 'orange-pip' theory now know that multihulls can compete with monohulls in this respect.

Unfortunately an appreciation of just this one aspect of the monohull-versus-multihull battle – which has been raging for some two decades – does

---

* The dictionary definition of primer, 'A small introductory book on a subject', is barely applicable when cats and tris are involved. I prefer the other meaning: 'One who, or that which, primes, esp. to ignite an explosive compound, etc.'

nothing to help the tyro into the game. Whether he is British, European, American, or lives in the Antipodes or wherever, the monohullist who wants to go multi, or the beginner who is sold on either cats or tris, is confronted by a world-wide array of designs which will one day inevitably surpass the bewildering display of current monohull offerings. So, first he must choose between a cat or a tri; then he must decide on a designer; finally, he must make up his mind whether he wants a ready-built, a one-off or a DIY multihull. The process of sorting out these extremely difficult matters is what this book is all about.

In one aspect we are rather fortunate. I have already admitted I know very little about catamarans, so you and I will be able to investigate this subject to our mutual advantage. On the other hand I have been sailing on and off for forty years – ever since I taught myself to sail a 14-ft clinker-built dinghy in the early thirties; so I have experience on my side. Since that first dinghy I have sailed a variety of sizes of craft up to my engineless, 115-ton Thames spritsail barge, *John & Mary*, in which my wife, son and I lived and cruised for eleven years just after the Second World War; so, in addition to sailing experience, I have both living-aboard and 'living-a-dream' experiences. During our investigation you will find that both of these items are also relevant to our subject.

This book is a primer for beginners in multihulls. As such, it does not contain technical arguments about the disadvantages and advantages of various hull forms. For those who wish to delve into the complexities of designing, I have listed in the appendix, with brief comments on each, all the books about cats and tris that I have been able to discover.

Finally, this book is not concerned with small, open multihull day-boats or racing dinghies, apart from their historical significance in the overall development pattern. I have never gone along with the suggestion that in order to gain experience for bigger craft one should first sail small open boats. A dinghy cat or tri (and I have sailed both) is different in virtually every aspect from a multihull large enough to contain a cabin to sleep two or more, just as my 14-ft dinghy differed enormously from my second yacht, which was a 12-ton gaff cutter. If you want to learn to handle a cabin multihull, then my advice is to start off as you mean to go on. You will inevitably be advised otherwise by other experts, which in the end means that you will have to make up your own mind, but then sailing has always been a highly controversial subject as you will soon find out if you are a stranger to this sport. So whatever you decide after reading this book, you can be quite sure that whether you select a tri, a cat, or go back to monohulls, there will be plenty of people to tell you why you have made the wrong choice!

1   The Chicken, or the Egg?

Knowledge of the historical facts about multihulls is of much greater importance for the newcomer into this branch of yachting than information about the development of monohulls was to his predecessors. We tend to think of catamarans and trimarans as sophisticated improvements by western civilisation of flimsy, native-conceived craft. This misconception arises from the belief that our culture must inevitably be superior to whatever occurred before us; yet the truth is that at least two thousand years before Columbus discovered America, men were already beginning to sail fast and to navigate accurately across the great ocean which we now call the Pacific. Only recently have we begun to concede that the ancient Polynesians must have been first-class boat-builders, seamen and navigators.

The main difficulty has been that old traditions die hard, and consequently our nineteenth- and early twentieth-century historians were unable to visualise the possibility that a race of people who had not invented writing could be anything else but backward. It was even suggested until quite recently that single- and double-outriggers were just simple, natural developments to hold upright the original hollowed log invented by primitive man, and that the Pacific was populated by drift and other types of accidental voyaging.

Nothing could be further from the truth!

The current theory of a possible connection between Phoenician boat-builders and white-skinned fugitives from the Tigris and Euphrates estuaries, who later mingled with the proto-Polynesians, is of interest only because it is said that the Phoenicians built their boats bottom-up from adzed-hollowed logs with risen-on planking, a method of construction which the Polynesians used. Whether or not the premise is true, it certainly reveals that the proto-Polynesians were well past the hollowed-log stage at this time.

We are told that the word catamaran derives from the Tamil, *kattumaram: kattu*, to tie or bind; *maram*, tree or trunk. In Malaya this originally meant a raft, generally of three logs (the centre one being the longest and curved up at the bow), propelled by paddles. It should not be thought that this word-root was exclusive to Indonesia. A surprising fact is that the Chinese sampan has virtually an identical origin and the word 'sampan' derives from *san*, meaning three, and *pan*, meaning planks. The oldest Chinese writing yet discovered, from the Shang Dynasty (1766–1122 BC), reveals that boats similar to the present-day sampan were in use for river trading, that they were sculled with an oar over the stern, and that the seams were caulked – all indicating that boat-building and usage had progressed well beyond the three-log stage some 3500 years ago. (Large ocean-going junks did not materialise until the end of the Liu Sung period, AD 420–479; they were five-masted, generally about 150 ft × 32 ft, carrying up to 180 tons of cargo. They soon conquered the Indian Ocean, sailing as far afield as Persia and the Red Sea.) In a paper entitled 'Twin Hull Ships'* P. Vajravelu, BE, MSc, an associate member of the Royal Institute of Naval Architects, added this interesting footnote:

> I would like to say a few words about our Indian history of the tenth–eleventh centuries, or even earlier. In those times, Raja Raja Chola and his son Rajendra Chola were the prominent kings in power over a major part of Southern India. They extended their reign overseas in the south and in the east. They were using 'catumarams' for their merchant and war fleets, in order to achieve stability and high speeds against the strong winds at sea. This name means, in the regional language Tamil, wooden beams which connect two big boats and was used to denote the complete arrangement.

Since the raft and the sampan came into existence long before these Indian 'catumarams', it would seem reasonable to assume that our present usage – meaning a twin-hulled vessel – originated approximately one thousand years ago, although the meaning then was centred on the beams which connected the hulls, and not, as we now assume, on the two hulls. I mention all this because I still cannot find out who first applied the word catamaran to the modern twin-hulled yacht – and it will be seen that the usage is not entirely correct, since three hulls were implied by the original derivation rather than two. However, the English language contains many such anomalies and I suppose we should be grateful that trimarans are not now called sampans!

Fortunately, it has been established that Russian-born, American-naturalised Victor Tchetchet was responsible for coining the word trimaran when he built his 24-ft, double-outrigger open day-boat in 1945. His first attempt with a multihull had been an 18-footer, specially assembled for the 1908 Imperial Yacht Club Regatta held at Kiev; he won the race; but inevitably lost – for he was told that his boat was not a boat; disqualification was not an unusual experience for multihull owners in the early days.

Although modern scientists have now proved, at least to their own satisfaction, that the Pacific was populated by white, or Caucasian, tribes from south-east Asia who had moved eastwards through Indonesia, Melanesia and Micronesia, such inspired newcomers as Thor Heyerdahl managed to introduce doubt by demonstrating that Polynesians could have migrated from

---

* Corlett, E. C. B. (1969) 'Twin Hull Ships', in *Quarterly Transactions of RINA*, **III**, 4.

the east (South America) by drifting on rafts. If the theory is doubtful, the Kon-Tiki expedition was certainly successful in one respect – it provided material for an overnight best-selling book. The French explorer, Eric de Bisschop, who in 1937–8 sailed his Polynesian double-canoe (catamaran), *Kaimiloa* (1) from Hawaii to Cannes in 264 days, countered this premise by proving that the Polynesians were quite capable of sailing rafts to windward. He demonstrated his belief in 1956–7 by navigating his raft *Tahiti-Nui* from Tahiti to near the Alexander Selkirk/Robinson Crusoe island of Juan Fernandez, sailing more than 5000 miles, much of the time against adverse currents and winds, in 6½ months.

From such theories and counter-theories several hard facts have emerged which should affect the thinking of modern multihull designers and yachtsmen.

Firstly, the large sailing double-canoes which the Polynesians used for long transoceanic voyaging were virtually extinct by the time Europeans sailed into the Pacific, a few years after Vasco Nunez de Balboa looked out on the South Seas from a peak in Darien on 26 September 1513. The earliest explorers, starting with Ferdinand Magellan, whose tiny 85-ton *Vittoria* completed the first successful circumnavigation in 1519–22, were too engrossed in survival to pay much attention to native-wrought miracles of boatbuilding, and it was not until much later that science came to the Pacific and began to record what remained after the initial rape.

They discovered multihulls of every shape and size. Small paddling outrigger canoes, 10–20 ft (LOA), were the most numerous, together with the slightly larger sailing version, generally about 20–30 ft (LOA). Larger still

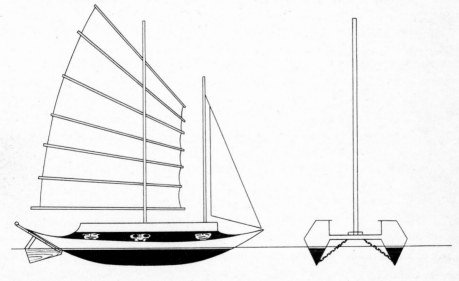

1 *Kaimiloa* (1937)

3

were the 30–50 ft inter-island, trading and passenger-carrying sailing out-riggers whose curves were pure delight to many an artist's eye. For heavy-duty passenger and cargo work within the safety of the reef, 20–40 ft (LOA) double-canoes were ideal, powered by paddles, by single or double Bermudan-type sails or by single or double, boomed lateen sails. The enormous – often over 100-ft (LOA) – war double-canoes of Tahiti and Hawaii were always paddled, but the giant Tongan double-canoes, which were the largest of all Polynesian craft and could carry as many as two hundred persons, were sailing vessels. So the idea behind the modern cruising catamaran comes from the *toniaki* and similar types of ocean-going double-canoes, more than from the lagoon-trading *tahifa* or the large inter-island sailing outriggers, although our present designs are actually based more upon the latter.

All of these craft were either twin-hulled or had a single hull fitted with an outrigger.

The third type, the double-rigger, was, and still is, peculiar to Indonesia. Nobody knows why, and we can only conjecture. Accepting the current scientific theory that the Pacific was populated via Indonesia, and reviewing the problem entirely from the point of view of a boat-builder and a seaman, I would guess that the sailing double-outrigger evolved before the single-outrigger, and that the double-canoe conception was developed last.

Look at it this way. Small, hollowed-log canoes with single outriggers were obviously the first development towards multihulls, but they were intended almost entirely for propulsion by paddles rather than sailing. The outrigger, or *ama*, to give it its correct name, was therefore a float. However, when a mast and sail were added, the problem became whether to use the *ama* as a float (i.e. sailing with it always on the leeward side), or as a counter-balance platform (i.e. with the *ama* always to windward). As a float, it could become a hazard in squalls or rough seas, since it could easily be driven under and thus capsize the canoe; as a counter-balance platform (the method most often used) constant attention to wind-shift, wind strength, etc. was essential by every person aboard. So the single-*ama* was not really suitable for ocean voyaging, whatever the overall length of the main hull. That the larger versions were used for inter-island trading throughout many centuries reveals (to my way of thinking) that they were much easier to build; this advantage, plus their undoubted speed, outweighed the potential fault in the design.

Out in the steady trade winds of the Pacific the single-*ama* performed beautifully whilst trading between islands, but in the very beginning, amongst the tightly-packed archipelago of Indonesia with its variable winds and rapidly changing weather conditions, such a vessel would have been at a considerable disadvantage. In these waters a double-*ama* would have been ideal.

The trimaran configuration obviously was never designed to be paddled – it could only be sailed. Here then, in Indonesia, the double-*ama* was evolved,

4

and here it still sails to this day, because it is fast and easily handled on both tacks. There are no records of the size of these early vessels, but it should be remembered that giant trees were plentiful in this area. Later, the single-hull war canoes of the Maoris were hollowed from a single trunk over 100 ft long because the forests of New Zealand, like those of Indonesia, grew such monsters. However, it is extremely doubtful whether double-outriggers were ever built as big as the double-canoes, or were used for transoceanic sailing.

It is said that around 2000 BC the proto-Polynesians began to creep eastwards. Some however went to the west – across the Indian ocean as far as Madagascar; they retained the double-outrigger but otherwise they are of no particular interest to us. Over the centuries the bulk went through Melanesia (which was already populated by the Papuans), through Micronesia, and into Fiji, Samoa and Tonga. There they settled for a time, but something – adventure? conquest? escape? – drove them onwards into the vastness of the Pacific. These were the voyages, say the scientists, which were made in the huge sailing double-canoes. Radiocarbon dating indicates that they were in the Marquesas in 124 BC and Easter Island in AD 536 – nearly 500 years before the Vikings discovered America by taking comparatively short hops from Norway to Iceland to Greenland to Newfoundland to America.

Of course, the de Bisschop theory – that many of these voyages were made in steerable bamboo rafts, capable of sailing to windward – remains. Since he physically proved that this was possible, and because his discovery affects our inquiry, we must take note of what he learned.

It should not be thought that this Frenchman imitated the *Kon-Tiki* voyage in the hope of producing another best-selling book. He had already sailed in square-riggers, been commissioned in the French naval reserve, captained his own trading schooner, sailed Chinese junks into the Pacific from Ningpo and Amoy, voyaged from Hawaii to Cannes in the double-canoe *Kaimiloa*, (which he had designed and built virtually unaided), and experimented with a double-outrigger, *Kaimiloa Akea*, in the Mediterranean. By sailing his catamaran more than halfway round the world (his sole companion was a temperamental Breton, Joseph Tatibouet, who seemingly only rarely gave physical assistance to his skipper) de Bisschop proved to his satisfaction that use of the Polynesian sailing double-canoe for long voyages of exploration was unlikely. His argument is simple: a steerable bamboo raft could carry a greater load with a much better margin of safety and seaworthiness than the huge double-canoes which were supposed to have been used. These, argued de Bisschop, were employed only for major transoceanic voyages to known landfalls, when speed was of prime importance.

His argument is not unreasonable. When the early Polynesians migrated eastwards, they left behind them the wet forests and the giant trees of Indonesia. Large logs became unobtainable, so the ingenious boat-builders

5

actually sewed logs together, and fastened any additional planking with fibres obtained from the coconut palm. The exact process does not concern us here, but for those who are interested, I recommend *Polynesian Seafaring**. It will not come as a surprise to learn that vessels with fastenings such as these inevitably leaked – so much, in fact, that the bailer, or *tata*, was always a beautifully carved masterpiece of religious and magical importance. Without the bailer, the vessel became a wallowing raft – though it should be stressed that even in this state it would not sink, and could still be sailed. It was not necessary for the Polynesians to invent lifeboats and life rafts as we had to; when our wooden ships leaked they frequently foundered, whereas the Pacific multihulls were always capable of supporting their crews. Only in recent years have we returned to the greater safety of unballasted craft and their consequent unsinkability.

Compared with the toil involved in selecting and felling the best trees, dragging them to the canoe shed (generally the largest and most imposing building in the village; a size quoted in the eighteenth century as 150 ft × 30 ft, and 24 ft to the eaves, was said to be 'middling') and shaping and assembling the hulls, building a raft of large bamboo logs would be a simple matter. Long voyages of exploration are notoriously costly in both manpower and vessels, as the Europeans discovered when they began to investigate the world of water. It seems logical that if a raft could be made to work to windward, then it would serve admirably for initial explorations of unknown seas.

According to de Bisschop, two Spanish officers first described the Polynesian *guara*, or multiple dagger-boards as we call them now, in 1736. The *Kon-Tiki* was fitted with this device, but for some reason the boards were fixed; *Tahiti-Nui* had five such boards along the fore-and-aft centreline, but these could be raised and lowered as required. The difference, as every yachtsman should know, meant that *Kon-Tiki* had to be controlled with a steering oar, whereas de Bisschop's raft was at all times self-steering, since adjustments could be made to the depths of the five dagger-boards to balance the forces of wind and sea against the hull, and thus achieve a straight course in the direction required. It seems evident that this invention was being used centuries, if not millennia, ago on rafts of various types around most of the coasts of the north-western and south-eastern Pacific; different forms can still be seen in such antipodean areas as Formosa and Ecuador, Vietnam and Peru. The early Chinese junks (and sailing rafts – for the invention was not exclusive to the Polynesians) used both dagger-boards and rudder.

Well, de Bisschop and his crew sailed *Tahiti-Nui* towards South America and proved that it could be done. Possibly, too, he showed that sailing double-canoes did not achieve quite as much as we had been led to believe, for they

* Dodd, Edward (1972) *Polynesian Seafaring*, Dodd, Mead Inc. USA and Nautical Publishing Ltd, UK.

must have needed a great deal of care and attention, both in maintenance and handling, and therefore they may have been reserved only for important and known sailing routes.

That is merely speculation (we shall probably never know the whole truth about the colonisation of the Pacific), but from the facts stated some interesting information emerges. Neither the modern cat nor the tri is derived from transoceanic sailing double-canoes or double-outriggers. Eric de Bisschop made the point quite clearly in his book *Tahiti-Nui* (Collins, 1958):

> Although my long voyages in *Kaimiloa* in the Pacific, Indian and Atlantic Oceans proved that the Polynesian double-canoe was perfectly capable of sailing anywhere in the open sea [*he refers to the inter-island vessels, not the transoceanic giants*], it would be wrong to draw hasty conclusions... For between my *Kaimiloa* and the ancient Polynesian canoes lies a world of difference. They have in common only the principle of joining twin hulls together to make a fast and stable sailing craft, but that is all.

In other words, modern multihulls are at best, very broadly based on inter-island native craft, so this translation into ocean- and world-cruising yachts is really a very recent invention.

I have made this point because I believed what I was told when I decided to begin what I knew would be a long battle: converting yachtsmen to multihulls – in my particular case, trimarans. At the back of my mind was the idea of resurrecting proven ocean-going vessels, for if the Polynesians could cross the Pacific in such flimsy craft obviously we could do even better with modern materials and equipment. Needless to say, my faith was entirely misplaced; transoceanic sailing double-canoes had rotted away on coral beaches long before the Europeans arrived, and if large transoceanic sailing double-outriggers ever existed they had certainly disappeared before we could catalogue them. Double-outriggers (or trimarans) had probably never been used at all for transoceanic voyages.

So much for popular misconceptions.

But the *guaras* are a different matter. I do not know who first conceived the idea of eliminating the clumsy leeboards which had been used by Europeans for centuries, and replacing them with a central hinged plate, but it could not have been so very long ago – probably no more than 150 years or so. The mechanically-obvious principle of multiple drop-boards to balance the forces which beset a sailing vessel were seldom used, and British RNLI sailing lifeboats, nearly all of which have now disappeared, were among the very rare examples to use multiple hinged-plates. Yet, surprisingly, the first trimaran to cross the Atlantic used movable dagger-boards in order to maintain some control over what was otherwise an awkward vessel. I have often wondered about the source of the inventor's information.

7

Nonpareil (2) could perhaps be more accurately described as a raft than a trimaran. Her three hulls were cylinders of natural rubber, each 25 ft long with a 30-in diameter. On these was built a wooden platform, 20 ft × 11 ft 6 in, which stepped two masts, schooner-rigged. A tent, of all things, was erected between the masts to accommodate the crew of three: John Mikes, American, the inventor, builder and skipper, with George Miller and Jerry Mallene, Prussians, as crew. They sailed from New York on 4 June and arrived at Southampton on 25 July, 1868: 51 days for the voyage. Not a bad time really, for many larger ships often took much longer, and a month was reckoned a fairly average crossing time.

As so often happens when yachtsmen are confronted with strange craft, scorn and derision was all that Mikes achieved in Britain. Although most yacht historians acknowledge that *Nonpareil* was hove-to on seven occasions, the general consensus is that this voyage only proved that it is possible to drift from west to east across the Atlantic on anything – a haystack would do equally as well. But if this were so, why bother to mention the ability of the raft/trimaran to heave-to? John MacGregor, of Rob Roy canoe fame, made some caustic remarks about American visitors wishing to see Europe at a cheap rate, but neglected to mention such elementary construction details as how the platform was attached to the rubber hulls. Nothing at all was

2   The experimental life-saving trimaran-raft *Nonpareil* which crossed the
   Atlantic from New York to Southampton in 51 days in 1867

said about the movable dagger-boards fore and aft, slotted in the 2-ft gaps between the cylinders, which enabled this vessel to heave-to on seven occasions, to self-steer for most of the time, and to make the crossing in an unspectacular but average time for small boats of that period. (Some west to east crossings between 1868–99 recorded 64, 51, 49, 46, 45, 69, 55 and 60 days in craft ranging in length from 14 ft 6 in to 30 ft.) I cannot entirely subscribe to *Nonpareil* being a trimaran, but certainly she was not just a raft. So, since she had three hulls, and was obviously controllable, this was the first transatlantic crossing by a three-hulled sailing vessel.

Actually, history tells us that the catamaran configuration preceded the trimaran in Europe by more than 200 years. On 20 December 1662, Sir William Petty launched *Invention II*, a 30-ton clinker-built vessel which he had designed; it had two bottoms, or keels, carried thirty men and ten guns, and had exceptionally good accommodation. She was also described as being very seaworthy and extremely fast, although I find it hard to believe that such a new invention, carrying a large crew and 5 tons of cannon, could really merit such a description. However, she was reported to have won a wager of £50 by beating the pacquett-boat *Ossary* ('... the best ship or vessel the King hath there', wrote diarist Samuel Pepys) from Holyhead to Dublin by the surprisingly large margin of 15 hours, although nothing is said of the wind speed and direction at the time. Probably a single reach across the Irish Sea in a stiff breeze aided her on this occasion, because it must be pointed out that the working ships of this period could hardly be regarded as fast competitors – even to a slow catamaran, which evidence indicates was square-rigged!

It seems unlikely that Sir William Petty had copied the idea from Polynesian sailing double-canoes. It is true that Francis Drake and Thomas Cavendish had circumnavigated during the latter half of the previous century (1577–80 and 1586–88 respectively), and brought back tales of their many strange adventures, but it was not until the middle of the eighteenth century that George Anson returned from his famous circumnavigation with an actual example of a Micronesian proa (5).

It should also be remembered that yachting did not come to Britain until 1660, when the Burgomaster of Amsterdam presented King Charles II with the 52-ft × 19-ft × 10-ft *Mary* – generally accepted as the first-ever British yacht. By the summer of 1661, two British-built yachts, *Anne* and *Catherine*, were launched, and the Dutch added to this fleet by sending another *jaght*, *Bezan*, which the famous diarist Samuel Pepys soon claimed for himself. It is not so very surprising that on 1 October of that same year the King wagered £100 that his *Mary* was faster than his brother's *Anne*; and so in less than a year the British had invented yacht racing – a sport which apparently had not occurred to the Dutch originators of the *jaght-schip*. This seems to be a likely reason for the King's sudden interest in speed.

9

On 22 September 1662, Petty had launched in Dublin a little 1·64-ton, 30-ft × 10-ft × 10-in spritsail-rigged cat, *Simon & Jude* (3, 4), which King Charles II misleading renamed *The Experiment*, and is still sometimes called *Invention I*. This was undoubtedly his best creation. She was thoroughly tested in a race on 12 January 1663, organised by no less an authority than the recently formed (1646) Royal Society. She was fitted with shallow straight keels, extending five inches below her two hulls, which were cylindrical; so perhaps she was the basis of the idea for *Nonpareil* some 206 years later. Although she easily beat the three small boats which opposed her, it is significant that she managed to do so in spite of a bad moment when she missed stays, got into irons and drifted ashore, breaking one of her rudders. It is interesting to speculate what might have been the result to British, and ultimately to international yachting, if Sir William Petty had known about *guaras*, although it must be admitted that he had proposed the design of a hinged drop-plate in 1661. He built two more catamarans: one, *Experiment*, which carried a total crew of 50, was lost in a gale in the Bay of Biscay in 1665; the other, *St Michael the Archangel*, built in 1684, was a total failure. His contribution is significant not only because he designed the world's first yacht multihull, but because she actually proved to be fast (recording up to 20 mph); however, like most out-of-phase inventors, his conception was only partially sound, and he seemed to lack the determination to invent a completely new rig and to develop his undoubtedly original ideas for getting a sailing vessel to windward with a minimum of leeway. Twin hulls alone, no matter how fast they sailed, were not enough to sway opinion in favour of his design.

If Petty had copied the idea from descriptions of multihulls brought back from the South Seas by various explorers, raiders and traders, then surely he would either have taken note of how the Polynesians rigged their craft and of their methods for achieving windward performance, or, when he was only partially successful with western-type rigging of that period, would have surely turned to the Polynesian inventions for inspiration. That he made no attempt to do so seems to indicate that the catamaran was entirely his own invention – or else that he refused to copy from people who were at that time regarded as ignorant savages.

In fact, those savages were nothing like as ignorant as the Europeans when it came to boat design and aerodynamic efficiency – and navigation too, although I cannot argue this point here. Sometimes I wonder whether the cranky modern theory about spacemen visiting this planet and being stranded here is not indeed a fact! How else did the men of the Pacific evolve such ideas as asymmetrical hulls, planeing surfaces, controllable-camber sails and, above all, the delicate balance of a vessel which could very nearly fly (5)? Against such craft, Petty's 'inventions' and 'experiments' were like First World War tanks.

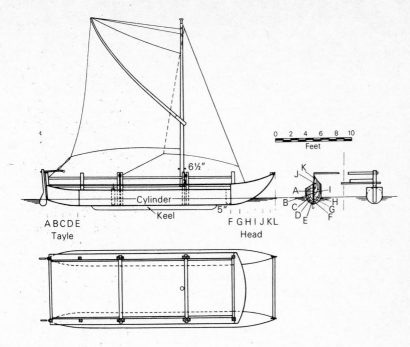

6½"

Cylinder

Keel

5"

A B C D E
Tayle

F G H I J K L
Head

0 2 4 6 8 10
Feet

K
J
A I
B H
C G
D F
E

3 *Simon & Jude* – plans

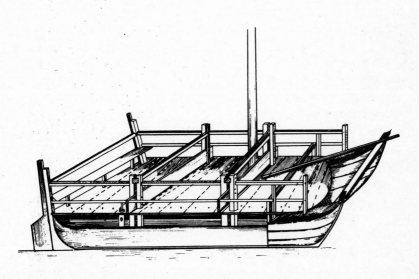

4 *Simon & Jude* (1662)

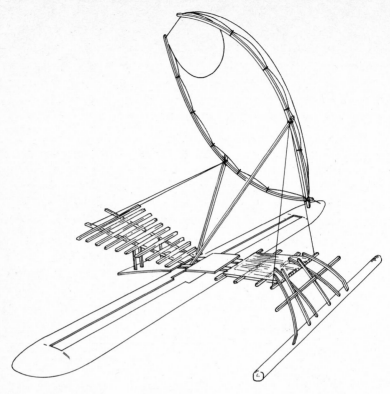

5　A proa, 'a vessel which could very nearly fly'

Why, for example, do we continue to retain the rudder in its present form? To this day the outriggers still use a free-floating steering oar (if they are not powered by the ubiquitous outboard). It is not just another paddle, but is specially designed for this purpose; above all it is efficient at all times, in a flat calm or a gale. Unlike the early steering oar of western civilisation, it was never fixed; consequently it could be moved from one end of the vessel to the other when tacking, or be positioned anywhere along the lee side as a balance to avoid unnecessary steering; in this case the steering oar became a *guara*. Such versatility can scarcely be considered as a crude accidental discovery!

As to rigging and sails (6), much could and has been written on the subject. High-aspect ratio, Bermudan-like sails, sloop- or schooner-rigged without headsails, with a battened or perhaps more correctly, boomed leech, were standard for lagoon handling; for inter-island sailing, the enormous flexible-boomed lateen mainsail was the most popular rig. Its similarity in shape to the loose-footed lateen sails of the Arab felucca tends to support the theory that Polynesians originated from the Eastern Mediterranean, but more likely it is a coincidence. The Tonga version looks rather like a Viking squaresail

12

but I don't really believe that the Norsemen copied it from them; neither do I think the Bermudan leg-o'mutton design was conceived from the boomed-leech, high-aspect-ratio, windward-performing rig of the Society Islands. To be frank, the Polynesian conceptions in both cases must have been easily the superior, and their greater control over the giant lateen sail (through adding a flexible boom) undoubtedly was an improvement on the Mediterranean/Nile versions. But how did they rig their giant, ocean-going double-canoes? Alas, nobody knows for sure.

With the underwater hull lines, multihull builders of 2000 or more years ago prescribed modern yacht architecture on virtually every point: vee, single-chine, elliptical, flared-chine, round bilge, flat-oval bilge, and vee curved into a pronounced tumble-home or heart-shaped (7), are among the many different shapes which they evolved. However, although asymmetrical or one-sided curved main hulls in single outriggers were commonplace long before they became a drawing-board delight, the reversed hulls of some of their sailing double-canoe designs were more of an unfortunate necessity, promoted

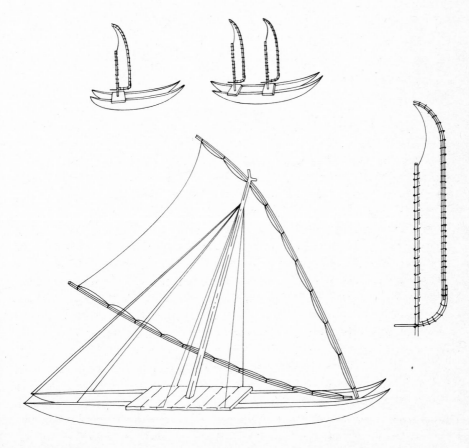

6 Polynesian sails

by their cumbersome method of tacking. Instead of going about through the eye of the wind as we do, they reversed direction across the wind (8) by lowering and then rehoisting the mainsail so that the tack of the sail, and the helmsman, changed ends. This method was always used, particularly in single-outriggers which could only sail on one tack (with the single *ama* either to leeward or to windward, depending on the preference in specific areas), and undoubtedly it was the weakest link in the overall design; I shudder to think of the panic in the event of a surprise squall catching aback a large outrigger or a double-canoe – but I suppose that in those mostly-steady and favourable breezes this did not happen very often. In the event, only those areas which were subject to variable winds, or were more mountainous than the sea-level coral islands, produced reversed-direction hulls in double-canoes.

In spite of claims by multihull enthusiasts that many successful two-hulled and three-hulled vessels were designed between Sir William Petty's *Simon & Jude* and the end of the Second World War, little of any particular significance actually occurred during these 285 years.

In New York, in 1814, a steam-driven, two-hull warship was launched, the main idea being that a paddlewheel between the hulls would not be vulnerable to crippling by gunfire. It seems that this power-in-the-middle theory, with or without military considerations, seized the imagination of a number of designers on both sides of the Atlantic. In Scotland, in 1821, the 92 ft × 34 ft 6 in *Union* operated successfully as a Tay ferry, and in Britain the 157 ft × 26 ft 6 in *Gemini* was built for the Great Exhibition of 1851, although she failed to complete her trials through lack of power; a similar fate awaited *Alliance*, launched in 1862. *Castalia* (9) (Plate 1), 290 ft × 60 ft × 7 ft, had some success in 1875 as a cross-channel steamer, for her wide decks were popular; however her two steam-engines, which gave an indicated horsepower of 1516 when driving the tandem paddle-wheels between the hulls, were supposed to give her a commercial speed of 14 knots, but only produced a maximum of 11. She was withdrawn within a year. Her owners tried a second time, but ran out of money before the vessel was completed; her Newcastle builders finished the job and sold her to the London, Chatham and Dover Railway Company, who named her *Calais Douvres*. In spite of the poor performance of *Castalia*, undoubtedly caused by the considerable turbulence and resulting loss of power through having paddle-wheels in the tunnel between the hulls, this new catamaran followed the same pattern, although her engines were increased to a total of 4300 hp. She achieved slightly better than 14 knots, but at the cost of high fuel bills, and needlessly expensive maintenance; also the excessive heat from her engine-rooms drove the passengers on deck, where they were promptly seasick. Nevertheless, *Calais Douvres* survived eleven years until 1887 and can probably claim to have been at least a partial success. An even more freakish version of

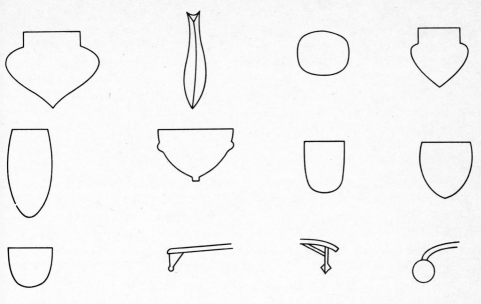

7   Hull shapes

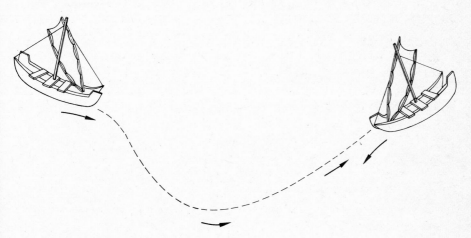

8   Method of tacking across the wind

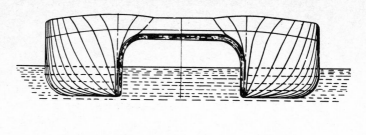

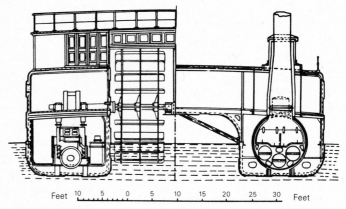

Feet   10   5   0   5   10   15   20   25   30   Feet

Scale for midship section

9   Cross-sections of *Castalia* (1875)

power-in-the-tunnel was the American catamaran tug *Rosse*, which operated on the Hudson from 1882: she had an endless belt of buckets between the hulls, which made her look more like a dredger than a tug; her manoeuvrability was said to be very poor and no doubt she was as unsuccessful as most of the other vessels mentioned.

The Victorians ran through a gamut of multihull ideas, which included another infamous cross-Channel passenger ship, the 302-ft × 183-ft giant *Pas-de-Calais*, which had such an appalling motion in a seaway that a gimballed saloon was fitted in an attempt to save the passengers from violent seasickness; needless to say, the modification did not succeed. Other multihull freaks included Robert Fryer's steam-driven tri-ball *Alice* (10), of 1882, which looked (and must have behaved) exactly like a giant steamroller on three enormous balls. Then, in 1896, came an even greater freak: *Bazin*, designed by Frenchman Ernest Bazin, which was neither cat nor tri because it consisted of a steel girder platform, 126 ft × 40 ft, supported on three pairs of 33-ft diameter wheels each of which were driven by a 50-hp engine; in addition, a 550-hp engine provided a sort of long-shaft outboard power. Designed to achieve 30 knots, in fact it failed to make even half that speed, so like most of the others I have mentioned it was a failure. But I must say I have a certain sympathy for the inventors of that period; they were prepared

16

to build anything – but anything – and test it! And there were many more than I have named.

On the yachting side, Patrick Miller of Glasgow produced some multihull designs as long ago as 1786, but only *Scotland*, a five-masted catamaran is known to have been constructed. The Stevens Brothers of Hoboken, generally recognised as the builders of the first American yacht (the 56-ft two-masted, canoe-like pirogue *Trouble*, launched in 1816), probably had their interest in multihulls aroused by the trials of the centre-paddlewheel warship which, as previously mentioned, had been launched in New York two years earlier in 1814, on the opposite bank of the river to their yard. This would seem the only explanation why, in 1820, they built a catamaran *Double Trouble*, which, since they very soon discovered that *Trouble* was the faster of the two, registered its sole victory as an historic first.

The person generally credited with building the first successful modern catamaran is the American yacht designer, Nathaniel Herreshoff. Much has been made of his multihulls, particularly his 25-ft *Amaryllis* which is reputed to have beaten a whole fleet of monohulls at the Centennial Regatta in 1876 off the Battery in New York harbour. This was the same year that Alfred Johnson became the first man to sail singlehanded across the Atlantic; it took

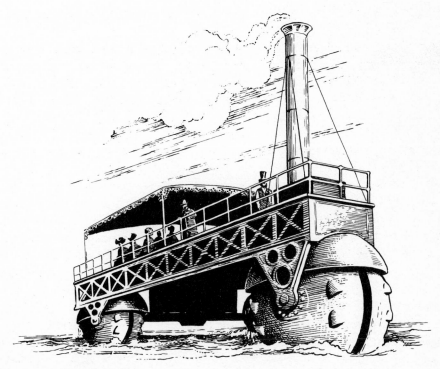

10   Fryer's Tri-ball (1882)

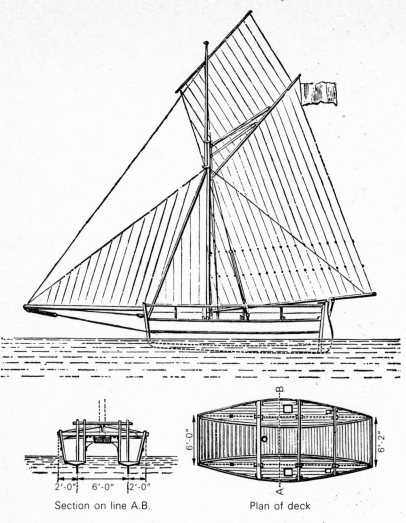

Section on line A.B.   Plan of deck

2'-0" 6'-0" 2'-0"   6'-0"   6'-2"

11 This 21-ft asymmetrical catamaran, built by John MacKenzie of Belfast
in 1868, clearly shows the weight and rig limitations imposed by the
accepted trend of the period

him 55 sailing days to reach Liverpool from Gloucester, Mass. in his tiny
20-ft gaff cutter-rigged dory, *Centennial* – eight years after the successful
crossing by the trimaran raft *Nonpareil*.

As is now repeated *ad nauseum* by multihull enthusiasts, Herreshoff's two-hull
designs were called freaks, and banned from racing at the New York Yacht
Club. The excuse generally quoted is that *Amaryllis* was so fast that the current
racing yachts were hopelessly outclassed. Personally, I doubt if this was the
real reason. His catamaran may have been faster off the wind but she was
almost certainly a poor performer to windward and, because the hulls had

18

almost no rocker fore or aft and the beam was too wide, she was probably as temperamental going about as Petty's *Simon & Jude*. It wasn't that she was too fast – much more likely that the conception of a miniature non-yacht offended the general feeling of yachtiness peculiar to that period, when prestige was measured in large tonnages and big crews rather than in simple speed alone.

Herreshoff however was not deterred, and continued to experiment with the catamaran configuration. The very next year, 1877, he built *Tarantella*, although it is said that he had to be content with racing her against steamships off Narragansett. Probably another apocryphal story! He also was responsible for *Orion*, *Teaser* and *John Gilpin* (1878) (12), and *Lodola* (1879). Later he returned to monohulls and became more famous for his America's Cup designs.

Once again, I very much doubt if Herreshoff really thought overmuch about the Polynesian conception of a double-canoe, even although he is reputed to have been inspired by the flying proas of the Ladrone Islands. That he maintained a stubborn preference for the long straight keel, and for the rig of the day, seems to indicate that his ideas were as bogged down as those of Sir William Petty. In other words, both attempted to westernise a specialist native craft without studying the philosophy of the original creators. This probably has been the major stumbling-block for western imitations of native multihulls over the centuries.

And so the many and varied experimenters continued unsuccessfully to

12 Nathaniel Herreshoff's *John Gilpin* (1878)

attempt to convert the Micronesian, Melanesian and Polynesian concepts into modern creations by using grossly overweight materials. We had to wait 400 or so years from the time that Europeans first set eyes upon the delicate beauty of Polynesian sailing multihulls before suitable lightweight materials were invented and, almost simultaneously, until American servicemen fought their way across the Pacific and saw for themselves the remnants of the beautiful craft which once had flitted from island to island like so many birds of paradise. By the end of the Second World War most of the larger out-riggers and virtually all the double-canoes had disappeared for ever; now, after something like 3000 years, the time was ripe for a new multihull to arise from the nest of the old. It was, I think, right and proper that such an egg was laid in the Pacific.

But I hope I have shown that the parentage of this mutated chick is as dubious as the controversy it was about to arouse in the new world of competition into which it had been born. There seems no doubt that the chill from the cold waters of the Atlantic, which began to enter its soul in the seventeenth century, had, by the Second World War, virtually eliminated the last vestiges of happiness from a paradise lost. And yet the image of this past bliss somehow continued to linger as an aura of hope for the dreamers from the western civilisation which had all but replaced the ignorant savages of those earlier, happier times – and so a little South Sea island magic was retained. Perhaps this is the reason why the new chicken survived its perilous formative years, which have still to be related.

2 The First Modern Transoceanic Multihulls

The end of the Second World War produced an expansion of interest in the sport of yachting. Although money was tight, paradoxically it was not difficult to amass a large amount once one had overcome the initial financial difficulties of starting a new business. Fortunes were made, and lost – if not overnight, certainly within the short period of a year or two. And as money began to pour into the pockets of the successful few, the market for status-symbols such as yachts grew; more and more people turned towards yachting for realisation of their dreams. So although this particular breed of status-seeking yachtsmen may not be of any interest to us in this book, the money they spent in the yacht industry of Britain, Europe, America and elsewhere certainly helped to restore equilibrium after its abrupt rundown from the cessation of hostilities. But in the beginning money was tight...

The first postwar transoceanic voyage in a multihull therefore comes as a surprise, for it was accomplished by a French trimaran which crossed the Atlantic in 1946 – long before the first catamaran ocean crossings (the Atlantic in 1950–1, and the Pacific in 1955). She was the *Ananda* (13), measuring 42 ft 10 in × 34 ft 3 in × 9 ft 1 in on the centre hull, supported by two 22 ft 9 in × 3 ft 3 in floats; the overall beam was 22 ft 1 in. As with so many of these early multihull designs, *Ananda* was an unsuccessful success. I mean by this that, although she achieved what was expected of her by her owner, André Sadrin, the world of yachting almost totally ignored her voyage; it seems that she was regarded as just another freak. Even Humphrey Barton, in his excellent book *Atlantic Adventurers* (Adlard Coles, 1962), lumps her in the same chapter as Franz Romer's *Deutscheir Sport* (first modern canoe transatlantic) and Alain Bombard's *l'Hérétique* (first transatlantic rubber dinghy, ex-food and water), under the title, *Three Curious Craft*. Poor *Ananda* – she deserved a better description than that.

If the subsequent multihull designers had researched this voyage they would have discovered in advance many of the difficulties which, seemingly, came to them as a surprise. Of these, I regard *Ananda*'s motion in a seaway as being the most interesting. During the shakedown section of her voyage, from Sète in the south of France to Casablanca, the original crew became so violently seasick that Sadrin had to replace them with Frenchmen Didier Petit and Nick Scherer for the actual Atlantic crossing. I greatly admire

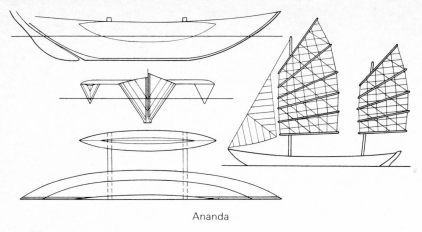

Ananda

13   *Ananda* (1946)

Sadrin's spirit in pressing on in such circumstances, and I will go into this subject of multihull motion causing seasickness in more detail in a later chapter.

Ananda was solidly built of mahogany on oak, displacing 8·7 tons – certainly she was not the type of lightweight multihull we have come to recognise as the best for blue-water cruising and racing. Her first leg from Casablanca to the Cape Verde Islands, although made in strong fair winds, only averaged 90 miles per day. Undoubtedly she was much too heavy for fast passage-making. Eight days after arriving at Porto Grande, she departed for Martinique – on 9 October. A fortnight later, in mid-Atlantic, she was struck by a violent squall which developed into a full gale. Because of her weight, low freeboard and short, beamy floats, she was continually swept by the heavy seas, and during the night she was thrown on her starboard beam. She also became almost unsteerable, and a large foresail had to be hoisted and two emergency drags streamed astern, to assist in keeping her on course. On 30 October the weather improved, and on 7 November she arrived at Fort de France, Martinique, having sailed 2100 miles in 20 days, averaging 4·37 knots – a record that was to stand for some time.

In his description of this voyage, Humphrey Barton concludes:

A curious result of the violent motion was that all the crew were suffering from eyesight trouble. One of the floats had a great deal of water in it, which they had been unable to pump out as it had spent most of its time awash. They were all decided that it would be unwise to continue the voyage and *Ananda* was therefore laid up. It had been an interesting but expensive experiment which clearly proved that a trimaran may not be a suitable craft for ocean cruising.

Well, as recently as 1965 the world-famous scientist, Dr T. E. W. Schuman, misguidedly remarked: 'During the present century no human being will land on the moon and return safely to earth'. In these days of rapid development it is inadvisable to be too dogmatic.

At about this time Woodbridge P. Brown, an ex-US serviceman who had been stationed in the Pacific during the Second World War, began experimenting with Polynesian outriggers with a view to building a yacht version of these craft. Woody Brown was therefore the first westerner to conceive the idea of ocean-going catamaran yachts based to some extent on Polynesian principles. He rediscovered, amongst other things, the asymmetrical hull which had been evolved so many centuries before; and contrary to the opinion of Eric de Bisschop (and later in the fifties, Jim Wharram), he decried the theoretical flexibility of the fastenings of the crossarms: in his view, after experiments, the so-called built-in flexibility was merely a by-product of age and inadequate materials for the job. After further experiments with a 16-ft model, Woody joined forces with Alfred Kumalae, a boat-builder, and Rudy Choy, a young up-and-coming yacht designer. Together, they built the 38 ft 6 in beach catamaran, *Manu Kai* (14), and launched her in 1947. They claimed that she was the first successful modern catamaran in yachting history, and I cannot find any historical facts to disprove their right to this claim. Certainly she was the first large postwar cat, but as we will see, the French *Copula* (15), which also had asymmetrical hulls, followed this first only a few months later on the other side of the world.

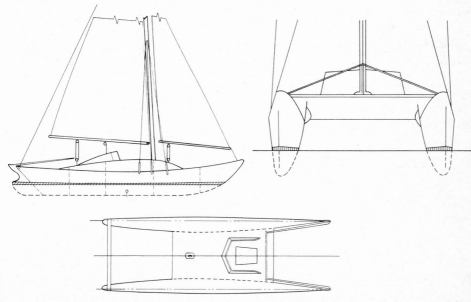

14   Woody Brown's *Manu Kai* (1947)

Although this book is concerned primarily with sea-going multihulls, for the record I should mention some of the pioneers of multihulls who developed their ideas from smaller beginnings than *Manu Kai*. That there were quite a number of them when compared with the big boys, indicates the scarcity of capital which I mentioned at the beginning of this chapter. Shortage of funds for experimental development was, and still is, more responsible than anything else for all the anti-multihull stories you have heard. Either an enthusiastic designer spent his own money on building his dream-ship, or he formed a multihull-building company and sold his products to unsuspecting yachtsmen, hoping to make enough profit and reap sufficient experience to improve gradually on his basic design. They used this method in the early days of automobiles and aircraft, and although it has the great advantage of being (theoretically) self-supporting, it can also result in some very adverse publicity. So there were those who built big from the start, and those who built small.

Of the latter, undoubtedly Roland and Francis Prout of Canvey Island in the Thames Estuary were the first commercially-successful catamaran dinghy designers and boat-builders. They began in 1947 by joining together two of the paddling canoes which they had been manufacturing since the end of the war. (They were national canoe champions for several years and were chosen to represent Britain at the Olympic Games at Helsinki in 1952.) So their first 16 ft 6 in × 6 ft 6 in double-canoe was probably nearer to a genuine double-canoe than most other early catamarans, not forgetting that de Bisschop's *Kaimiloa* (1), was copied more directly from Polynesian craft. The Prout brothers continued to experiment and eventually came up with the 18 ft × 9 ft 6 in *Sheerwater II* in 1954. It was in one of these, named *Endeavour*, that racing helmsman Ken Pearce achieved a radar-measured $22\frac{1}{2}$ knots over one third of a mile at Cowes in 1955. The highly successful 16 ft 6 in *Sheerwater III* followed shortly afterwards, and has continued to sell in large numbers to the present day as a restricted-design racing dinghy.

In 1946, shortly before the Prout brothers began to experiment, the American boat-builder, F. H. Creger, after spending many years in the Pacific, also began to build catamarans on a commercial footing, based on Polynesian designs. However, if I began to list all of the early designers and builders of multihulls who materialised – and who frequently disappeared just as mysteriously – we would not get very far. Suffice it to say that the majority were either non-commercial (i.e. they built one-offs for their own interest) or they concentrated on dinghy designs or small day-cruisers suitable for selling in quantity. 'Skip' Creger was very successful in the latter class, but many other names which became familiar during the late forties and throughout the fifties are now almost forgotten.

In my opinion too much emphasis was placed on speed during the formative period, and very little on cruising. The result was that both catamarans

24

and trimarans were looked upon as fast freaks, which could be controlled only by skilled helmsmen and crews. It is true that several beach cats were built on similar lines to *Manu Kai*, and that these carried many hundreds of tourists without accident on day trips out of Waikiki, but for the most part racing rather than cruising was the predominant feature. British designer Erick J. Manners produced the *Catamanner*, a comfortable day-cruising dinghy with sit-up side benches, but although popular for a time she soon faded into oblivion. Even *Manu Kai* was reported to have achieved 28 knots in a wind of 30–35 knots, so although she was not actually designed for racing, an interest in top speed was aroused. And once the yachting public have such figures in their collective heads, they expect this sort of performance at all times. Therein lay the early folly of suggesting what was possible; I decry nobody, for I made exactly the same mistake myself in the early sixties, as we shall see.

Woody Brown's most famous cat, the 40-ft *Waikiki Surf*, is generally credited as being the first to cross an ocean (or, rather, part of an ocean) since Eric de Bisschop's Pacific, Indian and Atlantic Ocean crossings in *Kaimiloa* in 1937–8. During 1955 she made the passage from Hawaii to Los Angeles in what was then the very fast time of 16 days. However, as I have already shown, misconceptions abound in anything to do with multihulls.

Five years before *Waikiki Surf*'s first, a French-designed catamaran made a successful crossing of the Atlantic from Tenerife to Martinique in 31 days – and thereby became the first postwar catamaran actually to cross an ocean. It does seem strange that although both cat and tri transoceanic firsts were French inspired, nobody in that country bothered to develop these initial designs for some time afterwards; but the fact remains that *Ananda* was the first postwar trimaran, and now, in 1950–1, *Copula* was the first modern catamaran to cross an ocean.

She was based initially on the 23-ft cat, *Marie-Celine*, which earlier had cruised successfully in the Mediterranean. It is interesting to note that once again cylindrical hulls came into the picture, for the designer of this small cat, M. Castella, used 20-in diameter cylinders to support the platform on which was built a cabin – and the engine room, for *Marie Celine* was driven only by a 20-hp petrol engine. That was in 1947.

In November of that year, as a result of a request for further information from an adventurous Frenchman, Raoul Christianen, who had studied Eric de Bisschop's voyages with considerable interest, M. Castella constructed a two-foot model which was tank-tested and found to be satisfactory. Early in 1948, construction of an all-steel 46 ft 8 in × 17 ft 9 in × 5 ft catamaran began in earnest. *Copula* (15), so named to symbolise the mating of her two floats, was unique in that she was the first ocean cruiser with asymmetrical hulls. Unfortunately, she was also probably the heaviest catamaran of her dimensions ever to be built – she displaced over 22 tons! Ketch-rigged with

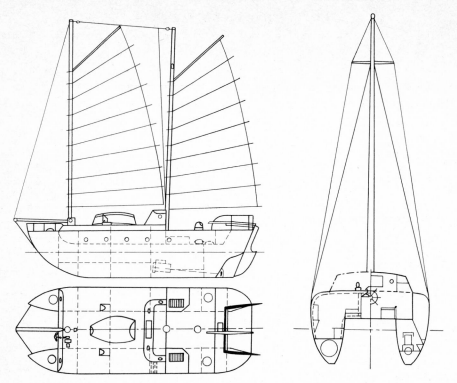

15 *Copula* (1948)

fully-battened, junk-oriented gaff sails and a headsail, it must be admitted
that she looked a bit of a mess, but she was launched at Toulouse in 1948
and completed a very satisfactory shakedown cruise from Sète to Casablanca
and back in that same year – a voyage of over 3000 miles. In 1949 she
cruised along the French and Spanish shores to Algiers and Majorca
(another 3000 miles), and in 1950 her owner took his wife, Josette, and a
crew of two out of Bordeaux on a scientific voyage across the Atlantic. In
order to record observations and collect specimens for the National
Meteorological Society and the Oceanographic Institute of France, *Copula*
was overloaded with equipment such as an air compressor, diving suits, a
large generator and a fully-stocked laboratory and workshop, in addition to
her twin 18-hp diesel engines. Surprisingly, considering her all-up weight,
she still managed to achieve some reasonable fast noon-to-noon runs of 156,
150 and 138 miles on her transatlantic crossing from Santa Cruz, Canary
Islands, to Fort de France, Martinique, where she arrived on 10 January
1951. Finally, she cruised northwards through the islands to Morehead City
on the North Carolina coast (where she ran aground on a sandbar and was
nearly lost); there she entered the Intercoastal canal for New York.
Altogether she covered 9000 miles in 90 sailing days, giving an average speed
of 4·17 knots – not at all a bad effort, all things considered.

26

Three years later in Britain, a Welsh multihull enthusiast, James Wharram, designed and built the 23 ft 6 in *Tangaroa* (16) (Plate 21), which was just about as different from *Waikiki Surf* and *Copula* as it is possible to imagine. Of those two cats, the former was undoubtedly a yacht within the fullest meaning of the word, and the latter a floating laboratory, but *Tangaroa* was as near to the Polynesian conception of a double-canoe as de Bisschop's *Kaimiloa*, which means that she can only be described as a yacht because she was being used for recreation, pleasure or racing – although none of these activities was totally applicable to the case.

Jim's contribution to ocean-cruising multihulls is much more practical for those who dream of getting-away-from-it-all than the expensive developments created by the American builders, which originated with Woody Brown, Rudy Choy and Alfred Kumalae – later joined by Warren Seaman, to become Catamarans by C/S/K: Choy, Seaman and Kumalae. The C/S/K dealt in thousands, often tens of thousands, of dollars per yacht; Jim Wharram thought, and still deals, mostly in hundreds. This great gap between two developing ideas with the same ultimate object of commercial success makes for some fascinating comparisons.

Jim built *Tangaroa* for $420, or just over £100, and crossed about 2400 miles of wild ocean in her (1957 was notorious for the irregular trade winds which developed into some very bad storms over the Atlantic); Woody Brown and Rudy Choy sailed their expensive creation across 2300 miles of the Pacific, against the prevailing wind, and achieved the same result. The moral is that you don't have to be wealthy to take up yachting.

In 1954, with a crew of two German girls, Ruth Merseberger, navigator, and Jutta Schultze-Rhonof, cook, Jim sailed *Tangaroa* (16) from England

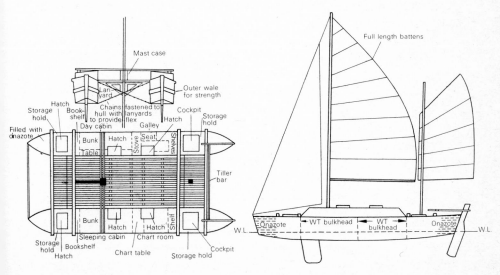

16   *Tangaroa* (1954)

across the North Sea and up the Rhine to Düsseldorf, returning in 1955 to cruise along the Channel to Falmouth, and finally in September crossing the Bay of Biscay to Ribadeo in North Spain. In 1956, *Tangaroa* continued her cruise down the Portuguese coastline to Cascaia, and from there she was shipped to Las Palmas in the Canary Islands. In the final week of December 1956, Jim Wharram and his two-girl crew set out for the West Indies. A report, published by the Slocum Society in the December 1957 edition of their magazine *The Spray*, was written shortly after their arrival in Trinidad on 2 February 1957. It is, therefore, an accurate assessment without frills of what Jim thought and believed about catamarans at the time.

When this bright year of 1957 began, I was aboard my 23-foot catamaran *Tangaroa*, one week out from Las Palmas, 100 miles from the Cape Verde Islands and approximately 2400 miles to go to Trinidad. We heard over the radio the New York beginning, but none of us felt any particular excitement. The wind was up to force 7 to 8. *Tangaroa* was driving before it with her twin spinnakers lashed to the tillers, steering a straight and accurate course. Life in her cabins was none too comfortable. Spray was spouting up through her slatted platform and driving in gouts through the ventilation slits. Inside the cabin, with only $\frac{5}{8}$-in pine between us and the ocean outside, the noise was terrific. As I lay in the bunk I could feel the sides working and bending under the strain.

When the morning came, things appeared much better. The waves could not be described as mountainous, as newspapers always love to describe them. They could have been no more than 12 to 15 feet high. But they were incredibly steep, and there was an occasional cross wave due to the South Equatorial Current mingling with the Canary Current, so that the serried lines of waves crashed into one swirling mass of water. After an anxious night it was pleasant to relax and watch *Tangaroa* getting on with her job, rising to the top of a pinnacle of water, then dancing away from it before it dissolved into chaos.

The pleasure was interrupted by the abrupt flogging of the port spinnaker. I jumped to the spinnaker sheets to find out where they had broken. There was a confused few seconds before I realised that it was not a spinnaker sheet that had parted, but the port rudder that had broken loose from the hull. The rudder rod had snapped under the strain of the constantly working spinnakers. It was a complete mess: the broken rudder attached to its tiller, the tiller attached to the tiller bar connecting it to the other rudder, and the sheets of both spinnakers fastened to the tiller bar – all mixed up together; the spinnaker sheets taut under the strain of the wind and the broken rudder fish-tailing through the water. Before we had got the mess in and cleaned up, *Tangaroa* swung beam on to the seas, and we took some nasty breaking crests on board.

The advantage of the open slatted deck for deep-sea cruising was amply proved. Had we had a high built-up deck structure, now fashionable in catamarans, I fear that the windage and wave pressure would have turned us completely over.

28

Unfortunately this rudder trouble was to continue throughout the voyage, turning what should have been an exhilarating experience, and for me the fulfilment of a dream of many years standing, into a nightmare.

In Las Palmas I had replaced my rudder rods with new ones. Most Spanish-manufactured goods are third-rate. With a slight play in the gudgeons it took approximately three to five days for the rod to crystallise and the rudder to break free. So, at any hour of the day or night could come the cry Rudders! and then would follow the desperate struggle to recover and to repair.

I was in this state for five weeks because, due to the weak rudders I did not dare drive on in all weather. Since the Trades were running at an average of force 6 to 7 it meant that we had to feel our way across the Atlantic, taking a total of six weeks instead of 30 days.

During this time I vowed again and again that I would never travel the high seas on a catamaran. A wave would deluge me and my thoughts would run on: What a fool am I! Why should I risk my life in boat experiments? In a few years catamarans would be extensively tested out along the coasts. Then, out of the sum total of knowledge, one might be able to design an ocean catamaran.

Within twenty-four hours of landing in Trinidad I was inquiring about the price of timber, and now, six months after landing, I have large quantities of plywood on order and I am looking for a place to build our new 40-ft catamaran *Rongo* (Plate 22).

The reason is, after level-headed thinking, that the behaviour of the *Tangaroa* was superb.

After landing we heard that ships were running three to four days behind schedule due to the bad Atlantic weather. *Tangaroa* rose over all seas, the only water coming aboard being the three-foot breaking crests, and with only two-foot freeboard, there was nothing to stop the one-foot. In all weather the boat was absolutely stable. The two-burner paraffin stove is simply placed on a shelf, held in position by a half-inch ledge. Any pan or kettle placed on top of the stove was completely safe without lashing. As long as the two rudders were in position steering was beautifully easy. The wide deck space, the separate hulls, allowed the three of us to live together in comfort and in privacy that a single huller of the same length could not possibly have. Indeed, my two-girl crew had more faith in the craft than in the skipper, and told me quite emphatically that the only boat they wanted to go to sea in was a catamaran.

My problem now is: what will be the final design of the 40-ft *Rongo*? When I designed and built the *Tangaroa* in 1954, apart from one short article on *Manu Kai* there was nothing in English yachting magazines to give a lead. So I designed the *Tangaroa* on the lines of a Polynesian fishing boat. Considering the load she carried, the voyage she made, and that she cost only about $420 to build, she was a roaring success. Since the dark days of 1954 catamarans have come to the fore, particularly in Europe.

Besides *Tangaroa*, Europe has produced five cruising catamarans, three French, one English and one German. The German *Gerumpel* seems to have been a safe boat, but too heavy, with too much wetted surface and was, I suspect, a very wet ship. The only other English catamaran, called *Ebb and Flo*, was a 40-ft chine boat, built in 1954. The designer forecast that she would reach a speed of 30 knots. However, in a race for the fastest sailing boat she was beaten by an Uffa Fox *Jollyboat* and made no more than approximately 12 knots. As a cruising yacht, she seemed to have great possibilities, each hull having a beam of seven feet. Accommodation in her must have been good, which is most important in a cruising boat. The two hulls were united by the usual wing. It was longer than I consider safe, but was relatively high off the surface of the water.

To turn to French catamarans: the *Kaimiloa*, built in 1936 in Hawaii, is the parent of all modern ocean-cruising catamarans. I can find very little information about her, but she appears to have been about 25 ft [actually 38 ft] overall, massively built, and the hulls were flexibly fastened together. Precisely how this was done I cannot find out. This boat seems to have had the solid attributes in self-steering and strength that the old *Spray* had. Her voyage from Hawaii to Cannes via the Cape of Good Hope has yet to be equalled.

The next French catamaran that I know of is the *Copula*. I read the book about her by Jean Filloux, and, perhaps more to the point, I met one of her crew in Las Palmas who advised me not to cross the Atlantic in *Tangaroa*. On seeing our quiet persistence, he assured us that if we lived we would never wish to go to sea in a catamaran again. I gathered from this statement that life on the *Copula* was not too happy. But on looking at the drawings of her it is easy to understand why. That massive centre platform, so close to the water, was bound to suffer from the pounding of rising waves. Likewise there was too much wetted surface.

The other French catamaran, the *Tohu-Bohu*, built like the *Copula* in steel, impressed Las Palmas yachtsmen with her very comfortable deckhouse. She impressed a Dutch friend of mine with her poor welding and has, I believe, been abandoned in Martinique. Europe's attempts at catamaran designing, with the exception of *Kaimiloa*, have nothing to teach us.

The home of the modern catamaran is America, beginning with N. Herreshoff and on to the numerous modern designers. Undoubtedly the finest and most successful one is Woody Brown with *Manu Kai* (14) and *Waikiki Surf*. I doubt that faster ocean-racing catamarans than those two boats will ever be built.

While I think that the *Manu Kai* and the *Waikiki Surf* are superb sailing craft, neither is any use for my purpose. I have seen the *Waikiki Surf* described as a cruising catamaran, but what is meant by cruising I am not quite sure. A week's camping out, holiday racing from port to port, and eating in hotels is possible in her. But with a displacement of 3000 lb I cannot see how she can be a true cruising boat in the fullest sense. One way of taking a cheap ocean cruise is to buy food in bulk. For example, on the north coast of Spain I would buy anchovies, sardines, bottled olives and wine; in England wheat, tinned dairy products, etc. By large-scale buying one can save a considerable amount of money. A displacement of 3000 lb is simply not sufficient.

Having discussed available catamaran designs that I know of, what will the *Rongo* probably be like? First of all I would like her to be like the *Kaimiloa* or

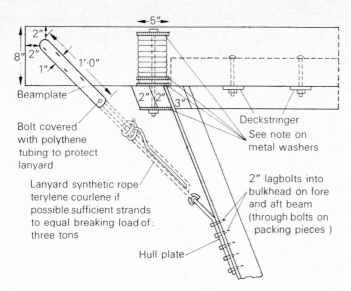

17 Wharram's method of attaching hulls to cross-arms allows for six inches flexibility out of true

the *Tangaroa* with two separate hulls, connected by cross-beams on some kind of a flexible mounting. On *Tangaroa* this was achieved by sponge rubber washers and rope lanyards, but on a 40-ft catamaran this is not practical. The *Kaimiloa* was fastened by tram car springs; quite how, I don't know.

I prefer flexible mountings for the following reasons:

1 It is so easy to overload one section of the hull and, due to the large surface of water covered by the boat, to have what amounts to a built-in strain. When the two hulls are flexible, they can float out of line to each other.
2 On two independent hulls, particularly when made of plywood or steel, the noise must be considerably less.
3 The looseness between the two hulls takes the jerk out when rolling at anchor.
4 A rigid boat is easier to flip over than a flexible one. The difficulty is to devise a cheap, simple and (as far as the public is concerned), attractive flexible system. *Tangaroa*'s system was efficient, but looked crude, which frequently led to her abilities being underestimated.

It seems that a cross between the *Waikiki Surf* and the *Ebb and Flo* would perhaps be the best design. I like the short wing section of the *Waikiki Surf* and the broad hulls of the *Ebb and Flo*. If I built a wheelhouse on the wing section I would have the equivalent of bomb-bay doors underneath it on a weak fastening. If the wheelhouse flooded, the doors would burst open. (Before anybody writes a letter, there would be a grating above the door so that we would not go out with the water.)

As a cross-section I will not have a chine or a flat bottom, but a semicircle, in profile, with a good rocker to the keel. To get extra lateral resistance I would have a centreboard in each hull and deep rudders, made of glued plywood.

By virtue of having sold the *Tangaroa* story to the popular press we have enough money to start building. Our immediate problem is to find a place to build, the best place on the island being the American base.

So to continue the list of initial problems, which began with *Ananda*, we have: excessive noise (also reported by the other transoceanic multihulls), rudder troubles (a common complaint), and the necessity for control over all-up weight. The other catamarans which Jim mentions are of little interest to our investigation since all of them were built of overweight materials – an obvious hangover from the strength construction of monohulls and a mistake which should have been learned from both the *Ananda* and *Copula* experiments.

For the most part rigs were reasonably normal in America, but there were some strange developments on the eastern side of the Atlantic. *Ebb and Flo*, for example, carried a Bermudan sloop rig on each hull. This 41 ft × 25 ft 3 in hybrid was designed by Thomas Tothill, and, like all other similar mono/multi compromises of the changeover period, she was neither one thing nor the other. In her case, the wide floats, the heavy all-up weight and the rather obvious fact that the lee sail was blanketed by the windward one, produced, during the same trials that Ken Pearce beat all comers in his *Endeavour*, the very poor performance mentioned by Jim Wharram. *Ananda*, and most of the other early tris and cats seemed to follow the de Bisschop lead of a variation of the Chinese fully-battened junk rig. This slowly dissipated over the years to become fully-battened, then part-battened, then normal Bermudan sails. By the time multihulls had settled down to a normal rig, Blondie Hasler had aroused monohull interest in the junk rig with his *Jester*, in the 1960 OSTAR.

On the eastern side of the Atlantic, then, we could lay claim to only one cat that had achieved any real success on a transoceanic passage – the Wharram-designed *Tangaroa*. In the Pacific Rudy Choy had launched the first cat designed entirely by himself: the 46-ft × 16-ft *Aikane*. That same year, 1957, this very handsome cat beat all previous speed records by winning the Newport to Ensenada race in 14 hours 1 minute over a distance of 125 miles. (Ten years later, she won in 14 hours 42 minutes, giving her the second-fastest time ever, as well as the fastest time in a decade.) She was also the first yacht home in the 1957 Trans-Pac, although officially she was not allowed to enter this all-monohull event; she beat the 83-ft leader, *Barlovento*, by 26 hours. Again, in 1959, she won this race unofficially (this time beating a 161-ft schooner by 17 hours), and in 1961 she achieved the following remarkable speeds:

1 Los Angeles to Marquesas: 2972 miles in 16 days 17 hours (7·41 knots average).

2 Tahiti to Hawaii: 2400 miles in 12 days (8·44 knots average).
3 On passage: 122 miles in 8 hours (15·25 knots average).
  She didn't only look good: she sailed good!

Nevertheless *Aikane* was an expensive yacht, whereas Jim Wharram was still counting his pennies while he built the 40-ft V-bottomed *Rongo* (Plate 22). In 1958 he sailed her, with his same crew, from St Thomas to New York – 1500 miles in 19 days averaging 3·3 knots – and in 1959 from there to Conway, North Wales, in 50 days (averaging 2·5 knots); not a fast passage, but an amazing achievement on a strictly limited purse. Nobody was interested, as this letter which I received from Ruth Merseberger showed:

Jim is now working hard on our *Rongo* to prepare her for her next trip. He was very pleased to hear from you, for there were months after our landing when we wondered whether it was worthwhile coming here at all. The welcome we got in New York was quite a different one, and we had only come up from St Thomas! Here, the British press could see only the sensational side of our story, and the yachtsmen ignored it altogether. It is hard if you think you are coming home after having succeeded in what you set out to do against the prophecies of all the 'experts', and then you are treated as if you did not exist at all.

Although he was not interested in fast or record passages, Jim Wharram again crossed the Atlantic in *Rongo* in 1961, returning in 1962, and thus became the first man to make a double crossing, or rather a double-double crossing, in a catamaran. This, on a shoestring, is no mean record! It should be noted that when Jim was making his second double-crossing, *Aikane* was doing virtually the same in the Pacific; in 1961 she was the first modern catamaran to sail out into the South Seas: Los Angeles–Marquesas–Tuamotus–Tahiti–Hawaii–Los Angeles.

Returning again to multihull dinghies, in 1955 an ex-pilot turned trade-journal publisher and a hobbyist multihull designer, Arthur Piver of Mill Valley, California, came up with his 20-ft *Pi-Cat*, fully prepared to sweep the board of all competition. There were no half-measures about Art – enthusiastically he emulated the proverbial bull in a china-shop, shattering in more ways than one the sanctity of monohull yachting. However, his dinghy cats were not a success, in spite of his claim in 1959 that a 17-ft version of *Pi-Cat* once reached a speed of nearly 40 knots. During this phase of his introduction, he also designed and built two monohull dinghies: the 15-ft *Nutshell*, which he claimed would plane when closehauled ('... a performance formerly considered impossible'), and the 10-ft *Scooter* ('... which has a double-curvature hull which gives a great speed when upright but increased effective beam and stability when heeled'). Piver was seldom at a loss for words when describing his products.

In 1957 Dr John Morwood of the Amateur Yacht Research Society in Britain (formed in 1955) made contact with Art and, as a result of many letters which passed between them, the 16-ft × 8-ft trimaran *Frolic* was born, described by Morwood as 'the first perfect trimaran configuration'. Next came the 24-ft × 14-ft *Nugget* which became a design popular with impoverished but determined deep-water adventurers, and finally, early in 1960, Piver launched the 30-ft × 18-ft *Nimble* – and probably the largest dollop of controversy to descend on the yachting world since Bermudan sails were introduced to replace the old gaff rig. 'Many people in boating take themselves seriously', Art observed in those early days, 'but the truth of the matter is that no one knows much about boat design, regardless of the many technical terms he may reel off or the mountains of mathematical data he may produce.' He continued to expound similar outrageous statements for the next eight years – until his tragic disappearance in an amateur-built 25-ft *Mariner* trimaran of his own design in March 1968.

Disregarding the controversy which Arthur Piver succeeded in arousing, there can be no doubt that he managed to achieve a delicate balance between affluence (represented in the early stages by Catamarans by C/S/K) and frugality (Jim Wharram's approach), which is the main reason why his trimaran designs became so popular during the sixties. If my own efforts on the eastern side of the Atlantic assisted the sudden explosion of popularity of Piver tris, it was because I have always believed that sailing is the cheapest method of escapism available to anybody who wants to get away from it all for a while. It will be seen that, although many designers tackled the problems of cruising and racing multihulls during the forties and fifties, only Arthur Piver reached the happy balance of a vessel which could be constructed cheaply and easily by amateur and professional builder alike. No wonder the world of yachting complained about the intrusion!

And so, in 1960, in company with George Benello and Bill Goodman, Art towed the first *Nimble* 3600 miles by road from San Francisco to Swansea, Massachusetts, and sailed her 3800 miles from there to Plymouth, England, via the Azores, averaging 5·67 knots. His purpose was to enter the Single-handed Transatlantic Race, organised by the British Sunday newspaper, *The Observer*, in conjunction with the Royal Western Yacht Club of Plymouth and the Slocum Society in America. Adverse gales in mid-Atlantic upset his calculations, and he arrived too late to take part; it is interesting to speculate how much sooner multihulls would have become accepted as ocean racers if he had managed to get to the start-line on time.

Of the lessons learned during this first west to east crossing by a modern trimaran, it is difficult to sort the grains of factual knowledge from the euphoria of chaff contained in Art's first book, *Transatlantic Trimaran*. 'How will the new 35-ft *Lodestar* look when she's doing 40 knots?' he asked ecstatically, thereby summing up how he hot-gospelled trimarans throughout the world in a spate of enthusiasm. The professionals were not impressed, but amateur builders, potential race winners and escapists were. Whether the Establishment approved or not, Arthur Piver had arrived – and so had the trimaran. The new revolution in yachting had begun!

Footnote. For those who are interested in the history of small boat voyaging, the only organisation in the world which specialises in the subject, mentioned in this chapter, is: The Slocum Society; R. G. McCloskey (secretary), 9206 Northeast 180th Street, Bothell, Washington 98011, USA.

3   Ogre Capsize

It will be seen from the previous chapter that apart from the interest aroused by C/S/K catamarans, which was mostly localised on the western seaboard of America, all other blue-water voyages by multihulls were largely ignored (even though record-breaking was reported from time to time in most yachting journals throughout the world). That is, until Piver crossed the Atlantic in the first *Nimble*. Thanks to his undoubted ability for arousing controversy, 1960 was the year when the yachting public really began to wake up to the fact that a major revolution was taking place.

Of course, during the previous decade small dinghy-type racing and cruising cats and tris had already made quite an impression, but this development was on entirely different lines from that of the bigger, potential ocean cruisers and racers. By the end of the fifties there were quite a number of multihull dinghy classes in Britain, America, Australia and elsewhere which were steadily amassing a following, but until Piver crossed the Atlantic nobody had seriously thought about multihulls as cheap ocean cruisers. Certainly the C/S/K reputation had done nothing to give anybody the impression that large multihulls could be built at a low price, and at that time very few people knew anything about the successful experiments of Eric de Bisschop and Jim Wharram. I very much doubt if any inventor of a totally new design of boat or ship could have chosen a better moment to display his wares – or a worse time to fumble his grand entrance. For Piver arrived at Plymouth too late to take part in the 1960 Singlehanded Transatlantic Race, and therefore missed the chance of a lifetime to prove the superiority of his design. Any other person would no doubt have despaired, but Piver seemed always to thrive on adversity.

'The insular people of Britain are far more interested in boating than is the average American,' he wrote, 'and the publicity given this race was extensive. Television crews, photographers and journalists in large numbers had swarmed about the boats for days. A number of newspaper accounts had speculated on our possible arrival in time for the race. In typical newspaperese, none of them said when *Nimble* arrives – they invariably said if *Nimble* arrives.'

Although he arrived after the race had started, and the journalists etc. had long since stopped 'swarming', and had returned to their respective newspapers, Piver managed somehow to spread the word that if the gales had not been against him all the way across the Atlantic he would certainly have shown the monohull contestants the quickest route back to the States. You can't keep a good man down!

'The passage had converted the Skipper,' he observed about himself, 'making him a dedicated cruising man. Before, he had only wanted to sail like mad, whooping and hollering in exhilaration, and his little day-sailers had provided all the required thrills. Now he had discovered that he could still whoop and holler, have the same sailing fun and live in comfort besides.'

Unfortunately, Art misread 'the insular people of Britain' and, I suspect, the yachting public of most other countries, including his own. Certainly he collected an enormous following of devotees, but he also antagonised the established and sacred yachting traditions in each and every country he visited. There were the pros and the cons – and in the early sixties the cons worked extremely hard to bring multihulls of every type into disrepute. There was even a period of two or three years when the catamaran followers fought the tri-mariners, and vice-versa. It was not a happy time.

I attended the start of the Transatlantic Race at Plymouth as the Slocum Society's representative in Britain, but I left long before Art arrived. So I never saw the first *Nimble*. At the time I was engaged in selling a range of ply dinghies, rowing and non-class sailing, built by P. & W. Craft Ltd of Ipswich, for the newly-formed Cox Marine Ltd. A year passed. I came to the conclusion that we needed to market some larger craft than dinghies if we were to stay in business – for many other firms had followed my lead, and the market was becoming saturated – and in due course I happened to read in the Slocum Society's magazine *Spray* about Piver's transpacific exploits in his 35-ft × 20-ft *Lodestar*, which with typical gusto he was tackling in 1961. If he could cross the Atlantic, I argued, and he was now on the Pacific high seas, then the design must have considerable merit. Why not market this new design of – what was it called? – trimaran. I discovered that in Britain the plans were in the hands of one Phil Patterson of Kirkby-in-Furness; I paid £30 for the working drawings of *Nimble*, and in this simple way Cox Marine moved into trimarans.

Of the difficulties in finding a suitable builder (for P. & W. Craft lacked the necessary space), and the decisions which I had to make during her construction (for Piver's plans left a great deal to the imagination), I will say nothing more. Contour Craft Ltd, then of Gorleston, made a first-class job of *Nimble Eve* (Plate 3), and I happily signed a cheque for £1500 after she was launched in heavy rain on 1 December 1961. When I sailed her down the coast from Great Yarmouth to Ipswich a few days later – a distance of about 65 miles – I was not quite so joyful.

It is a rather remarkable experience to handle for the first time something made by man which is very different from anything produced before. I had

had some similar adventures in my earlier flying days – such as being one of the original pilots to shoot off a seaborne rocket catapult in a Hurricane fighter – and I soon discovered that sailing *Nimble Eve* for the first time was in many ways as adventurous as my introduction in 1941 to the suicidal Merchant Ship Fighter Unit. In order, my *Nimble* disillusionments were as follows:

1 *Nimble Eve* was NOT as fast as I had expected.
2 She seemed incredibly flimsy.
3 She vibrated when under way.
4 She had a peculiar motion which was very sick-making.
5 Even in force 3–4 (which we had on that first voyage) the triple-diamond, single-shrouds-supported mast bent alarmingly.
6 The cockpit was too small, and even with just two crew in it the stern was immersed too much.
7 The reefing gear was inadequate – even in force 4.
8 She was excessively noisy below when under way.
9 The Perkins 30 hp outboard which I had thought would be necessary to power her was much too big and heavy – and was quite useless in a seaway of even the mildest swell, because the prop was more often out of the water than in.
10 To be honest, after many years of sailing heavily-constructed monohulls (and particularly after 11 years in my Thames barge), I just couldn't trust her not to fall apart in high winds and heavy seas.

On the credit side, however, I had to admit to the following:

1 I loved her wide, spacious decks.
2 She tacked easily and positively. There was absolutely no thought about her missing stays.
3 She worked well to windward – much better than I had thought possible.
4 Although her motion was, well, peculiar, we soon discovered that down below cups could be left on the cabin table, and that even if they were full they didn't spill their contents.
5 There was an indefinable something about her which from the beginning produced a mutual affection. This did not only happen to me – many others who have sailed or owned Nimbles have noted it. I believe it is the mark of a thoroughbred, although I have never understood where her 'breeding' could have come from.
6 To me, she looked good. Many other people have told me that she looked bloody awful, but I can only say that I didn't, and still don't agree. 'Some like 'em fat, and some like 'em thin, but the boat of my

dreams is the one in between.' In a manner of speaking, *Nimble* was in between just about everything – including every discussion and argument.

Well, I didn't argue – then. Cox Marine's expenditure of £1500 represented the profit on a large number of dinghies, and I had to get this back as quickly as possible. I worked *Nimble Eve* and myself extremely hard: from the tail end of 1961, until she was replaced by a considerably modified version, *Nimble Days*, in November 1962, I sailed the prototype on 63 demonstrations, regardless of weather conditions; she and I survived seven major gales at sea during these trips, the highest costguard-reported windspeed being 60 mph.

I could write a book about those 63 very varied experiences. That was the period when yachting and newspaper journalists did their utmost to decry, and give the minimum of support to multihulls. Advertising managers vied for my trade, but they had to admit that their editors were not exactly helping them to gain my confidence. 'You'd think,' one such manager once told me, 'that we were competitors, instead of being mutually interested in increasing the sales of both magazine and ads. If only he'd print a normal article, instead of all bloody disasters.'

Those who are interested in the history of trimarans during this period should read my book *Trimaran Development* (Adlard Coles, 1972) which, in addition to the battle fought against the establishment, gives detailed descriptions of all the trimaran capsizes during the first decade after the launching of *Nimble Eve*, i.e. 1962–71 inclusive. I mention this, because although most yachtsmen are now aware that the disaster of capsize was largely a red herring

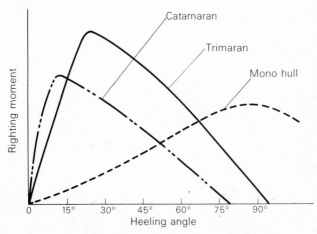

18 Static stability tests indicate the enormous initial righting moment of multihulls. Capsize would appear to be almost impossible, but this graph does not take into account the human element.

introduced by the anti-multihullists in those early days, the unpleasant thought still remains – and probably always will do. Mention trimarans, and to a lesser extent catamarans, and the ugly word 'capsize' will automatically be included in the conversation. Of all the disadvantages quoted against multihulls, the possibility of flipping over is easily the No. 1 threat – or is it in actual fact? The true answer is *no*, but since it is essential that the newcomer into multis really understands all the aspects of this new sport, I must now divert from development and analyse one of the most controversial subjects ever to be discussed in yachting. Let us begin at the beginning.

There were 17 trimaran capsizes during the ten-year period 1962–71:

1 Arthur Piver's 24-ft Nugget class. July 1964, Salcombe Bar, entrance to Salcombe, Devon, England. Gale conditions. Owner and crew had crossed the Channel to the French coast, where they broke their mast. They sailed back across the Channel, jury-rigged with half a mast. A gale sprang up and they tried to make Salcombe for shelter. The state of the tide was wrong for crossing the Bar, and a wave lifted the tri stern over bow and crashed her on the Bar. No lives were lost. The tri was amateur-built, and the owner and crew were said to be inexperienced with multis. Surprisingly, the tri was not structurally damaged.

2 Hedley Nicol's 35-ft *Vagabond*. September 1964, Moreton Bay, Queensland, Australia. Unreefed; genoa set. Windspeed (anemometer confirmed) 60 mph. Deliberate maximum speed attempt. This is the famous yacht-that-flew episode. Reached a height, confirmed by many eyewitnesses, of at least six feet before flipping over.

3 Arthur Piver's 30-ft *Nimble Jest*. February 1965, River Orwell, Suffolk, England. Unreefed. Windspeed (confirmed by coastguard and HMS *Ganges*) 55 mph. Special demo trip for yachting journalist enforced by time factor. Journalist lost way whilst tacking; tri capsized when severe sleet-squall overwhelmed her at this moment.

4 Hedley Nicol's 35-ft *Vagabond* (same one as No. 2 above). June 1965, Breaksea Spit, Sandy Cape, East Australia. Windspeed (confirmed by local fishing fleet) 50–60 mph for 72 hours. Two crew were attempting to sail from Gladstone to Brisbane after 1966 Brisbane–Gladstone ocean race at Easter. Restricted time period and adverse winds made them attempt dangerous passage through shallow Breaksea Spit against local advice. Mast and sail was discovered two days later; nearly three weeks after, HMAS *Sydney* found the capsized tri, still floating, but in badly holed and battered condition: she had been rolled over by heavy seas and smashed bodily against a coral bottom – almost certainly in a shallow channel through Breaksea Spit. Two lives lost.

5 Arthur Piver's 24-ft Nugget class, *Taa Roa*. September 1966, off Cape

Town. Unreefed. Windspeed 50 mph. Inexperienced owner tried to reach harbour in a 'buster' without reefing. He admitted: 'It was sheer stupidity on my part to let the float dig in so much. I should have reefed. I asked too much of the boat.'

6 Richard Hartley's 28 ft 6 in Sparkle class. December 1966, off Sydney, Australia. Owner admitted carrying too much sail in a full gale.

7 Richard Hartley's 28 ft 6 in Sparkle class. April 1967, off Victoria (Port Philip Bay), Australia. One float filled with water (hatch was loose) in gale conditions, so owner hove-to and bailed. The tri tacked, and then capsized when the partially filled float was driven under.

8 Robin Chaworth-Musters' 30-ft Triune class. 1967, Poole harbour, Dorset, England. Windspeed in excess of 60 mph (coastguard-confirmed: ... the worst equinoctial gale at Poole since 1932). Demo trip for obtaining photos. Reefed, but only with reduced headsail; mainsail unreefed, and so the tri was unbalanced with excessive lee helm.

9 Norman Cross's Cross 24 class. 1967, River Tiber, Italy. In gale conditions owner, with three crew, tried to make entrance over bar. Tri broached and capsized. One drowned.

10 Lock Crowther's Kraken 33 class, *Bandersnatch*. September 1967, on passage from Melbourne to Sydney. Strong cyclonic winds. Presumed to have hit a whale but this claim has been queried. Another suggestion is that she rammed an unlit steel buoy used by the oil rigs off the Victoria coast. She was found capsized with one float missing. Four lives lost.

11 Hedley Nicol's 25-ft Clipper class, *Clipper I*. March 1968, on passage from Cape Town to South America (having already crossed the Indian Ocean single-handed – the first tri-mariner to do so). Windspeed 50 mph. Lying ahull with no sail set and owner asleep, tri was rolled over by a wave. Owner admitted overloading (causing pooping the previous day – and the dangerous overload of water in the bilges had not been pumped out), and his own careless handling as reasons for this capsize. 'Deep down,' he wrote, 'I feel I failed her.'

12 Hedley Nicol's 35-ft Wanderer class. 1968, near Hobart, Tasmania. Windspeed estimated at 70 mph during squall. Owner on weekend cruise with wife and five children admitted: 'I should have concentrated on sailing rather than wasting one or two minutes trying to get the children into the cabin.' Tri drifted into sheltered waters after capsize, and those trapped in cabin escaped via the slot in the transom after the outboard was removed.

13 Arthur Piver's 46-ft Trident class, *Waka Toru*. August 1968, on passage towards Lord Howe Island from Sydney, Australia. Tri discovered capsized three months later by 800-ton trader, *Moanaraoi*. No bodies

found. From photographic evidence of the inverted hulls, I think this tri capsized by cartwheeling. Eight lives lost. (*Note:* it is interesting to record that the captain of *Moanaraoi* tried to sink the trimaran, first by fire – which was not successful – secondly by repeatedly ramming her. She was left in a shattered condition. The wreckage was reported from time to time by other ships, and nine months later an Australian correspondent, Bob Herd, told me that *Waka Toru* had finally drifted ashore in Northern Queensland. Here is satisfying evidence that even a large and heavily-loaded tri cannot sink!)

14 Richard Hartley's 35-ft Lively class, *Pathfinder*. May 1969, on passage from Hiroshima towards America. Windspeed given as cyclonic winds exceeding 50 knots in area. Owner was inexperienced, and had already been involved in two collisions: the first with a Japanese freighter in November 1967, which cost the company 4,800,000 yen, or about £5600 or 13,400 US dollars; and the second with a Japanese fishing boat which also caused extensive damage, although this was only partly repaired at a Japanese boatyard. Shortly afterwards the owner left Japan with three crew: two Japanese, who were experienced in dinghy sailing only, and a British merchant seaman who lived in Canada. They paid $500 each for the passage. The tri was discovered inverted, with the starboard float missing, seventeen days after departure. From evidence, it would seem that she had rammed a 35-gallon can which supported a fishing net. Four lives lost.

15 Hedley Nicol's 29-ft Islander class, *Wanderer* (not to be confused with Nicol's 35-ft Wanderer class). 21 June 1970, on passage down the Intercoastal Waterway inside the eastern coast of America, six hours' motoring/sailing south of Norfolk, Virginia. Windspeed, maximum of 84 mph (coastguard-confirmed) during violent thunderstorm. From the evidence, owner and crew of two were sufficiently inexperienced to ignore until the last second the well-known warning:

> When the rain's before the wind
> Tops'l sheet and halliard mind.
> When the wind's before the rain
> Set your tops'l up again.

'Rain began to fall, and one of the crew and I went below to put on rain gear', wrote the owner. 'Suddenly we were heeling badly...' Seconds later the tri capsized.

16 Norman Cross's Cross 24 class. 7 September 1970. Windspeed no more than 20 mph. On passage from Oceanside, north of San Diego, to Catalina Island, some 44 miles offshore. Owner and son (aged 22) noticed tri was 'feeling loggy' when about two-thirds on way. Discovered port float hatch (under stowed dinghy on deck) had floated

away and float was flooded. Tried to luff into wind, but float sank. Tri capsized 90°. Took to dinghy, but broke one rowlock. Then a wave capsized the small boat. Son drowned. Owner admitted it was not the fault of the tri; he had known about the loose hatch and had intended to fix it.

17 Arthur Piver's 33-ft Stiletto class, *Auriga*. 1971. Windspeed: gale. Capsized whilst racing off Rendondo Beach, California.

Summarising this total list of known trimaran capsizes over a period of ten years, we can apportion main causes as in Table 1:

Table 1

	DESIGNER	LOA	AREA	LIVES LOST	CAUSE
1	Piver	24 ft	Coastal	—	Bad seamanship – inexperience?
2	Nicol	35 ft	Coastal	—	Record attempt – overconfidence?
3	Piver	30 ft	Inland	—	Special demo plus inexperience
4	Nicol	35 ft	Coastal	2	Bad seamanship – overconfidence?
5	Piver	24 ft	Coastal	—	Bad seamanship – inexperience
6	Hartley	28 ft 6 in	Coastal	—	Bad seamanship – slackness?
7	Hartley	28 ft 6 in	Coastal	—	Possibly bad luck
8	Musters	30 ft	Coastal	—	Special for photos – overconfidence?
9	Cross	24 ft	Coastal	1	Bad seamanship – inexperience?
10	Crowther	33 ft	Coastal	4	Not known – bad luck?
11	Nicol	25 ft	Ocean	—	Bad seamanship – slackness
12	Nicol	35 ft	Coastal	—	Bad seamanship – slackness
13	Piver	46 ft	Ocean	8	Not known
14	Hartley	35 ft	Ocean	4	Not known – bad luck?
15	Nicol	29 ft	Inland	—	Bad seamanship – inexperience
16	Cross	24 ft	Coastal	1	Bad seamanship – slackness
17	Piver	33 ft	Coastal	—	Racing

Of these seventeen, the only really inexplicable accident, with seemingly unnecessary loss of life, was the large 46-ft × 24-ft Trident class, *Waka Toru*. I corresponded with the owner, Bill Shute, over a long period when he was building his dreamship, and I know she was carefully constructed and well equipped. Did she cartwheel, or did she ram something? About five feet of the starboard float bow had been wrenched off, which could indicate either misfortune – yet if it had been a case of ramming why was she found upside down, and why wasn't the radio used? This is the only really mysterious capsize I know about.

Of the rest, it is apparent that bad seamanship, often self-admitted, is the primary cause, either through inexperience, overconfidence or just general slackness. The ramming of unlit buoys, whales or whatever cannot be blamed on to multihulls (although it must be admitted that the possibility of so doing at high speed does increase the chance of disaster), and one capsize while racing can hardly be regarded as of major importance.

It is, I think, important to note that in every case when the windspeed was known, capsize occurred at, or over 50 mph. (The sole exception, No. 16, was more of a slow sinking than a wind-in-sails capsize.) This should indicate to all tri-mariners a red danger mark for their mental, self-computing anemometers. Whether the wind is squally or steady, be extra alert when it exceeds, say, 40 mph, and don't, whatever you do, allow your mind to be diverted from your duties to your ship at this stage.

Seventeen tri capsizes in ten years make an average of 1·7 per year; twenty deaths in the same period average 2 per year. But these figures are meaningless until they are set against monohull and/or catamaran equivalents. Alas, no such figures are available. During the same ten years, I know that there were at least a similar number of catamaran capsizes – in fact, I believe there were more; certainly more cats than tris capsized while racing (e.g., *Golden Cockerel* and *Imi Loa*: C/S/K designs; *Apache Sundancer*: Macalpine–Downie design).

In order to give some perspective even to the trimaran capsize figures it is necessary to make a guess at the total number of cabin tris sailing during the first decade. I went into this matter in some detail in *Trimaran Development*, and the result of my figuring indicated a world total of about 5500 trimarans, sleeping two or more, at the end of 1971. Other estimates in America give numbers as high as 200,000, and (slightly more realistically) 35,000. The American publication *Trimaran Magazine* estimated 7–9000 in November 1969, but this included day-cruising types. I think that my assessment is as accurate as it is possible to guess, bearing in mind that I had a sound knowledge of the market from 1961–6 inclusive.

Taking the average of 550 tris built per year, we arrive at a probability average of capsize of 0·31 per cent – in other words, you can expect one trimaran to capsize out of approximately every 300 launched. Three hundred to one is not bad odds against capsizing, and the loss of life probability odds must be considerably better since there is nearly always more than one person sailing on each trimaran. Assuming an average crew of three per trimaran (and I regard this as a low figure), the probability average of loss of life works out at 0·12 per cent – or getting on for odds of 1000–1 against a single death as a result of capsizing in a trimaran. During this same period, the chances of being killed or injured on British roads were about 0·7 per cent, or slightly worse than 150–1!

It will be seen, therefore, that the mighty ogre of trimaran capsize is really only a small, though ugly, elf. He needs watching – always! – because his ugliness has a dreadful fascination similar to the many fallacious stories which credit snakes, bats and toads with devil's work, but it does seem absurd that such a minute dwarf has been allowed for so long to control the destiny of all the vessels known as multihulls.

As long ago as 1955, Mike Henderson invented masthead buoyancy for a dinghy; later, in 1958, he incorporated the horrible excrescence which became known as a 'flying saucer', in his cat *Golden Miller*. She was followed by his twin-ballasted-keels-and-flying-saucer cat, *Misty Miller*, which in my opinion was a regression to *Copula*, or even further back to the lumbering Victorian steam-cats. In spite of the excessively overweight keels, *Misty Miller* could not always be relied on to self-right after a knockdown, and because her hulls had to be placed relatively close together to assist the self-righting moment, she suffered badly from wave pounding in the tunnel between them. Nevertheless, lawyer Michael Butterfield sailed her in the 1964 Singlehanded Transatlantic Race (losing one keel on the way, which very nearly sank her) and came 11th, taking 53 days. In the same race David Lewis, also with ballasted keels on his 40-ft × 17-ft *Rehu Moana*, came 7th in 38½ days, thereby qualifying as the first single-hander to cross the Atlantic in a multihull. Derek Kelsall, who, 500 miles on his way had had the misfortune to strike some flotsam, which badly damaged his rudder and broke the dagger-board so that he had to return to Plymouth for repairs, finally crossed in 35 days. That his 35-ft × 20-ft trimaran *Folatre* was unballasted – in fact she was deliberately lightened during construction by eliminating the large coachroof of the Lodestar class design – explains quite simply why his was the quickest crossing. These lessons had been learned on *Ananda*, *Copula* and others more than a decade before, but in 1964 Ogre Capsize was a giant of deception who all too often dictated ridiculous policies.

It is significant that David Lewis, who went on to sail round the world in *Rehu Moana* (west-about, via the Magellan Straits and the Cape of Good Hope, totalling 41,609 miles in 3 years 2 months: 1964–7), gradually abandoned Colin Mudie's original design of two excessively heavy dagger-plates, and finished up with a 17-ft wood keel bolted to each hull, 1 ft 3 in deep at the stern, tapering to 1 in at the bow. These gave a maximum loaded draught of 3 ft 3 in. In his book *Daughters of the Wind*, Lewis wrote: 'I have indicated in the text that worries about stability soon ceased to be a practical consideration. The combination of heavy keels with great beam to enhance stability appears to have been an attempt to marry two incompatible principles and the original keels were redundant.' In *Children of Three Oceans*, Lewis wrote: 'We gave away our automatic sheet release in New Zealand as redundant.' Since Lewis, with all his experience – and responsibilities, for he took his wife, Fiona, their two young children, Susie and Vicky, and a friend, Priscilla Cairns, with him on the circumnavigation –

reduced Ogre Capsize to reasonable proportions, why do others continue to persist in giant killing? The answer is, of course, that propaganda is insidious: once started, it creeps into the very souls of all those incapable of total self-reliance. If they need to be reassured by a skilled designer that their multihull is totally safe then they should forget about going to sea in small boats and take up knitting; at the very least they should never risk going afloat in either a cat or a tri, for it is fact of life that whatever you inwardly fear, nature, when challenged, will reveal your weakness by brutal demonstration.

I think Piver was the first multihull designer to invent the sheet-release principle, but I never used his idea, nor did I fit it on any of his trimarans which I ordered for my customers. I was often asked why. Since my reasons in those early days are still relevant, I will explain them again.

Piver was undoubtedly the first multihull designer to worry seriously about Ogre Capsize. In his original range of plans (24-ft Nugget; 30-ft Nimble; 35-ft Lodestar; 40-ft Victress), he drafted the total sail area of each tri to very safe margins, and rigged the mainmasts with single shrouds which, he claimed, would break if the sail area was not considerably reduced before the wind reached 40 mph. He also invented a quick-reefing foresail on a club-boom and, of course, the automatic sheet-release jamb-cleats. I must admit, however, that I was not impressed by these precautions.

Nimble Eve was equipped with all these devices except the sheet-releases. We didn't fit these because (a) of the cost (they would have to be specially made), and (b) I felt quite sure that the snatch-back caused by a sudden release in a strong wind would inevitably cause the poorly-stayed mainmast either to break, or to part a shroud. The whole concept of weaknesses in rigging was repugnant to me; as I have already admitted, this concept was the cause of many of my original dislikes for the design (items 1, 2, 5, 7, 10 on page 38). I refused to launch a second Nimble without making considerable improvements to clear these up, and as many of the other disillusionments as I was able.

By the time *Nimble Days* was launched in November 1962, I had persuaded Piver to increase slightly the size of the cockpit and improve the buoyancy in the stern (item 6); at the same time he made other structural alterations (for details, see *Trimaran Development*). On my part, I added shrouds to the middle diamond and to the masthead, fitted roller-reefing to the main boom which may have looked ridiculously superfluous but was only just powerful enough in a strong wind, increased the thickness of the mast by half an inch and the fore-and-aft depth by one inch, discarded the quick-reefing foresail, replaced the Perkins 30-hp outboard with a Crescent 8 hp ... I will not go on; there were many other modifications, but in this chapter we are concerned mostly with capsize problems.

Nimble Days revealed a whole host of new difficulties which I solved one by one in due course, but for the most part I never had cause to worry about

46

trimaran rigging again. That my method was overstrong I do not deny, but far better in my opinion not to have to worry at all about the main source of power than be in constant fear of the mast going overboard. Very well, now the helmsman could concentrate solely on sailing. (I should add that at this stage it had never occurred to me that a trimaran could be capsized by wind alone.)

Piver's plans were reasonably good, but many of his figures were inaccurate. The sail plan of Nimble gave a total main/foresail area of 325 sq ft; in fact, our sailmakers, Jeckells of Wroxham, worked out that the actual area was 287 sq ft – 38 sq ft less than what I had already regarded was an under-canvassed boat! As *Nimble Jest* capsized with this rig, clearly it can be argued that undercanvassing is not a safeguard against capsize – although it must be remembered that she was not reefed at the time. Other multihull designers have used this safeguard (e.g., Bill O'Brien's BOB-cats), but such measures are, in my opinion, more of a danger than a help as they tend to support a complacent it-can't-happen-to-me attitude.

There is no such thing as a non-capsizable boat or ship; the sooner yachtsmen learn this simple rule, the quicker they will learn seamanship, and thereby eliminate unnecessary foolishness. Even a 100 per cent guaranteed self-righting vessel cannot be relied on to save the lives of those who go to sea in her, as so many RNLI lifeboats have sadly proved. It is no good arguing that these brave men went out in conditions that no yachtsman would think of facing; freak seas and hurricane winds are not held in reserve especially for the brave or only for self-righting lifeboats! One day you will have to face this enemy, and it is better to do so with a basic knowledge of seamanship, rather than having learned to rely on a clutter of electronic and other gadgetry which may, and probably will, let you down when you need it most.

Designers of multihulls are beginning to concentrate on the problems of self-righting without using heavy weights or masthead buoyancy. The hang-over from monohulls of ballasting to prevent capsize is, I hope, now a thing of the past, and although the masthead buoyancy idea to prevent total inversion may have had some merit, it was soon discovered that a slap-down at speed, or in heavy seas, either battered the 'flying saucer' into small pieces, or more often broke the mast first! Over the years I have received many suggestions from both amateur and professional designers, and I include recent examples of each, with permission, to show the similarity of current thinking on the subject of self-righting trimarans.

The first, by Mr E. A. Leeb of London, was sent to me in 1974 with a brief note: 'Dear Mr Clarke, What do you think?' I replied as follows:

To your excellent set of drawings (19), and footnote question, I very nearly made the Eric Morecambe reply: Rubbish! However, a cliché reply to a stock phrase is not really what you require.

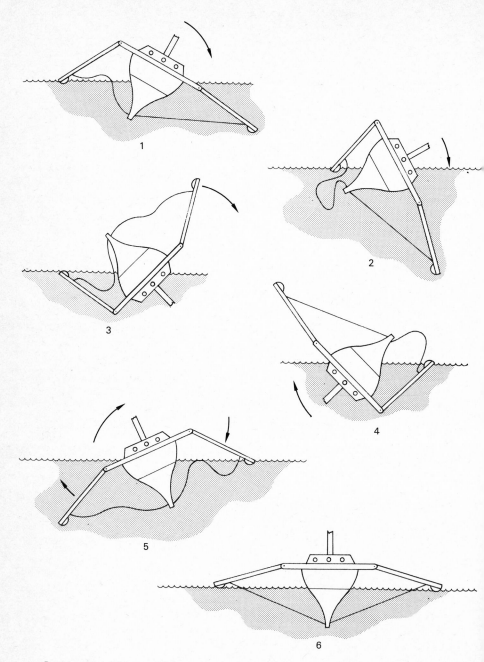

19 Leeb's self-righting trimaran

Seriously, such a scheme could never work for so many reasons that I just cannot be specific in a short letter. The idea is most ingenious, but if you have ever been out in a storm in a small boat you must realise that floats flopping around as per your drawings would soon reduce even an all-steel vessel to its component parts.

The multihull capsize has been a bugbear, invented by anti-multihullists, and continued by everybody who has followed this red herring. The facts are clearly described in my book *Trimaran Development*, and I recommend that you read it. The rumour of multihulls capsizing all over the world is a myth; the percentage is infinitesimal.

The simple answer is that if a person is constantly worried about the thought of capsize in a multihull, he or she should go to sea only in a monohull. This is the only 100 per cent safe invention to prevent multihulls from capsizing.

On the other hand, I corresponded at some length with professional designer Paul Winch, BSc, CEng, MRINA*, who had this to say about self-righting tris:

A professional designer is responsible for those who sail in his craft in so far as he can help them by good design. To this end, my main reason for developing self-righting trimarans is to combine the merits of trimarans with the safety in capsize of a good monohull. I am also aware of other influences.

These days are cramped days, in harbour, on moorings, and most of all in marinas. I cannot believe that the future lies with vessels the size of two, let alone three. Also these are days for careful investment in a product which is of wide appeal and which is durable; this rules out the exceptionally lightweight craft which win the odd race and are never heard of again. My mind has been active for ten years in the search for a new kind of vessel, light enough to be fast but built to last, and having variable beam with automatic self-righting. During the last five years the configuration shown in the plans (20) here has evolved. Earlier studies ranged from proas with wing masts through reversible catamarans to a range of folding trimarans with joints in all sorts of unlikely places.

Of course a sensible and alert seaman will shorten sail in good time; he will watch wind and weather, and he will have a hand on the sheets when working up to windward in a multihull. Perhaps he should take this precaution on all points of sailing, since the most unexpected things can happen. Unfortunately we are not all good seamen, and even those of us who are good seamen have lapses due to fatigue, unforeseen accidents, seasickness among the crew ... we may be seasick ourselves and even, just possibly, single-handed. So I for one am not interested in designing boats for perfect sailors who do everything right, but for the sort who make mistakes. Perhaps this is because I have met many of the latter, and none of the former!

My principles are that a yacht must look after her crew when they fail her. If they get her downwind in bad weather she must be able to fight her way

* Address: 31 Prince's Court, Wembley, Middlesex, England.

to windward again. If she is knocked on to her beam ends in the process she must self-right and be on her way again with a minimum of fuss. Her crew may be stretched to the uttermost in locating their seamarks, deciding their strategy and fighting off fatigue. Such stress is doubled and trebled at sea when so often the ship's company are unfit before the real trouble starts. They are liable to be least able to cope when the need is greatest.

A further dimension is added to the argument when ocean racing is considered. By the nature of the sport one is bound to press on with all speed possible night and day. But how can one do this when the margin between fast sailing in a confused sea and waterlogged sloshing upside-down is a matter of constant vigilance? Such vigilance is acceptable in a sport such as skiing or gliding or motor racing, or even dinghy racing. But at sea, since one cannot summon this degree of concentration, let alone see what is coming 24 hours a day, sometimes in dreadful conditions, one shortens sail for reasons of safety. Now if capsize is made a manageable thing instead of the ultimate disaster, what a strong position the skipper is in! He can carry more sail with confidence, and is under way again immediately after capsize, if this does occur, with next to no time lost as a result.

The self-righting trimaran illustrated below (20) embodies the most promising ideas I have developed. The principles and details of the design, and of a number of others of various configurations, are the subject of patent applications.

The smallest of the range illustrated is intended to be versatile, the one basic model serving several quite different customers. Probably the main appeal will be as a day-sailer in hot countries. In this case the large cockpit will be used for sunbathing, the floats for swimming and more sunbathing, and the cabin for changing and the privacy which all parties need at some time. A party will be able to sail considerable distances to their chosen beach or anchorage, and get home again in safety even if the weather takes a turn for the worse during the day.

I envisage the main demand in Britain and Europe will be from weekend yachtsmen – those with a family. They will sleep in the cabin while the children sleep in the cockpit under a fitted tent. There is room for the whole family to eat in the cabin and to shelter there in bad weather. The weight of the family is included in the designed displacement for the outboard motor version.

The inboard engine version is designed to sail with a crew of two or three, these being the likely complements for extended cruising and offshore racing respectively. The appropriate water, stores and fuel are of course included in the design displacement, as is all equipment anyone would need, such as cooker, mattresses, spare sails, change of clothes, etc.

The particular vessel illustrated here has been kept to the length and breadth permitted for caravans towed by ordinary saloon cars in the UK and on the Continent. Boats are frequently trailed which are both longer and wider than these limits, on the basis that they are loads on the trailer and not the structure of the trailer itself, but I cannot imagine trailing anything larger than these limits to be either a pleasure or even practicable in our congested streets.

Discussions are in hand at the time of writing with a view to this design going

1 and **2** The Past – and the Future?

1 The Victorian cross-Channel ferry, *Castalia*, 290 ft × 59 ft × 7ft, launched in 1875. Under-powered, she finished her brief working life as a floating isolation hospital.

2 A 52 ft × 36 ft × 3 ft suggestion by Planesail.

One hundred years separate these designs; sometimes I wonder whether we progress, regress – or just procrastinate too long.

3 *Nimble Eve* was an example of Piver's first successful ocean-cruising trimaran. Heavily overloaded, she was abandoned in a force 10 Channel gale in 1962. Her crew of five were saved; she survived two more days of gales, only to drift into the breakers off Andresselles, France, which smashed her to matchwood.

4 (*below*) A later version of Nimble, *Trinui*, which was the first trimaran, and the first multihull after de Bisschop's *Kaimiloa*, to cross two oceans. In 1962–3 Alec Grimes and Roy Garsides sailed her from England to New Zealand.

5 A good example of a modern cruising catamaran. This central-cockpit, 26-ft Heavenly Twins class was designed by Phil Patterson after considerable experience in sailing both tris and cats, including a transatlantic crossing in a Nimble. Very few multihull designers have such a history, and so it is advisable that you investigate the background of the designer of your choice before you commit yourself to any payments – unless, of course, he is already firmly established.

6 (*above*) and 7   One method of lifting a trimaran by crane (**6**). Note the
padded rope slings. (In the background, Ingeborg von
Heister's Lodestar *Ultima Ratio*; she was the first woman to
make a double single-handed crossing of the Atlantic – E–W in
1969, W–E in 1970.) The same boat is shown with wings folded
on a trailer (**7**) which was towed from England to the south of
France. Cruising cats are unable to reduce beam in this way
which is a decided advantage in favour of tris if you want to
explore places without the bother of having to sail to them.

into production after prototype testing and development. My hope is that my work, which has been spread over many years, will produce a breed of yachts which will provide enhanced efficiency and safety.

Although I have included Paul Winch's remarks in full, I do not entirely agree with his philosophy. However, since I particularly wanted to demonstrate both sides of this argument, I am extremely grateful to him for his help.

At the 1975 London Boat Show, I inquired around the catamaran stands to find out what cat designers had to say on the subject; the consensus of opinion was quite emphatic: *their* cats just didn't capsize. Roland Prout, who, let's face it, has accumulated twice my experience in multihulls, told me that he just could not envisage any cruising cats of Prout design capsizing. Furthermore, he went on to say that to the best of his knowledge none had. I found this hard to believe and said so; surely somebody, somewhere, had gone over?

I have already pointed out that there is no such thing as a non-capsizable boat, and the tyro will no doubt seize upon this statement in order to maintain the controversy. For myself, I would much rather believe in the proven facts that multihulls are not easily capsized, particularly in normal yachting weather, and that if and when conditions worsen into the abnormal, a multihull has as good, if not better chance of survival than a monohull. But more about this in Chapter 9.

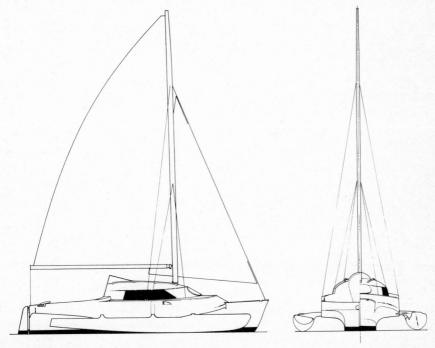

20   Paul Winch's self-righting trimaran

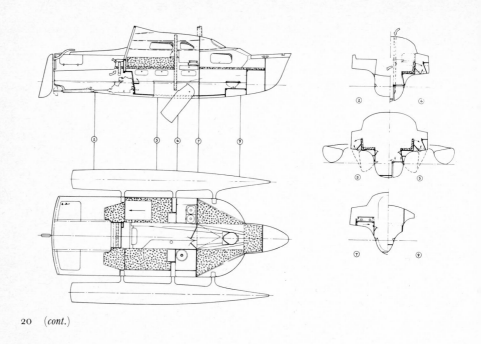

20   (cont.)

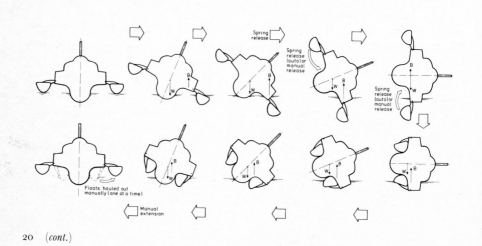

20   (cont.)

4 Cat or Tri?

Although I would not personally allow my choice between owning either a cat or a tri to be influenced by the questions Which is the safer? and Which is less likely to capsize?, I have a shrewd idea that in spite of what I have written in the previous chapter you may still be concerned about safety. I know this because I receive many letters each year about these two points, and generally the position is complicated even further because the correspondent goes on to outline his requirements (i.e. his dreamship), and then asks me, What would you buy if you were me?

Well, if I were you, I'd buy what I fancied most – which gets us nowhere. But if you want to know my personal preference, well, I'd buy only a trimaran for deep-water cruising or racing, but I would be prepared to own either a tri or a cat for coastal cruising or racing. I put this succinctly in *Trimarans – an Introduction*: 'Cats for coastal; tris for transocean.' Needless to say I was immediately accused of just about everything, including smart-alecky alliteration.

So how does one come to a decision on this prickly subject?

Well, it can be done by way of that modern abomination, a questionnaire – provided the person who is supposed to advise is not slanted in his views. After leaving Cox Marine I acted in the capacity of a multihull consultant, using details supplied by potential clients on a questionnaire which I had compiled. But this was only for selecting the most suitable sort of trimaran for customers' requirements, since I was not involved with the possibility of catamaran sales. Over a period of nearly four years – selling some thirty sets of plans, a dozen second-hand tris and seven new craft in the process – I gave advice to over 300 potential clients who had completed the Tri Selection Questionnaire. From this experience I learned that potential multihullists were badly in need of advice, and that I was the only freelance consultant available; I have never designed a multihull, and since leaving Cox Marine I have owned no allegiance to any multihull designer, therefore I can claim that I am entirely uncommitted to any particular design or designer. Bearing in mind that since my basic knowledge of multihulls stems principally from sailing tris (although I did sail a Prout Sheerwater dinghy-cat briefly in the fifties) I have a bias towards three hulls, let us examine first the advantages and disadvantages of these two types of craft.

53

I thought it best to let a multihull (cat *and* tri) designer set out the main points as he saw them; here, then, are the views of Norman A. Cross of San Diego, California.

Advantages of a trimaran over a catamaran

1T Lower centre of gravity and greater beam for stability
2T Weight concentrated amidships
3T Less wetted surface at low heeling angles; therefore faster in light winds
4T Less windage side profile
5T Less under-wing deck area and usually more clearance
6T Only one rudder and keel required
7T Not as stiff. Easier on rigging. More comfortable ride
8T Initial stability is less (heels easier), but ultimate stability is greater
9T Greater deck area
10T Easier to install inboard auxiliary engine
11T Wider platform for standing rigging and running rigging
12T Comes about faster
13T Better cabin accommodation in smaller sizes

Advantages of a catamaran over a trimaran

1C Less overall beam, therefore slightly easier to find berthing space
2C With two hulls to support the displacement, each hull will have only half the displacement/length ratio of a tri
   Note: The question arises whether two hulls with half the D/L ratio will each have less drag at high speed than the one hull of a tri
3C A large saloon can be built on the wing deck on sizes above about 36-ft LOA
4C Inboard motor can be mounted in a nacelle on the centre line of the wing deck with inboard/outboard drive. Propeller can be rotated up out of the water when not in use
5C Easier to beach
6C Two hulls to build instead of three

These pros and cons are fair enough as you read through them, but are they of any real help to you in making up your mind whether you are going to buy or build a tri, or a cat? I doubt it; and I don't absolutely agree with all Norman's points.

Take item 2C, for example. Now I'm not going to involve myself in a technical argument which even designers cannot agree about. But I do know that for the most part cats have been considered as beasts of burden, whereas tris have tended more towards becoming lightweight 'flyers'. For this latter trend, we have to thank Arthur Piver who was the first multihull designer (indeed, the first yacht designer) to bring to the attention of owners the simple fact that trimarans should not be overloaded. Of course everybody knows how Samuel Plimsoll did this for merchant shipping in 1876, and most yachtsmen have appreciated the reasons for a designed load-waterline; probably a reasonable percentage could describe the difference between Thames tonnage, deadweight tonnage, gross tonnage, net tonnage and displacement tonnage. But although I have never met a catamaran or a monohull owner who is particularly worried about his load tonnage (LT) – unless, of course, he is about to race, or he has just lost a race – I know a large number of trimaran skippers who are continually on the alert against overloading.

Piver started it all with his Loading Rule, which stated quite simply: 'My trimarans can carry three-quarters their built weight, which is the weight of the boat when it is launched without any fittings except for the mast, spars, sails and rigging.'

The confusion caused by this rule was, in the early days, sometimes hysterical, and more often than not chaotic. Some seemed to think that if a tri was overloaded it would fall apart in the first seaway it encountered; others found it difficult to accept that (for example) a Nimble could only carry 1500 lb, and that from this figure essentials had to be deducted as follows:

Deck
Pulpit, anchor, warps and lines, outboard, outboard bracket, boathook, deck broom, bucket, navigation lights and wiring, sail cover, bilge pump, small dinghy, etc. Say approximately 250 lb.
Interior
Cupboards and lockers, sink, water tank (empty), cooker and fuel, companionway, floor covering, shelves and Formica covering, mattresses and seat cushions, interior lighting and wiring, batteries, marine toilet. I used to reckon about 400 lb for all this.

This left only 850 lb for crew, water (remembering that 1 gallon of water weighs 10 lb), food, personal belongings, sleeping gear, charts and navigational gear, fuel for the outboard – and so on! It will be seen that two men each weighing 200 lb, plus 30 gallons of water and food and equipment for a fortnight, soon took care of the LT: the load which could be carried after deductions of essential interior and exterior fittings. So why, I was asked repeatedly, has Piver designed the interior to sleep six? The answer for that period, I regret to say, is that Nimble was originally designed to sleep four; *I* was responsible for doubling the forward bunk, and making the saloon side seats convertible to bunks, and I regret even more that although I soon reverted to four berths, later tri designers (including Piver) began to increase bunk capacity. But more about this later.

In due course I learned through experience that Piver's Loading Rule erred on the low side – which was good, not bad. After much deliberation (for I had to make the decision; Arthur was a poor correspondent), I

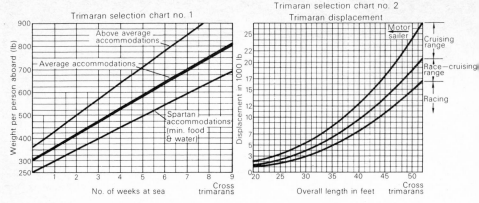

21 Multihullists often seem unable to grasp the importance of not overloading their yachts. Norman Cross's Trimaran Selection Charts will help
you determine (a) the load (LT) you require and (b) the size of trimaran needed to carry this load (see Appendix VI, page 182)

reassessed the LT figures for the original range of Piver's tris as follows:
24-ft Nugget, 550 lb; 30-ft Nimble, 1200 lb; 35-ft Lodestar, 2500 lb; 40-ft
Victress, 4400 lb. Remember that LT is the load which can be carried after
deductions of essential interior and exterior fittings. (Norman Cross's
Trimaran Selection Charts (21) provide a prospective owner with a means
of determining the load he requires and the size of trimaran required to
carry this load.)

Load Tonnage was my idea, evolved from the confusion of those early
days, but I don't think it really caught on. Multihull designers have generally
reverted to displacement tonnage, which gives little or no guidance to the
owner who wants to get the best out of his tri and who is anxious to give
his vessel every possible chance in the event of running into very bad to
impossible weather and sea conditions. This is unfortunate, because the propaganda against overloading which Piver pioneered has to some extent clung
to the tri image, whereas cats seem to load as they like. No matter; be
assured that a trimaran is all the safer, will give you a better ride, and is
faster and much more seaworthy if not overloaded. So it is up to you to find
out from the designer his recommended LT; I can't say more than that.

However, I think it would be true to say that Piver's Loading Rule resulted
in trimarans being considered rather more than they warranted as high speed
sailing machines, because in the early sixties in America several designers
and companies (excluding C/S/K) began to launch big catamarans, loaded
down to the marks with luxury extras, and seemingly with little or no regard
for overloading or performance (except under power). A new image began
to emerge: tris are delicate; cats are husky. When a potential American
customer in 1963 turned down a Lodestar in favour of a catamaran of a
similar size, he gave his reason as: 'Well, Nobby, I guess she just can't carry

all the essential cabin fitments I require'; I soon discovered that 'essential' in this case meant an inboard engine, a generator, an ice box, ship/shore radio, air conditioning, a shower – and a host of other items which were quite impractical for Lodestar. Yet they were all installed in a similar-sized catamaran – although I must report that this customer wrote to me a year or so later to say that he had sold her because she was such a poor performer under sail; later he bought a large tri!

So, the very first question you will probably ask yourself now when choosing between a cat and a tri is: how much load will I want to carry? A second question follows: do I want super luxury? And a third: do I want to 'whoop and holler', like Piver, when I'm sailing, or do I actually want only a reasonable 50/50 performance? It will be seen that these three questions can be reduced to one: why am I considering a multihull at all, instead of a monohull? If your answer is because there is so much more space on and in a multihull, then the chances are that whether you realise it or not you are going to make determined efforts to fill all that space, either with luxury, or with a clutter of excessive gear and gadgets, heads and bunks. Therefore it can be stated correctly that many people buy multihulls because of the additional space available; and why not? it is an excellent reason, providing they exercise some restraint when filling it. Alas, such caution is rare; as I have shown, I fell into the trap myself, and I know of one space-filler who actually planned fourteen berths for his Nimble (he intended to charter her).

So if your main reason for going multi is space, let us examine the differences between cat and tri. These can be stated as follows:

1 *Headroom* Most tris of 25-ft LOA and over have 6-ft headroom in the cabin, whereas cats in smaller sizes have this headroom in the floats only, and not in the 'midships saloon. Therefore, if good headroom is required, and money is restricted, only a tri will be suitable.

2 *Sleeping* Medium cats (say 30–36-ft LOA) generally are able to offer a more varied accommodation plan than tris, because the latter are restricted to a rather narrow central hull. For this reason, cats in this range are often more expensive than similar-sized tris. If you come into the middle price range, and you are seeking good to excellent accommodation, then a cat is the better choice.

3 *Galley* Again the cat wins in the medium-size class. Wives who have learned to be good galley slaves in monohulls will not object so much to the constant to-ing and fro-ing past the sacred area in the narrow hull of a tri, but untrained cooks cannot possibly grumble about the secluded galley space provided in an average cat.

4 *Heads* Where, oh where can the damned thing go in the narrow hull of a small tri? Cats win easily.

5 *Deck* This is more difficult. Young parents with children seem to prefer

the cat with its spacious cockpit even though the actual deck space is generally restricted to the foredeck. Tris on the other hand, generally have a cockpit which is much too small to contain children; but they have an excellent unrestricted deck space overall. I have found that many adults prefer trimaran decks, although whenever children are involved the catamaran cockpit becomes more popular.

What is your next reason for wanting a multihull?

The majority of people who write to me – and I have answered well over 30,000 inquiries since December 1961 – want a multi 'to get away from it all'. This may come as a surprise, but it is quite true. Very few indeed are after a fast cruiser; in fact a large percentage make a point of stating that seaworthiness and seakindliness are what they are seeking, and they will willingly sacrifice speed to achieve their aim. Since these correspondents were writing to me only about trimarans, I cannot be specific about their reactions to catamarans.

If you are an escaper, or otherwise require a multihull to cruise deep water, Chapter 8 goes into the subject in more detail; but choosing between a cat or a tri belongs here. The safest answer I can give is for you to take note of usage, for many more tris than cats have successfully crossed oceans.

I hasten to assure indignant catamaran designers that although they may think I am prejudiced, I am quoting only facts. The multihull designer whose many and varied vessels have logged the most deep-water voyages is Arthur Piver: up to the end of 1974, I estimate that around 400 of his designs completed at least one transoceanic voyage out of the 700 or so that started; these included four circumnavigations out of a total of at least seven to my knowledge – although probably there are several more I have not heard about. Cats, on the other hand, although many more have been launched than tris (I think it likely that the ratio is more than 2–1), have not achieved anything like the same total; in fact I very much doubt if they have done half as well. This does not prove conclusively that trimarans are necessarily better ocean cruisers than catamarans, but it does seem to indicate that yachtsmen regard the former as being more seaworthy – and faith, we are told, will move mountains. The reason why Piver's tris lead the fleet in this aspect of the sport is easily explained: he was the first to introduce uncomplicated designs which were capable of deep-water cruising, and which could be built by amateurs; I estimate that over half of his 400 craft that have sailed across an ocean were home-built, as were three of the four circumnavigating tris.

Although David Lewis completed the first-ever multihull circumnavigation in a catamaran in 1967, Eric de Bisschop the first crossing of three oceans in 1938, Raoul Christiaen the first cat transatlantic voyage in 1951, and Woody Brown the first part-transpacific crossing in 1955, seemingly the general feeling of multihull enthusiasts was that cats were all right for racing and coastal cruising, but for crossing oceans – no! There is no precedent for this that I am aware of; it has just happened that way. However, under test conditions sometimes it would appear that opinion has not been mistaken.

In the 1974 Round Britain Race, for example, 39 monohulls, 12 trimarans, 9 catamarans and 1 'foiler' crossed the start line at Plymouth: 61 starters in all. The weather conditions during the second leg from Crosshaven in South Eire to Castlebay in Barra, Outer Hebrides (and thereafter) can be described briefly as bad. About halfway through the race, the fleet was reduced to 46. The percentages of each type of vessel which dropped out are interesting: 23·1 per cent monohulls, 16·7 tris, 33·3 cats, 100 'foiler'. Of those who failed to finish, the percentages are even more fascinating: 33·3 per cent monohulls, 16·7 tris, 55·6 cats, 100 'foiler'. So of those that started, only 26 of the 39 monohulls and 4 of the 9 cats finished the race: but out of 12 trimarans, 10 remained to the end – 7 of them in the first 10 to cross the finishing line at Plymouth. The race was won by a cat – the sponsored 70-ft *British Oxygen*, said to have cost £80,000 – but tris came 2nd, 3rd, 4th, 5th, 8th, 9th and 10th. The 80-ft *Burton Cutter*, which came 6th, and the 53 ft 10 in *Quailo II*, which came 7th, did a little towards saving face for the monohull supporters; the second cat home, however, *Snow Goose of Wight*, which came 15th, could hardly qualify as a success for modern catamarans, as she had been built fifteen years before – in 1959 – by the Prout Brothers! The next cat home finished 25th: a 30-ft Iroquois, *Minnetaree*, designed by Macalpine–Downie and built in 1970. Although a cat won, it was undoubtedly a disastrous 2000 miles for the catamaran image.

Now one hard race does not prove very much – if anything. Certainly I do not intend to analyse the reasons why the various types failed to complete the course. My main object in including these figures is to set your mind working along similar lines, so that in due course you will look more closely at such testing matters as long races and begin to draw your own conclusions, unmarred by any slanted views of 'experts'. I have shown no doubt that my views are also slanted, for figures such as these make me even less inclined to consider cats for ocean cruising; it should also be borne in mind, however, that similar races in other parts of the world (e.g., the Trans-Pac) have produced very different results – for both speed and seaworthiness – in favour of catamarans.

The next point to consider when choosing between two and three hulls is speed. Which is the faster? The answer is simple: there is nothing in it. Out-and-out racing machines in either class can joust – and in one race the cat will win, in another the tri will succeed. This will, I expect, go on for many years before complete satisfaction is attained.

There is one point which has nothing much to do with theories of wetted surfaces, etc. It is that rigging a racing trimaran is considerably easier than rigging a racing catamaran. An obvious difficulty when setting up a very tall Bermudan mast between two hulls, however inflexible the spars may be that joint them together, is that they are going to 'work' in strong winds and a seaway. This means that the lee rigging will inevitably slacken and snatch to the pressure of wind and movement of hulls. A trimaran, however, nearly always carries the main shrouds to chainplates on the centre hull, with masthead shrouds only attached to the floats or sometimes to the crossarms; consequently, the working of the hulls does not affect the main rigging anything like as much as on a cat.

Few people can afford the high cost of having a special racing multihull designed and built for them, so I think it is reasonable to forget about these extremes. With standard classes of cats and tris, I don't think one can be any more dogmatic about speed than with the racers – there's not much in it, depending of course on the waterline length and on the basic purpose of each design in both classes. So when speed is considered, the choice is entirely yours; there is no real evidence as yet to support either contestant, and quite frankly I don't think there ever will be.

One point in favour of a trimaran which I should mention relates to the danger of hitting flotsam, or otherwise sustaining damage to a hull, or even to more than one hull. I know of many cases when this has happened to tris, and often repairs have been possible because of the buoyancy available in the other hulls. But if a cat is holed in one float, the situation is not nearly as simple, and I regard this factor as a positive disadvantage for ocean cruising, and something to be remembered when choosing between a tri and a cat even for simple coastwise cruising.

Another equally valid point on this subject, for those who demand maximum safety, is that the floats of a trimaran provide ample space for such reserve floatation as polystyrene (or even ping-pong balls). On the other hand, because most of a catamaran's hull space is taken up with accommodation there is generally not much left for safety precautions. So again, the three-hull configuration has the advantage over two hulls for ocean cruising when maximum safety precautions are taken into consideration.

It can quite rightly be argued that the two outer floats of a trimaran may be more vulnerable in a bad seaway, or when hitting flotsam, than the hulls of a cat. I am aware of six cases when a float has either been wrenched off completely, or has been damaged so badly that wave action has finally battered it from the crossarm. *Bandersnatch* has already been mentioned as an example of the former, and for the latter there was the extraordinary voyage of the Piver 35-ft Lodestar *Om*, who lost her port float in the Tasman Sea, but eventually made land, and saved her crew of three, by sailing on two hulls.* The risk, of course, is there, but I must point out that in three of the six cases the cause was almost certainly a design fault in the

* Full details in *Trimaran Development*.

method of connecting the floats to the crossarms. The Australian designer, Hedley Nicol, lost a float and his life with those of his crew in *Privateer*, a 36 ft 4 in Vagabond Mk II of his own design, in 1966*; a Nicol 29-ft Islander, *Triventure*, lost a float in the Mozambique Channel off East Africa in 1968*, and a Nicol 36 ft 4 in Cavalier, *Rub-a-Dub-Dub*, lost a float in the Baltic in 1969*. In each case the port float was involved, but this may only have been a coincidence.

Now, let us consider that questionnaire.

1 *Age?* This is important: e.g., at 50 you are more likely to seek comfort and safety than speed, and so on.
2 *Married or single? If married, give number, ages and sexes of children* Again more important than is generally considered. A wife without children will invariably choose the closest she can attain to home comforts; with children, this point immediately becomes a long list of 'must haves'.
3 *Cruising/racing requirements? Which will be your usual sailing area?* Local, coastal, deep-water or transoceanic? Never buy a yacht until you are quite sure you know what you are going to do with her.
4 *Crew: Singlehanded? Family only? Friends?* Apply logic similar to that required for question No. 3.
5 *Sail only? Auxiliary? 50–50? Power only?* Don't kid yourself. If answers to 1, 2, 3 and 4 are entirely honest, it may well be that your true requirement is at either end of this question. Don't waste your money on an engine if you want to make a sailing circumnavigation record attempt; similarly don't waste your money on expensive rigging and sails if you are a marina sailor, when one good diesel will do all the work you will ever require from your yacht.
6 *Which has always been your preference: cat or tri?* This may sound like a daft question, but in fact most people are biased before they realise it. If you discover or know that you have a preference, then I don't think you should switch unless there is a very good reason for it. If, for example, you have always thought that a cat is much better than a tri because of the spacious accommodation, but you purchase a tri because you believe it is more seaworthy, you will inevitably always be comparing the tri on unfavourable terms with your first love; whereas if you bought a cat you must compare it on favourable terms with a tri. As I say, this may sound ridiculous but experience has taught me that customers nearly always react in this manner (and so do their wives).
7 *Will you want to let or charter your multihull?* If so, your prime consideration must be what you think your customers will want most – not what you want. Accommodation is the obvious 'first', and in the small and medium sizes there can be only one choice.
8 *For how long a period will you want to live aboard?* This, too, may sound stupid if you have not thought about it before. The question, really, must be considered in relation to all the previous ones. At the extremes, the accommoda-

* Full details in *Trimaran Development*.

tion for a solo circumnavigation will be very different from that of a marina sailor; equally, normal yachting accommodation will bear no relation to the requirements of a family who intend to use the vessel as a floating home. So think about this before you answer.

9 *Do you want to buy new? Second-hand? Or build the multihull yourself?* This question is frequently connected with availability. There are fewer multihulls in the world than monohulls, and you may well discover that there is nothing suitable to meet your first choice in either the new or the second-hand market. A compromise here, however, must still stand up to self-searching questions 1–9. If your opinion has hardened on the side of three hulls, don't be side-tracked by the immediate availability of a cat which seems, 'as near as dammit', as good. The object of these questions is to help you to fix your choice between a cat and a tri; if you couldn't care less which you have, my advice is that you should go to the monohull market where you will find a much bigger variety to choose from.

10 *How much do you want to spend?* I've written one book on this subject (*The Lure of the Sea*; Adlard Coles, 1970), and I could easily write another. The final choice must depend on how much you can afford, balanced against all the previous questions.

Now let us see how this simple questionnaire works. For an example I'll pick a married man of 33, wife 31, with three children: two girls, 11 and 8, and boy 9. They have raced fast dinghies for six years, but the children are growing up and there is not really enough room for all five of them to enjoy it – even in an 18-footer. Father now has enough reserve cash to buy a new or second-hand vessel in the lower medium size-range – about a 30-footer. They have decided on a multihull because they have heard that multis are fast. But they are not so much interested in racing now, because mother is more inclined to think of the children's enjoyment; however, she has given her OK for father to enter an occasional race if he feels the urge. Father, on his part, is secretly worried about the skills required to handle a large multihull after a smallish racing dinghy. Conversations with friends (not multihullists) nearly convince him that he is a fool not to go for a well-ballasted monohull, but he has read about both cats and tris sailing across oceans, seemingly without difficulty, and he is determined to go multi; the fact that his wife has already decreed the route he will take, because she refuses to go to sea in a monohull which will behave in the same way as their racing dinghy, no doubt has aided his determination. They live near a large estuary in a densely populated area.

Our family have never had the space to take friends out in their racing dinghy, and consequently they can answer question 4 quite simply: the multi-hull will be mainly for their own use. There is no doubt either about their cruising grounds: the estuary and its offshoot creeks will last them a lifetime. Perhaps, when we get used to her, father suggests, a long coastal cruise or...? Well, perhaps, says mother.

Now the shallow waters of this estuary demand a boat which will dry out in safety (for even the best navigators go aground here), and father knows that in this respect a cat is slightly better than a tri. Trouble is that he has read all about Piver's whooping and hollering, and this has persuaded him that tris are faster than cats and also that they are less liable to capsize (he must have read my books); besides, he may want to win the odd race...

Well, one thing is certain: he needs an auxiliary engine to make sure he gets back to his moorings in time on Sundays – but this surely is a bit of a red herring. He knows that the estuary's spring tides are fierce, and suspects that wind-and-tide against a multihull may well slow progress under power to a stop. Perhaps an outboard will be adequate for light-air handling or flat-calm motoring – in other conditions it would be better to sail than motor. An outboard would certainly be cheaper to buy, install and maintain.

Then there is their annual three-week holiday to consider: a cruise to the rocky west, perhaps? Or to the sandy shallows of the east coast?

With these thoughts (and many more) father and mother have to choose between a cat or a tri. But surely they have already come to a decision without realising it?

They have three children, with ages placing the boy between the two girls. Maybe there has always been plenty of argument about the exact time brothers and sisters should be separated in their sleeping quarters, but they are growing fast and this really clinches the matter.

Father, still wanting his tri, is forced to abandon the search. It is true that if he could spare just a leetle more cash he could put his son in the forepeak of a tri of about 35-ft LOA, and his two daughters in the stern cabin, whilst his wife and himself sleep on the wing bunks in the saloon. But not in the size of trimaran he can afford. In a cat, however, with the girls in one float and the boy in the other, with husband and wife between them – well, he has to admit it is a good arrangement. I hope that this fictitious father found a suitably-priced cat, with a neat outboard arrangement, a fair handicap and... But there is no need for me to go on. In this example there can only be one satisfactory answer; in your case I have no doubt that a very similar ruling would apply.

To the out-and-out racing man, who has been expecting me to produce statistics to prove whether a cat or a tri is the better, I can only apologise – and tell him to consult a multihull designer. Even then I doubt if he'll get a really satisfactory answer. The same applies to the dedicated deep-water cruising man. It is not yet time to be too dogmatic about such matters, although I do not excuse myself for stating my personal preferences.

One last consideration you should give some thought to when making your choice is the purely aesthetic approach: which do you think looks better? To some, the two-hull configuration is the more beautiful, whereas others prefer the appearance of three hulls. Don't dismiss this idea as being irrelevant;

it is probably the most important, which is why I asked for your preference in Question 6.

Nobody knows much about the mental processes involved when a man is attracted visually to a particular female. 'God knows what he sees in her', is a two-way criticism implying visual and spiritual mysteries initially, and some male-like wonder at the thought of him waking up each morning and finding that on the pillow. This analogy can be applied to boats, or virtually anything else if it comes to that.

I have made the point in my other books, but it is worth repeating: in the word seamanship, man has been dropped, seemingly unwittingly, between sea and ship. Yet with love and understanding of both the sea and the ship, a threesome marriage is not too far distant – when sea, man and ship will merge as one to reveal an art which should be as delicate as the finest brushwork of an Old Master, or as tough as the building of a pyramid. As an art, seamanship can be taught, but the spirit of man cannot escape from his soul if there is neither love nor understanding within him to strive for perfection with his ability.

You have no choice in your selection of the sea; this you must accept, and at all times be wary of an unrelenting mistress. 'To face the elements is, to be sure, no light matter when the sea is in its grandest mood', wrote Joshua Slocum, the first-ever solo circumnavigator. 'You must then know the sea, and know that you know it, and not forget that it was made to be sailed over.'

But you do have the choice of a vessel, and as this part of the marriage is the only one you can control you should select wisely. If you believe that you love her, you have only to ask yourself one final question: are you prepared to face her on the moorings every morning? Or, to put it another way: will you be proud to show her off to your friends at all times?

When you come to think about it, this is probably the most important decision of all those you will have to make when you are selecting between a catamaran and a trimaran. So don't, whatever you do, sign the marriage certificate until you are quite, quite sure.

5 To Make You Think

When you have arrived at a firm decision as to whether you require a cat or a tri, your next problem is going to be which cat or which tri will be the most suitable for your requirements. The Trimaran Selection Questionnaire which I compiled in 1967 is equally applicable to both cases, so I reproduce it here for you to supply your answers.

1 Surname: 2 Christian Names:

3 Address: 4 Telephone:

5 Age:
Also, please state where you were born (this information may be required later for yacht registration procedure).

6 Height:

7 If married, please quote wife's height:

8 Children (age and sex):

9 Do you require a cat/tri mainly for: coastal cruising? short sea voyages? racing? transoceanic voyages? (cross out items not mainly wanted).

10 If for any of the first three purposes in No. 9, state usual sailing area:

11 And/or home port or moorings:

12 Do you intend to live aboard? (i.e. use the multihull as a houseboat when not cruising):

13 Do you intend to charter? If so, quote area:
Also (a) will you, and/or wife, act as skipper/crew?
      (b) or will you employ a skipper/crew?
      (c) or will you charter without skipper/crew?

14 How many persons do you wish to sleep at the most?

15 How many persons do you wish to sleep on average?

16 (for small multihulls) Is 6-ft headroom essential?

17 Do you wish to:
(a) build the complete multihull yourself?
(b) purchase professionally built hulls, or a semi-completed vessel, and complete the job yourself?
(c) purchase a professionally built multihull?

18 If (a) or (b) above, please state briefly any previous boat-building experience:

19 How much do you want to spend altogether? (quote your maximum figure):

20 Will you require a mortgage? If so, how much out of the maximum total quoted in the previous question?

21 Please state previous sailing experience:
22 Will you want the multihull selected for single-handed sailing at any time?
23 Do you have a preference for the type of building material? (e.g., GRP, sandwich foam, glassed ply, etc.)
24 Do you have a preference for any particular designer?
25 Do you have a preference for any particular builder?
   or do you insist on a multihull constructed in your country?
26 Do you have a preference for an outboard auxiliary, or inboard (petrol or diesel)?

As I have said, over 300 prospective clients used this questionnaire so that I could help them find a suitable craft. As a result of this experience I am able now to offer you some advice on how to do the same thing for yourself. If you follow this method, you should finish up with not more than three possibilities, and probably only one multihull which meets most of your requirements.

First, let me go to the nub of the matter – the vital question which just over 40 per cent of my form-fillers failed to answer. This *bête noire* was No. 19: how much do you want to spend altogether?

I was interested in the reasons why this particular question was dodged so often, and so I asked around. There were two conflicting ideas in people's minds: (1) that it would give me too much of a guide on how much money they had available, and therefore enable me to 'up' the price of a second-hand boat; (2) for a similar psychological reason it could reveal the minimum they were prepared to spend, so that I might be inclined to offer a new boat which would be priced at over this figure in the hope that they would be tempted. (I actually changed the question to read: quote your minimum figure; it made no difference!) Such is the state of the average yachtsman's mind, no doubt as a direct result of big business taking over the boat market!

Now, fortunately, there is nobody to twist you but yourself – and the surprising factor is that the average yachtsman will do just this if he is not very careful. In order to make sure that the same rules are still applicable, I checked at the 1975 London Boat Show; oh yes! nothing much had changed in the nine years since I last exhibited there – apart from the prices of course. The method, however, was much the same, and it is still being worked (as really it must be) to the benefit of boat-builders and to the detriment of yachtsmen. Some call it the 'extras racket', but this is not fair criticism; the motor-car industry has been doing it for many more years with its 'accessories', and the public have continued to purchase unnecessary items for their cars at enormous cost without complaining overmuch – even though they have always known that the profit margins on such goods are very high. But it is different with a boat, isn't it? Or so most of my customers have told me in the past. Many expected me to supply them with all the extras within the quoted price bracket for that design, but it is significant that although I refused they went ahead and ordered a fair proportion of them anyway.

It will be seen that I am leading up to the subject of how much (maximum) you want to spend, by showing you that if your figure is, say £5000, you will automatically think of paying this amount only for the multihull of your choice – whether it is new or second-hand. Unfortunately, you will still be open to the temptation of extras, which is where you will begin to twist yourself. Some months later, when you find that your £5000 multi has actually cost you £6579 you will realise precisely what I have been getting at.

In order to drive this lesson home, I am going to quote retail figures for a Piver trimaran built in 1965, together with a 1965 list of extras. In order to appreciate fully the amount of money which a sales organisation has to make, I am also quoting the figure which I paid to the builders. Now they, too, must make a profit, and because their figure for building a standard trimaran was kept under tight control, I allowed them considerable latitude with their prices for the extras; not only did they charge me the full retail price (collecting, of course, the difference between this and their bulk-buying wholesale price), but they added their labour and overheads, with a profit margin, to this figure. On top of this, I added *my* profit margin. This is what you had to pay for your extras – and I shall never understand why so many yachtsmen, who were (and still are) constantly complaining about the high prices of yachts, continue literally to waste their money on the vast range of extras currently available.

For this example I have chosen a 35 ft × 20 ft × 2 ft 6 in Piver-designed Lodestar (22). In 1965 she cost £3350 (I paid my builders £2550); here is her specification in full at this price:

Standard specification

All our trimarans are built of WBP Phenol-bonded mahogany marine plywood (BSS 1088) on prime selected Columbian Pine frames, chines, gunwales and stringers. Aerolite 300 glue is used throughout with silicon bronze 'Gripfast' nail fastenings. In each case the three hulls and undersurface of the wings are fibreglassed (6 oz cloth) to deck level. A false keel is fastened over the fibreglass under the centre hull to prevent damage when drying out, etc. Unless otherwise stated, all standard craft are supplied with the following fittings: Terylene or Dacron foresail and mainsail (and mizzen), stainless steel rigging (Talurit or Nicopress splices) with SS mast bolts and tangs and SS chainplates with SS bolts, galvanised turnbuckles, Tufnol blocks, yacht sisal halliards and cotton sheets, burgee halliard, pulpit, CQR anchor and 3 fm galv. chain, with 12 fm nylon line, galv. stem fairlead, galv. bollards, cleats and fender eyeplates, galv. fore and main (and mizzen) horses, Tufnol jamb cleats to fore (and mizzen) and mainsheets. Roller reefing to main (and mizzen); reef points to foresail.

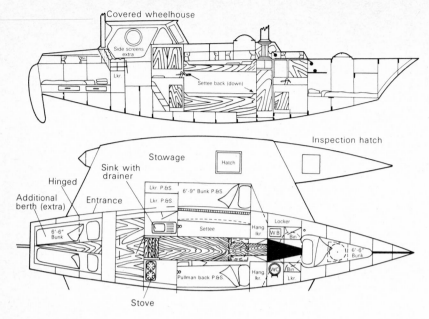

Covered wheelhouse

Side screens extra

Lkr

Settee back (down)

Inspection hatch

Stowage

Hatch

Sink with drainer

Hinged

Additional berth (extra)

Entrance

Lkr. P.&S
Lkr. P.&S
Lkr. P.&S

6'-9" Bunk P.&S

6'-6" Bunk

Settee

Locker

Hang lkr

W.B

Bin

6'-6" Bunk

Hang lkr

WC

Bin

Lkr.

Pullman back P.&S.

Stove

22   Lodestar G/A

Exterior finished with Cerrux marine paint to owner's colour choice, including antifouling, boot-topping, non-slip deck paint on deck and coachroof(s) (if decks and coachroof are fibreglassed as an extra, pigment and sand will be incorporated in the final coat of resin so that the decks need not be repainted), varnish trim, mast(s) and spars. Cockpit sole fibreglassed throughout. Interiors all include: $\frac{1}{4}$-in Perspex windows, Marley Consort flooring (light grained brown), Lionide covered plastic foam seats and backs (red) with plastic foam bunk mattresses (red ticking). Hydra marine toilet with seacocks, varnished mahogany table, black Formica covered sink and cooker surround; white plastic sink with draining board and pump tap, Calor cooker with two burners and grill, Calor 10 lb bottle with regulator, fibreglass water tank(s); wired and fitted with electric lights in saloon, foc's'le (and aft cabin), with lights to all bunks (batteries extra); cupboards, lockers, stowage, etc.

It will be noted that apart from an outboard or inboard auxiliary engine, and batteries for the electric cabin lights, this trimaran only needed her water tanks filled to be ready to go to sea for inshore daytime sailing.

For those who wanted to save money by doing some of the work for themselves, and thereby saving labour charges, I offered Lodestar as a 'shell' (i.e. completed in all respects outside, including sails, but with nothing inside except loose floorboards) for £2800 (cost to me £2175); or just as three hulls

68

and crossarms for £790 (£600), and with the three hulls fibreglassed, £1150 (£860).

Now for the extras which tempted so many. I have extracted these from the standard list which I priced for 1965 in November 1964. I quote only those items which were applicable to Lodestar. The price I paid to the builders for each item is in brackets.

		£	£
1	Supply and wire stern, port and starboard navigation lights	42.50	(31.75)
2	Supply and wire steaming light (required with auxiliary power)	9.50	(7.12)
3	Supply and wire riding light	11.50	(8.21)
4	(a) Fit outboard well in cockpit	16.50	(12.00)
	(b) Supply and fit split plug	26.00	(20.00)
7	Supply and fit 3½-in Kelvin-White compass, with light and built-in corrector	13.50	(11.50)
8	Fit beam shelves and ½-in double rail round decks	82.00	(61.50)
9	Sail covers	20.00	(15.60)
10	Completely sheath deck, coachroof, wheelhouse, etc. in fibreglass	264.00	(198.00)
11	Granulated polystyrene in plastic bags in bow and stern of floats	90.00	(67.00)
12	Henderson diaphragm pump with seacock (2 tons per hour)	22.50	(18.50)
13	Whale gusher pump with seacock (5 tons per hour)	24.50	(19.00)
14	Vortex rotary pump with seacock (8½ tons per hour)	32.00	(28.00)
15	Electric Jabsco Water Puppy pump	26.00	(21.00)
16	(a) Fit extra shrouds to upper spreaders, with SS chain-plates, turnbuckles, etc.	33.00	(28.00)
	(b) Ditto extra masthead shrouds for carrying genoa	36.00	(27.50)
17	Register ship, carve number, paint name	30.50	(28.50)
18	(a) 2 × 70 amp/hr heavy duty 6V lead/acid batteries	16.50	(12.25)
	(b) 2 × 135 amp/hr heavy duty 6V lead/acid batteries in hardwood cases	36.00	(24.25)
20	Extra for polyurethane finish instead of yacht enamel	36.00	(28.00)
21	Supply and fit icebox	29.00	(22.00)
22	Warps or lines (1 × 15 fm 2½-in sisal; 1 × 15 fm 2-in sisal; 1 × 15 fm 3½-in coir; 1 × 5 fm 2½-in and 1 × 5 fm 2-in sisal)	14.50	(12.00)
23	6 plastic foam fenders	6.50	(6.50)
24	5 Roll-a-boat inflatable fenders	10.50	(10.00)

		£	£
25	Supply and fit Sumlog speed and distance indicator	40.00	(40.00)
26	Supply synthetic sheets and halliards	35.00	(28.00)
27	Supply and fit 4 removable screw-type cowl vents at fore and aft of each float	33.50	(25.00)
29	Additional 2 gal plastic water containers (each)	0.50	(0.50)
30	Supply genoa, incl. sheet winches, synthetic sheets and halliards, etc.		
31	Supply nylon spinnaker, with synthetic sheets and halliards, etc.	136.00	(102.00)
32	Supply and fit sail nets (between floats)	35.50	(26.50)
33	Fit hinged flap to seat to make additional single bunk	8.75	(7.00)
35	Steps up mast	4.00	(3.00)
36	Fit signal halliards to both upper spreaders	8.50	(6.50)
37	Fit additional raised bunk in aft cabin of Lodestar, incl. mattress	18.50	(14.00)
38	PVC sidescreens and backscreen (with windows) for covered wheelhouse	28.50	(21.00)
39	Taylor *Para-fin* two-burner stove with grilling oven and fiddle in place of standard Calor arrangement	11.15	(10.15)
40	(a) Fit sliding windows on sides of coachroof	35.00	(27.90)
	(b) Ditto on sides of aft cabin	20.50	(14.50)
41	Fit drip-proof, transparent Skyvents for cabin ventilation		
	6-in inside diameter, each	7.25	(6.35)
	12-in inside diameter, each	25.75	(23.25)
42	Additional cost of alloy anodised and sound-proofed masts and booms instead of standard wood	295.00	(246.00)
43	Supplying club-boom for foresail, complete with galv. forehorse and pedestal	19.00	(14.00)
45	Cockpit cover for open type wheelhouse	36.00	(27.00)
46	Insulators incorporated in backstay for using as aerial	2.00	(1.50)
47	SS turnbuckles, thimbles and shackles throughout, instead of standard galvanised	40.00	(30.00)
48	Additional flipper pump in galley for salt water supply, incl. piping and seacock	15.50	(12.00)
49	Marley Spacesaver doors between toilet and saloon	11.50	(11.00)
50	Supply and fit Shoreway Mk 2 echo-sounder	38.00	(38.00)
	Totals:	£2019.40	£1592.32

If an average customer in 1965 ordered a Lodestar, purchased a 25 hp outboard, accepted some of the items listed here, and added several more of his own devising (which happened frequently), the final bill could easily exceed £5000. As prices have more than trebled in the decade since these figures were compiled, we can assume that for such a Lodestar the price will now be in excess of £11,000, and an average customer will therefore spend in the region of £5000 in extras. So the person who enters £12,000 in answer to Question 19, and then decides that Lodestar is the multihull for him, will almost inevitably finish up by mortgaging his tri in order to pay for the extras. This may be good for boat-builders and sales organisations, but the inevitability of the process should be constantly borne in mind – particularly by those who are new to the sport. And do not forget that since those happy days of my low-priced trimarans the Government now also take their cut in the form of taxes; so in addition to the builder's profit and the salesman's profit and the excessive overheads and the high labour costs... But no doubt you will now answer Question 19 accurately, and never exceed the maximum you have allowed yourself.

It is a safe rule to accept that most people never buy a yacht which subsequently proves to be too big for them. Almost always the reverse is true. Of course, nowadays lack of money can be blamed, but in fact even in the most favourable periods the tendency – particularly amongst newcomers to the sport – seems to be not to commit oneself to too large a yacht. Although to some extent my advice is contrary to the previous paragraph, it is as well to remember that the process of keeping wives and/or children happy on a small yacht depends very much on the space available on deck and down below.

So Question 7 is important, and so are 8, 12, 13 (for somewhat different reasons), 14, 15 and 16. The last five need to be answered with the same degree of thought and honesty as Question 19; once again, avoid cheating yourself.

Having absorbed my remarks so far – and you do not necessarily have to agree with me – your next step is to answer the questionnaire to the best of your ability on a sheet of paper. And there she is! That is the multihull which will most suit your requirements. You can't see her? Well, not to worry. On to the next step.

In the absence of an adviser who, from experience, could immediately begin to visualise the type of multihull you require from these details, you must now begin to collect data on builders and designers of cats or tris (depending on your choice from the previous chapter). From this moment you should begin my Selection Marking System.

On the whole, the human race is a collection of remarkably tolerant people. When they are forced to come to a firm decision about somebody or something, almost always they will compromise somewhere along the line. Perhaps this doesn't apply to politicians, or maybe it does (you see? I'm being tolerant), but if a positive decision were made ignoring tolerance, there is no doubt that we would surprise ourselves with our likes and dislikes. My method is simple; mark everything on a particular project from 1 to 9, but discard the 'tolerance' mark of 5. That is to say:

$$1 \quad 2 \quad 3 \quad 4 \quad - \quad 6 \quad 7 \quad 8 \quad 9$$

So when you write off to various firms and designers for brochures or information, begin your selection procedure by giving marks for the prompt-ness of their replies: 9 if they answer by return of post, 8 within three days, and so on to 1 if they take more than three weeks. Check postmarks: was the letter posted on the same day as it was typed? Check contents: was the reply standard, or was an attempt made to answer all the questions you asked? Check signature: was the letter signed by a director? or manager? or merely 'p.p.'? In your opinion, did they care about your enquiry? Mark accordingly. For the record, my own average for these markings seldom exceeds 4.

I have assumed that, as you are going to spend a fair amount of money on a multihull, you will be aware of the methods of obtaining the names and addresses of various tri/cat builders and/or designers. To those who are puzzled, I suggest they begin by buying some British, American or European (depending on where you live) yachting magazines and taking it from there. However, I will relent to the extent of suggesting that wherever you live in the world, you won't go far wrong if you join the Amateur Yacht Research Society; the subscription is small, their multihull knowledge is great, and they will always be pleased to help those who are lost in the wilderness (see Appendix I for address).

When you are satisfied that you have collected sufficient data to begin the serious marking of your project, you must go through each item in my questionnaire and award it a suitable mark.

For example, take your first self-answerable question, No. 6: your height? Perhaps you are a very short man – let us assume 5 ft 2 in. Obviously you will have no problems about headroom, but I wonder if the designs you are looking at have made allowances enabling a short person to see over the coach-roof when he is standing at the helm? Are the steps up to the deck convenient for your height? Are the winches too high on the mast? And so on. Or if you are 6 ft 8 in, reverse the process. Award your marks to each design accordingly; you will find it easiest to write them on the actual brochure or letter you received.

Already we have three marks, thus:

R	(for speed of Reply)	3
I	(for Interest by firm)	4
6	(answering Question 6)	7

Now continue through the questionnaire marking each multihull according to its suitability for your requirements. Some of the questions will call for more letter-writing to the designer or manufacturers: No. 9, for example, will require a good deal of thought on your part; Nos 18 and 21 should cause some considerable soul-searching. No. 20 depends on your current financial position: if you have to borrow to the maximum, mark low; minimum borrowing (or none) mark high. The same applies to No. 19; if your maximum estimated expenditure is, say, £10,000, and you find a multihull which generally suits your requirements for considerably less, mark high; mark 1 if she costs a penny over your maximum (because you can't really afford her).

The end product of this marking system – if you have been honest with yourself – will consist of a total for each multihull, the highest being the most suitable compromise. Remember, please, that every vessel ever designed by man is essentially a compromise, and the chance of your finding any type of yacht which meets your every requirement is nil. But by using this method, the inexperienced, and even the experienced multihullist can reach a much more satisfactory conclusion than by the haphazard method of scanning brochures and scrounging, or paying for, day trips in various craft. Unfortunately for you, there is still a good deal of work to do before you begin this last, and most pleasant task.

Having isolated the top three or four most suitable multihulls, you must now price each one according to the extras you decide you must have. This, you will soon discover, can be frustrating, since builders vary enormously on how much they 'give' with a standard boat. More letter-writing almost certainly will be required, in which case adjustments to your first marks for 'reply' and 'interest' may be necessary; similarly, you may find that marks given in the questionnaire will also have to be revised.

This second marking will be just as necessary if you are buying a second-hand multihull and not a new boat. In this case, the equipment which goes with each vessel varies a great deal, and it is more than likely that you will have to buy items (or pay for repairs or maintenance) before you can take her to sea. Find out the cost, and add it to the price of the boat in the same way as extras are added to a new vessel. Mark accordingly.

Your heap of brochures (or broker's details in the case of second-hand craft) should now have been reduced hopefully to one, and certainly not more than three possibilities. At long last you are free to investigate the options, sail them, and otherwise deal with them as your fancy dictates. In most respects she will be what you are seeking, but only from visual contact can you begin to be sure. *Never* buy an unsighted boat of any sort: photogenic actresses seldom look as delicious in the flesh, and although as a young man you may have fallen in love with a picture, in later years you will be very glad that you were not one of her several husbands!

We come now to a rather delicate point: from whom do you seek advice before committing yourself to such a large investment? It is no use asking the builder of the multihull you have selected; with the best will in the world, he cannot help being biased. In my experience, asking a multihull designer to discuss his, or other designs, is even worse; designers, like most other professionals in the arts, tend to live in a world of their own. I keep on admitting that I am biased, but I am certainly in a more neutral position than most since I neither design nor build.

In the case of either a new or a second-hand cat or tri I believe you have only one satisfactory course of action: employ a fully-qualified yacht surveyor. I'm afraid there is a chance that he, too, will be biased, but since you are paying for his professional advice I believe he is unlikely to let this creep into his report. Don't, whatever you do, go to a monohull yachtsman (no matter how experienced), a yacht club, a longshoreman or fisherman, a naval officer, or anybody who is 'connected with the sea'. I imply no disrespect, but such men of the sea are only experienced in the particular ability for which they have been trained. And don't expect unbiased criticism from a multihull yachtsman – again, no matter how experienced; he will certainly know what he is talking about, but the chances are that he will be either cat- or tri-oriented, and therefore he will undoubtedly want to convert you to his way of thinking. No, a qualified surveyor is easily your best bet.

Most people expect to employ a surveyor if they are buying a second-hand boat, but I suspect that not many give much thought to the idea when the vessel is new. After all, when you are paying a great deal of money for a multihull you are bound to think that she is in all respects fit to go to sea. I regret that this is seldom the case. Big business in western countries has titivated yachts, both externally and internally, to such a degree that even experienced yachtsmen have fallen for their charms – and forgotten to look deeper than the visible skin beauty. This, as every motorist should know, is exactly the same process as has been applied to automobiles; employ a qualified engineer to inspect your expensive, brand-new car before you drive away from the showrooms, and you will receive an unpleasant surprise!

So I suggest that whether you are buying a new or a second-hand multihull, you employ a professional to survey fully the boat of your choice. His charges for all the work involved are nowhere near as high as labour costs in other industries, and although it is inadvisable to visit him during the survey, afterwards he will be glad to answer any questions about the vessel you may want to put to him. *Don't attempt to obtain such information on the cheap.* There are many 'experts' and unqualified surveyors who will always be wasting your money. I have been asked many times by customers to survey tris for them, but I have always refused to carry out a full survey, even when I have been responsible for the building. I am not a trained surveyor, and I value my reputation. For a small sum I have occasionally given a tri I know the 'once-over', to see whether a detailed investigation is worthwhile, and on one special occasion I completed a top survey; but knowing something of the complexities of the skill incorporated in the art, I'd have to be given exceptional reasons before becoming involved. Make no mistake about it, yacht surveying is a skill which is worth every penny charged; don't cheat yourself here.

Another temptation may be the apparently low price of a second-hand multihull. Since I have given the financial facts about Lodestar, I will continue in the same vein. Seven were launched in Britain during 1965, five were privately owned, and two were for a charter firm based in the Mediterranean. I have seen three of these seven offered on the second-hand market, one of which was priced at more than double its original cost; another at substantially more than was paid in the first place; the third for just over its new price, seven years later. It can be argued that these figures are excellent reasons for looking for bargains in the second-hand market. Of the three I have quoted, you may well believe that the last might be worth investigating. But what you don't know, and what even a surveyor is unlikely to find out, are that these seven 'standard' Lodestars were all very different from each other.

To start with, one, *Three Wishes*, was specifically built for the 1965 London Boat Show. Since we were showing her on the Pool, I can vouch that the builders excelled themselves with the finish (although I must say that *all* tris they launched were both well-built and beautifully finished), and I know that the boat contains most of the extras quoted in my list. So this particular tri (actually launched just before Christmas 1964, sailed to London docks, taken by road to Earls Court, re-launched after the Show and sailed to Sweden for her new owner during January 1965) was an exceptional example. At the other end of the scale was a 'shell' which was sailed across the Channel to Europe for completion by her owner. Now he may well have made an excellent job of the interior, and installed a lightweight engine, but it is more than likely that in spite of my dire warnings he over-elaborated the inside furnishings and fitted a substantial diesel auxiliary; I don't know if it was so in this case, but I do know that this was the general trend at that time both in Europe and America.

If you were offered the latter tri second-hand, it could quite correctly be described as 'built by British craftsmen experienced in trimaran construction over many years', or something like that. If this Lodestar had been 'converted' as I have suggested, you would undoubtedly be buying a pig in a poke – and what is worse, this pig could by now be suffering internal ailments not easily discernible, unless the facts were realised by the surveyor you employed as a result of my advice. He could not be well-versed in the history of each and every multihull which has been launched; even I cannot remember the building histories of each of the 162 trimarans which I ordered during the 1961–6 period when I was responsible for so doing. Of the 326 plans sold to amateur builders during these five years I can say very little since nobody knows how many trimarans were actually completed, or were part-built, resold, and finished by someone else or even a third party – and so on. I have seen conversions of 'conversions' and, worse, trimarans 'based' on designers' plans. A qualified surveyor will certainly be of considerable help with any of these cases.

It should also be noted that in the early days of multihull building both cats and tris suffered a great deal from 'modifications' – a disease inherent in the development of almost any man-made object, particularly when capital is lacking. It should be remembered that with the best will in the world a modification is not necessarily an improvement. The designer, the builders, or even a bystander such as myself may think of a modification which will improve the boat, and build it into the next one off the production line. When tested, however, the 'mod' may not be quite as good as was expected, and so the production line is changed once again, or reverts to the original. There is one Lodestar still sailing which has... No! wild horses will not make me reveal the horrible truth which hasn't yet been discovered, and probably never will be – even by a qualified surveyor. I will only state categorically that this particular 'mod' was not, and never will be, harmful to either the tri or the owner – my builders' and my conscience is clear on that point; but when I think about what we did...

I hope I have shown that buying a second-hand multihull is not necessarily the best route for the impecunious to follow. Even with monohulls there are many difficulties and pitfalls, but long experience has enabled qualified surveyors to establish a routine which, while not 100 per cent foolproof, can be regarded as an above-average or excellent guide. I don't think multihulls have been around long enough for surveyors to be able to give more than average to slightly-above-average guidance. In percentages, I would expect around 95 per cent accuracy of opinion from a monohull survey, but only 50–70 per cent from the same surveyor after working on a multihull. I do not intend this in any derogatory sense; sea time is an essential adjunct to becoming a qualified surveyor, and I cannot believe that sufficient knowledge has yet been gained from this section of training in the few years since tris and cats have become established. Nevertheless 50–70 per cent guidance from a professional is better than all the opinions you can get for nothing, or the price of a drink, at any yacht club bar or similar place.

A common mistake made by many who are new to multihulls is to buy on the reputation of a name – either of the designer or the builder. For obvious reasons I cannot go into details, but the lessons learned from the changing fortunes of the car industry in any country in the world can be cited as good examples. Rolls-Royce, for instance, are no longer controlled by the men who made the name famous; are the equivalents in the multihull (or the monohull) world as good as they were before big business (or nationalisation) took over? I do not think so, but it is more than likely that your reasoning on this subject will be different from mine. I mention the point so that you will give it some thought – according to your standards, not mine.

Finally, we come to the problems which beset the home builder. I submit that the best way of selecting a plan for a tri or a cat is to follow the marking procedure I have described as though he were buying a new boat. Three additional questions, however, will make a slight difference to the total marks for each design considered.

HB.1   Can you clearly understand the plans and building instructions?
HB.2   What undercover space do you have available for building?
HB.3   Suitability of design to distance from water and launching facilities?

Home builders' question No. 1 is certainly up to you. HB2 and 3 could mean that you will have to go back to Chapter 4 and reconsider whether a catamaran or a folding-wing trimaran would not be more manageable in the circumstances. It is always advisable to build a boat under cover, even in the sort of climate that precludes worry about wind, rain, sleet and snow: modern glues, plastic/resin application, building materials (including timber), and even the casual workforce, require some degree of temperature control which cannot usually be attained in the open air. You may have enough ready money to build a 60-footer, but if you do not have the space, suitably wide roads to the sea or launching facilities, there is not really much point in building her. This may sound a rather stupid and obvious factor, but it is surprising how often the obvious takes amateur builders unawares.

There was the sad case of one such person who built a Lodestar on the banks of the Upper Congo twelve years ago, only to discover that some impossible-to-shoot rapids lay between his new creation and the sea, and that the forest-fringed roads in the area prevented transport by land. What could he do? He asked me this over a lunchtime beer on one of his infrequent visits to England.

'Well, you can't sail her, and you can't trail her – so you'll have to fly her', I told him, fortified by the beer and secure in the knowledge that for once it wasn't my can to carry. 'Ask the Americans if they have a helicopter handy.'

That Lodestar was flown to the nearest section of river which was navigable to the sea, and the customer was delighted with my perspicacity. As a result, the streamlined design of Lodestar can now be marked as 9 in answer to Question HB.3 if the air is your only possible means of transport!

It makes you think.

I hope it does, because the contents of this chapter were written with this object in view, and it is from these thoughts that your entirely suitable cat or tri should in due course materialise.

6　The Amateur Builder

By far the greatest proportion of enquiries which I receive about trimarans comes from potential amateur builders. The phenomenon does not occur nearly as much with catamarans, except in a few isolated cases (e.g., Jim Wharram's range of Polynesian designs). I suspect that the main reason for this is the enormous interest in home building which Piver's designs instigated; so tris led the field from the beginning.

It is, of course, much cheaper for you to build your own multihull than to have it built for you. Wages throughout the world have risen to such an extent that you can safely reckon on at least halving the retail price if you are able to cut costs by doing the work yourself. But is your work free? We shall see.

The average person's knowledge of carpentry and joinery is no better than the average yachtsman's knowledge of shipwrighting. At best it is barely professionally average; below this standard it could be considered as positively dangerous – except that so many amateurs, completely unskilled, have not only built tris and cats, but have sailed them successfully across oceans. So the pundits have been proved wrong over and over again.

I admire an enthusiast who cannot afford the price of a new boat and is prepared to roll up his sleeves and devote anything up to five years (and occasionally more) to the oh-so-long-process of building his own multihull. I know that his satisfaction as a result of completing the task will greatly increase his joy of ownership, and the process will certainly improve his self-reliance, but – and the big snag lies with that one word 'but' – from the many multihull plans sold to amateur builders I estimate that less than half are actually completed; and of these probably as many as 50 per cent did not even get started. Why does this happen? Why that 'but'?

The answer is that all too often dreamers are not very practical about their approach to home building; they tend to think in terms of completion when they approach the initial stages, with the result that when the actual hard work has to begin they are horrified at the enormity and the cost of the task still ahead. It happens something like this. First they read about somebody who has built a multihull, sailed to the South Seas, and written an article or a book on it. They begin to think how nice it would be to do the same thing and get away from it all. At this stage they usually dream about escaping for ever, but later practicalities generally tie them down to 'a few years'.

Almost always this type of dreamer then goes to the designer of the multi-hull he has read about, and in the early years this invariably meant Arthur Piver or Jim Wharram. Enquiries about the cost of plans and/or a completed craft make it clear that the latter is a financial impossibility (even if the house, the car, and all the other assets are sold), but... 'well, let's buy the plans and have a look at them'. Plans spread all about the living-room floor, especially in mid-winter with crises all around and warning fingers of doom being wagged, are conducive to excellent escapist dreaming. 'When she's finished', he says – whether he's head of a family, or a loner makes no difference – 'we'll get to hell out of this mess and sail away to...' The multi-hull is already built in his mind. 'Can't start her now', he mumbles as an icy gale rattles the windows, 'but next spring...' Launch her, and sail away in the autumn, he thinks, before the equinoctial gales... Money, he muses, well I've enough to buy some timber; make a start, that's the idea, but keep on with my job till the last possible moment... Just wait until I tell the boss what he can do with his job... No, I won't tell him, I'll just walk out... By golly! he dreams, I'll send him photographs of how we're enjoying life in the South Seas; I'll make him so bloody jealous that...

There is no need for me to go on; you can see why he will never make it.

Don't be misled by your dreams. At the same time do not be afraid to use your imagination. Your survival, whether you intend to get away from it all, or merely build a yacht for weekend sailing, depends enormously on your imagination, since this is your only method of pre-viewing the many stages between the conception and the conclusion of your self-determined ambition. However, there is nothing airy-fairy about the process of building your own boat; regard it simply as a business venture and maybe – maybe! – you'll succeed. (It is as well to remember that not all businesses, even with seemingly excellent ideas, necessarily make good.)

So back to the beginning: as a result of reading a book, an article, or for any other reason, you have begun to dream...

Well, you are lucky in one respect because you have this book in your hands, and you have only to turn back to Chapters 4 and 5 in order to work out whether it is a cat or a tri that you want, and what class of cat or tri best meets your requirements. You can begin this task at once, and it won't cost you very much either. Mark you, it will be several weeks before you can finally reach a decision and the initial frustrations caused by tardy correspondence will begin to temper your self-control, an essential quality in a seaman. Nature has a habit of teaching this lesson by harsher methods.

The item in my Multihull Selection Questionnaire which will give you some difficulty is – once again – No. 19: How much do you want to spend altogether? At this stage you need a rough idea of how much it is going to cost you to complete the multihull of your choice. While it is difficult to suggest rules about pricing in these inflationary days, you will not be far out if you cost initially, cat or tri, on the following rising scale, the totals including a suitable auxiliary engine, professionally made sails and a reasonable (but not fancy) inventory.

LOA(in feet)	£ per foot	$US per foot
20–25	60	150
26–30	100	250
31–35	150	400
36–40	200	500
41–46	300	750
over 46	400	1000

This price scale is based on the largest multihull in each section, e.g., a 30-footer will cost about £3000 or $US7500 to complete. A 28-footer will cost proportionately less, around £84 per foot; total, in round figures (always round upwards, never down), £2400 or $US6000. I stress that this method of pricing is only for initial guidance; it is by no means accurate, and by the time this book is published the figures quoted may well be too low. But the rise in cost according to size will still give a general idea of the pattern, which will enable you to award at least a provisional mark when answering Question 19.

A common mistake during these initial stages is either to think prices down, or to avoid the obvious. For example, the cost of building a 30-ft multihull which is intended only for local sailing and occasional short coastal cruises is not going to be nearly as much as that of a similar vessel built specifically for, say, a circumnavigation which will include rounding Cape Horn. Yet an optimistic dreamer in the latter class will invariably avoid such unpleasant details. I recommend adding 20 per cent to the price estimated in my tables if your intentions are to sail in deep water. Equally, those who build 'to get away from it all' hardly ever consider that there is a price for everything, and although the actual process of sailing across an ocean may cost them nothing, they will certainly have to pay a lot of money before they depart, with more expenditure when they get to their destination. Therefore, the escapist home-builder should begin now by adding an arbitrary figure to the estimated cost of building his multihull. He is going to have to pay sometime; it is as well to have some idea of the costs at the outset.

Since, at this stage, I am dealing only with approximations, the following table will enable you to put a figure on your intentions.

Intention	Boat expenses only (per year) (% of estimated cost obtained from table on page 81)	Personal expenses per year – cost solo
1 Local (50-mile radius)	4–8	1 unit
2 Short coastal cruises	5–10	1·7 units
3 Short foreign cruises	10–15	2·3 units
4 'Away from it all'	5–20	2·7 units

(NOTE: I have used a 'unit' to indicate the cost for a single-hander in order to avoid currency complications. You should have no difficulty in arriving at a figure to represent one unit if you ask around wherever you live and average out all the answers you receive.)

I will concede that these figures are arbitrary, but the amateur builder must understand clearly that pricing up timber, fittings and accessories is only a small part of his commitment. I have only quoted the average cost per year solo because this is the lowest possible denominator; perhaps two can live as cheaply as one – that is up to you. These figures, too, only apply to multihulls based in the Temperate Zone; it is impracticable to quote here for every eventuality. And even then I have assumed the lowest practical cost of keeping a boat and living cheaply. Insurance is not included, nor are expensive marina facilities. Numbers 1, 2 and 3 in the above table relate to seasonal yachting (e.g. 6 months afloat, 6 months laid up). Number 4 needs further explanation.

As a result of reading many hundreds of books about blue-water cruising over a period of some forty years, I discovered that in the past a reasonably safe rule for a rough costing of a low-priced circumnavigation for two persons could be quoted as double the price of a second-hand or home-built boat, or the cost again of a new boat. I doubt if this rule is still applicable, since materials and wages have risen more than the average costs of living afloat. For example, a professionally-built 30-ft trimaran is currently priced at much more than you would have to pay to sail her round the world in company with another person. Yet only ten years ago a protracted four-year circumnavigation by two people would have cost as much as they would have spent on their new 30-ft ocean cruiser.

So now, using my table, you will see that a four-year 'away-from-it-all' cruise for two on a 30-ft multihull would cost a minimum of £600 ($US1500), 4 × 5 per cent of £3000, plus 4 × 2·7 units (assuming that two can live as cheaply as one, which I don't believe). In fact, to be on the safe side you

8 A 32 ft 6 in ×
19 ft Herald

9 A 35 ft × 20 ft
Lodestar

8 and 9 When wings
cannot be folded,
transport is still
possible – with or
without special
permission. For
road haulage in
these circum-
stances a catama-
ran has a slight
advantage with its
narrower beam,
but for fair
distribution of
physical effort a
tri has more hull
area for spacing
out volunteer
lifters.

10 A 37 ft 4 in × 17 ft 6 in MacLear & Harris Bahama cat demonstrates why multihulls have to pay more at Marinas – in this case two monohulls of the same length could obviously fit into this dock.

11 (*below*) British designer John Westell proved that a berthed tri need be no wider than a cat with his manually operated variable-beam Ocean Bird 30 of 1966. His latest version, 37 ft 6 in *Wings*, reduces the beam of 27 ft to 17 ft in two minutes by hydraulic pumps – and so she takes up fractionally less space than the Bahama catamaran.

12 and 13   Two good reasons why a tri is a safer ocean
cruiser than a cat.

12 (*above*)   This 42-ft Hedley Nicol
design was run down
at night by a 150-ft
Mexican fishing boat
travelling at 10–15
knots. Nobody was
hurt, and the tri made
port under her own
power.

13   The story of the Lodestar *Om*
is told in *Trimaran Development*;
this picture was taken shortly
after her 1500-mile voyage to
salvation after a cyclone had
smashed off the port float in
the middle of the Tasman Sea.

14　Excellent evidence of the ability of multihulls to remain afloat – even when holed in all hulls. In 1973, New Zealand owner Gerald Hunter (aged 68) sailed his Nimble *Clansman* towards the mainland after she had been accidentally holed on some offshore rocks. Later she was towed into Whangarei, where this picture was taken.

should work throughout to the maximum figures: 4 × 20 per cent of estimated price of boat plus 2 (persons) × 4 (years) × 2·7 (units). In other words, it will probably cost something like £6000 ($US15,000), for two people to sail in reasonable comfort around the world. And even now you have only been working from the estimated figure for building a standard cruising multihull. I recommend adding 20 per cent to the cost for building an ocean cruiser; so by rounding *up* these figures you will need about £10,000 ($US25,000) for this little venture, and even with this amount you will be a long way from doing it in luxury. However, more about this subject in Chapter 7.

The enthusiast who is building only because he cannot afford a new cat or tri does not have quite so many financial problems. A 30-footer for local and short coastal cruises will currently cost him around £3000 ($US7500) to build, plus about 10 per cent of this figure per year to maintain (including laying up and launching), and probably not much more again for his partner and himself to enjoy an average total of 40–45 complete days afloat in every year. If he does all or most of the maintenance himself, this amount may be sufficient to include insurance cover as well as the many other small items such as fuel for the auxiliary and/or generator, bottled gas, etc. A simple sum will show this owner that his pleasure is probably going to cost him about 50 pence, or $US1.25, an hour, day and night, for his 45 days of sport, not including the depreciation on his £3000 investment (which, incidentally, will very nearly double the running cost!).

It can be seen from these examples why the dreamer can never succeed, except in his own mind. The cost of building and sailing your own boat is always more than you thought it would be. On the assumption that a few intelligent readers have not yet given up because they had already come to similar conclusions, the time has arrived to get on with the job of building the multihull of your choice. Or has it?

I'm sorry to say that we're nowhere near that stage yet, for although I may have sorted out some dreamers by quoting cash facts, it is now necessary to weed our budding shipwrights by mentioning working-hours facts.

Although he would never admit it, the average man is a very sheep-like person. By that I mean he generally prefers to abide by indoctrinated habits rather than his own self-discipline. Needless to say, the average man may not agree with such an outrageous statement. Nevertheless, the moment he is on his own he tends to strip off the rigid bands which so far have kept his nose to the grindstone, and unless he imposes self-discipline even more firmly than the enforced routine applied by his previous masters, he stands a good chance of getting precisely nowhere.

Some designers of multihulls quote the approximate man-hours it takes to build each of their designs. Since I have been mentioning 30-footers in this chapter, I will keep to this size. The average time quoted for an amateur to build a 30-footer, either cat or tri, is approaching 1500 man-hours. This may not sound too bad at first, but translated into normal working time it represents 190 eight-hour days for one man, or 95 for two men. Letters I have received from home builders indicate that nearly all the multihull designers are rather optimistic about the time they allow for doing the job. A knowledgeable amateur who understands how to organise his labour can certainly come close to the designer's building time, but the beginner – no! I advise him to add half as much again. For it is not only work on the multihull that you have to accomplish, there is also the tedious and patience-testing task of chasing up materials, etc. And that alone will add many a long weary hour.

Then again, what about the place which you are going to call your building shed? How many man-hours (and how much money) will you have to expend here? At the other end of your task, how much time will it take to restore the shed to its original condition after you have left (assuming you have had to rent the place); and while we're on the subject don't forget the considerable number of man-hours (and expenditure) which will be needed for the process of taking your boat to water.

Let us assume you are satisfied that you can include all this in a grand total of 250 working days. Are you going to work seven days a week? Even at this pace it is going to take you nine months; on a six-day week it will be more than ten months. What are you going to live on during this period? Your capital? If this is your decision I sincerely hope that you have remembered to add it to the cost of your boat. If you are married, with children, and are building in your back yard, this figure will be high; if you are a loner, building in a borrowed shed and living in rooms, the figure may well be proportionally higher. Work it out and see.

How much is your 'free' time costing now?

But you're not going to give up your job until the boat is built? Fair enough; yet have you considered the appalling task of working at two jobs? An eight-hour normal working day, followed by a meal, a brief rest and, say, a four-hour working evening, with eight hours each on Saturdays and Sundays, means that this 30-footer is going to take you over fifteen months of unrelenting work. By halving the hours on 178 full days, and thereby having to double the overall time to 356 days, you have automatically also doubled the time wastage per shift in starting and cleaning up, thereby extending the estimated completion date even further. And when are you going to find time to chase supplies, choose chandlery, order sails and an auxiliary, and otherwise complete the extensive paperwork with which you must become involved? Without any doubt, your total time will be eighteen months or more if you take all these matters into consideration.

Before you consider the next step, you should in all seriousness ask yourself: Is it worth it? If you think it is, ask yourself this: Have I the self-discipline to force myself to work like this continuously for eighteen months? Another way of looking at it: Could I take an eighteen-month prison sentence in my stride? If you are married, with or without children: Will your wife resent becoming a grass widow? or Will your wife maintain interest, and patience, for all this time? Whether she helps you on the job or not, this last question is equally applicable. Perhaps the best judgement can be made if you consider the ultimate question faced by so many husbands in this situation: Do I care if my wife divorces me as a result of this venture? If your answer is an emphatic No, then I think you should go ahead and build your dream-multihull – undoubtedly you are seeking a dramatic change, and I have no doubt that you will find it. If your answer is Yes, you should have a very careful rethink of the whole project.

And so at last we have arrived at the moment of truth when you are nearly ready to order the plans which my selection questionnaire and marking system have revealed as the best for your requirements. Now is the time to write off to the designers of the highest-marked selections and obtain from them a materials list.

For those readers who have never seen one, here is a Norman A. Cross materials list for a Cross 30 chine trimaran (23). I have picked the design

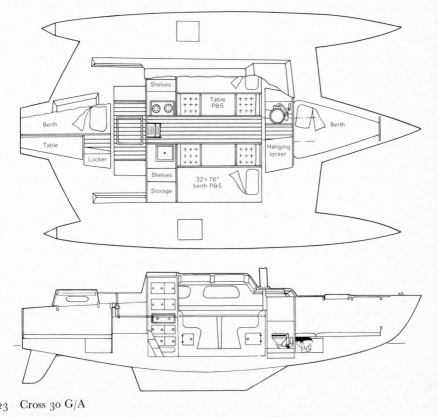

23 Cross 30 G/A

because in this chapter I have been using a 30-footer as an example, because these plans are now obsolete and therefore I will not be accused of favouritism, and because the chine configuration, built with ply, is the cheapest to construct of all the many alternatives on the market. Here, then, if you want to practise costing, is one of the lowest-priced 30-ft trimarans you could have found on the market.

Plywood: Marine Grade

$\frac{1}{4}$ in × 4 ft × 8 ft	14 sheets
$\frac{1}{4}$ in × 4 ft × 10 ft	4 sheets
$\frac{3}{8}$ in × 4 ft × 10 ft	12 sheets
$\frac{1}{2}$ in × 4 ft × 8 ft	1 sheet
$\frac{1}{2}$ in × 4 ft × 10 ft	3 sheets

Plywood: Exterior AB Grade (Marine Optional)

$\frac{1}{4}$ in × 4 ft × 8 ft	6 sheets
$\frac{3}{8}$ in × 4 ft × 8 ft	30 sheets
$\frac{3}{8}$ in × 4 ft × 10 ft	2 sheets
$\frac{1}{2}$ in × 4 ft × 8 ft	3 sheets
$\frac{1}{2}$ in × 4 ft × 10 ft	3 sheets
$\frac{3}{4}$ in × 4 ft × 8 ft	2 sheets
$\frac{3}{4}$ in × 4 ft × 10 ft	1 sheet

Douglas Fir or other light boat-building lumber

Size (finished)	Linear feet
$\frac{3}{4}$ in × $\frac{3}{4}$ in	36
$\frac{3}{4}$ in × 1 in	100
$\frac{3}{4}$ in × $1\frac{1}{2}$ in	200
$\frac{3}{4}$ in × 2 in	150
$\frac{3}{4}$ in × $2\frac{1}{2}$ in	645
$\frac{3}{4}$ in × $3\frac{1}{2}$ in	150
$\frac{3}{4}$ in × $5\frac{1}{2}$ in	120
$\frac{3}{4}$ in × $7\frac{1}{2}$ in	8
1 in × 1 in	60
1 in × 2 in	120
1 in × $2\frac{1}{2}$ in	60
1 in × $3\frac{1}{8}$ in	60
$1\frac{5}{8}$ in × $1\frac{5}{8}$ in	80
$1\frac{5}{8}$ in × $3\frac{5}{8}$ in	50
2 in × 3 in	10

Boom   2 pieces $1\frac{1}{8}$ in × $4\frac{1}{4}$ in × 16 ft
Mast   2 pieces $\frac{13}{16}$ in × $6\frac{1}{4}$ in × 33 ft
Jib Boom   2 pieces $2\frac{1}{4}$ in × $2\frac{1}{4}$ in × 9 ft

Tiller: Mahogany   1 in × 6 in × 7 ft
Glass   6 oz 50 in wide 150 lin yd
Resin   30 gal
Glue-Resorcinal or Urac; Nails (anchorfast or galvanised)

Alternatives in catamarans are rare. Easily the most popular do-it-yourself cats are those designed by James Wharram. Here is a materials list for his 34 ft × 15 ft 6 in × 1 ft 6 in Tangaroa class (24) (not to be confused with the 23 ft 6 in *Tangaroa* in which he crossed the Atlantic in 1956–7). With a waterline length of 28 ft 6 in to Cross 30's 27 ft 2 in (30 ft × 17 ft 6 in × 3 ft 3 in), the comparison is reasonably close.

Plywood: Marine Grade
$\frac{3}{8}$ in × 4 ft × 8 ft   55 sheets

Douglas Fir or Canadian Red Pine

	Linear feet
1 in × 1 in	20
1½ in × 1 in	520
2 in × 1 in	1040
2½ in × 1 in	140
3 in × 1 in	1586
4 in × 1 in	490

	Quantity
3½ in × 1½ in × 7 ft 6 in	4
4 in × 3 in × 4 ft	8
6 in × 1 in × 28 ft	2
7 in × 1 in × 6 ft	2
8 in × 1 in × 28 ft	4
8 in × 1 in × 6 ft	2
8 in × 1 in × 8 ft	2
8½ in × 1 in × 5 ft	2
8½ in × 1 in × 3 ft 6 in	2
9 in × 1 in × 8 ft	2
9 in × 1 in × 6 ft	2
9 in × 1 in × 28 ft	2
10 in × 1 in × 8 ft	2
10 in × 1 in × 6 ft	2

Masts (Bermudan rig)
5½ in × 5½ in × 30 ft
4 ft × 4 ft × 26 ft

Booms

$$4\tfrac{1}{2} \text{ in} \times 2 \text{ in} \times 12 \text{ ft } 3 \text{ in}$$
$$3\tfrac{1}{2} \text{ in} \times 1\tfrac{1}{2} \text{ in} \times 11 \text{ ft}$$

Various

	Quantity
$5 \text{ in} \times 1\tfrac{1}{2} \text{ in} \times 12 \text{ ft}$	2
$2 \text{ in} \times 1 \text{ in} \times 10 \text{ ft}$	2
$8 \text{ in} \times 3 \text{ in} \times 5 \text{ ft } 8 \text{ in}$	2
$6 \text{ in} \times 1\tfrac{1}{2} \text{ in} \times 1 \text{ ft } 11 \text{ in}$	4
$5 \text{ in} \times 1\tfrac{1}{2} \text{ in} \times 1 \text{ ft } 1 \text{ in}$	2
$2 \text{ in} \times 2 \text{ in} \times 2 \text{ ft}$	4

Anchorfast Nails (or similar)

$$48 \text{ lb of } 1\tfrac{1}{4} \text{ in}$$
$$18 \text{ lb of } 2\tfrac{1}{4} \text{ in}$$

Work it out, and remember that the cost is only for the bare shell: paint, sails, rope, fittings – a seemingly endless list of necessities will have to be added in due course. But if you cost the basic materials for the fittings which you have discovered by means of completing my questionnaire, you should be able to come to a final decision.

So this is it, and there should be no lingering doubt now: send off your cheque to the designer for the plans of your choice.

It could be argued that it would be more sensible for an amateur builder to work out the total cost before he sends off for the plans. I don't agree. The awful warnings I have listed in the first part of this chapter should be sufficient to make even the most unthinking amateur wary of rising costs. Since he cannot really visualise his requirements until he studies the plans, he must realise by now that the price he has worked out so far is a long way from the grand total he is going to have to pay in the end. After all, his expenditure so far is not very great: the cost of envelopes and writing paper, stamps, telephone calls, and mileage for his car, plus the price of the plans.

You have now reached a crossroads on your personal route through life: to build or not to build? That is the question.

Once the timber and essential materials are ordered, delivered and paid for, you are on the losing side until the boat is built. This capital expenditure will lie as financial dead meat, rotting, for as long as you care to dither and procrastinate. It cannot turn into an asset until you have sweated life into it. So this is a genuine moment of truth for you: to build or not to build?

Have you made your decision? I wonder if you realise that whether you have committed yourself to yea or nay, you have just made what will probably turn out to be one of the most momentous decisions of your life. I hope you will not regret it.

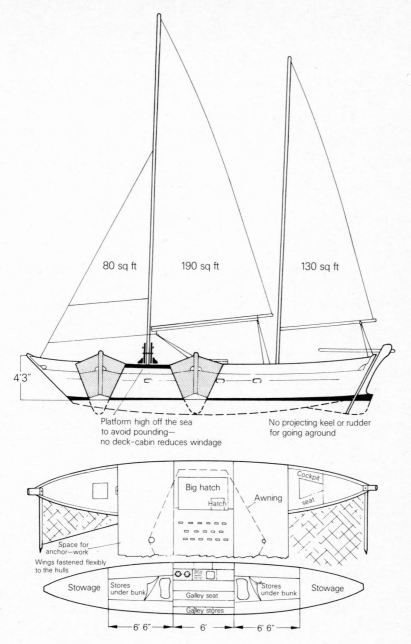

80 sq ft　190 sq ft　130 sq ft

4'3"

Platform high off the sea
to avoid pounding—
no deck-cabin reduces windage

No projecting keel or rudder
for going aground

Cockpit

Big hatch

Hatch

Awning

seat

Space for
anchor—work

Wings fastened flexibly
to the hulls

Stowage

Stores
under bunk

Galley seat

Stores
under bunk

Stowage

Galley stores

6' 6"　6'　6' 6"

24　Tangaroa 34 G/A

A few tips

I am not going to tell you how to build your multihull. In the first place
I have never attempted this frightful task, and I only know building from
a professional supervisory point of view; in the second place, I assume that
your 'yea' included an assessment of your capabilities in the woodworking
craft – particularly since you have had every opportunity to study the plans.
I will not even recommend a book on the subject, because only you can decide
what is best for you. If you have discovered already that you made the wrong
choice, your only hope is to go to evening classes and learn the subject
thoroughly while your timber rots.

There are, however, a few general tips, only indirectly connected with
building, which books and evening classes are unlikely to give you.

Insurance. It is a surprising fact that few home builders bother to insure
against the considerable risks of constructing a multihull in their own grounds.
Inevitably, friends come to have a look, but a good pal can quickly turn
into a nasty-minded enemy if he, or she (or worse, a child belonging to them)
gets injured by any one of the several hundred hazards which will be lying
around your project awaiting the unwary. You, too, could succumb! Three
months in hospital will upset your careful calculations more than somewhat.
And what about your wife? your children? fire? shed (or temporary plastic
erection) collapsing? And so on.

Then again, if you are not building in your own place, what about theft?
third-party accidents? damage during unloading of materials? damage to
rented (or loaned) property? And so on.

Don't forget about insurance, and even if you decide not to have yourself
and your risks covered, make sure that you take out common law coverage
for third parties to at least ten times the annual salary you would like to
be earning. It need not be expensive, but wherever you are in the world
it is as well to remember that there are certain 'third parties' who regard
people who can afford to build their own yachts as fair game for 'accidents'.
If you are the unlucky victim of such a plot, you will not survive their financial
demands unless you are adequately insured.

Tools. I very nearly left this subject alone, since the only tools I have ever
used with any enjoyment are a sailmaker's palm and needle, a rigger's spike,
and a pen. I have used just about every other type of tool in a large number
of different jobs, but of the three I have loved only the pen remains. And
this can scarcely count as 'working with my hands'. So who am I to tell
you what you should do?

Almost every household has a collection of tools which, even if not handed
down over the years, are near-useless junk. Don't try to save money by using
them. Your requirements for building a multihull which in due course may
be worth a lot of money are surprisingly few. I am not going to list them

because they vary, but I recommend that you begin by buying the essentials, and that you pay a good price for the best. You will never regret it.

Specialist tools (e.g., stapling gun for double diagonal ply construction) can often be rented. Any reputable tool shop will put you on the right track for this sort of item, or your timber suppliers may be able to help.

Building shed. I have already mentioned that in my opinion building under cover is essential, even if the weather in your part of the world is perfect. The direct rays of the sun can be as damaging to modern materials as rain and frost. If you have no alternative but to construct a temporary shed of plastic sheeting, do not be misled by the apparent strength of this material; some wind, some chafe, some sun (and the temptation to small boys) will soon reduce even nylon-reinforced plastic to tatters. A tilt, or canvas sheeting, at least over the top, will prevent insidious attacks by rain and sun. Such tilts can be hired, but the cost is high. An alternative is to slat the roof section closely with laths which can be obtained cheaply in the form of offcuts from any large timber yard; then cover with black plastic sheeting and secure by nailing through more laths on top. The sides can be shielded with quite thin-gauge clear plastic sheeting which is cheap and can therefore be renewed from time to time.

Never try to save money by building in a shed that is too small for the completed boat – you'll only lose working hours. A 30-ft × 18-ft trimaran needs a working space of 40 ft × 24 ft (minimum) – although 50 ft × 30 ft would be more suitable. If the area is restricted a good deal of pre-planning is necessary, since the raw materials will take up a surprising amount of room. In a small shed you will find that most of the timber has to be stored outside. Stack it level, with air gaps, and cover it. Better still, build another temporary shed for it.

All synthetic glues and resins give best results in certain temperatures, clearly stated by the manufacturers. Temperature control will therefore become a serious problem unless you bear it in mind right from the beginning. This applies particularly to all types of construction where glass-fibre is used: glassed ply, sandwich-foam, etc.

It is quite possible that building-shed problems will force you to reconsider a catamaran in lieu of a tri, since their beam in relation to their length can make quite a difference when space is restricted, or if transport to the sea is along narrow, twisty lanes. Adequate building space you must have; transport can nearly always be sorted out in one way or another. So don't begin to look for a place in which to build after you have bought the plans!

People often write to me asking if they can build the three hulls of a tri (or the two hulls of a cat) separately in a narrow shed in their garden, and then assemble them at a convenient launching place. It should be obvious that most, if not all, tris and cats must be completely assembled on the building site. Do not make the mistake of thinking that when your hulls are built

91

the job is nearly completed; in fact, you are less than one-third of your way through the task. Separate hulls can be built and moved elsewhere for joining, but you will still need a building shed, temperature control, etc. as before. I think my correspondents have in mind completing everything, including accommodation, on and in each hull, and then moving the hulls singly to the launching site for a quick joining together before the bottle is swung and the champagne drunk; this is virtually impossible, so forget about it – unless you are prepared to pay a designer a large fee to make the feat a practicality.

Transport and launching. Because the task of building a multihull is so great, many amateurs neglect to investigate thoroughly this seemingly trivial matter before they buy the plans. Don't be misled by my remarks in the previous section; transport *can* nearly always be sorted out, but it is better to make sure that the 'nearly' is not an uncrossable barrier in your case.

Although the police in various parts of the world may differ in their helpfulness, I have found that motoring organisations in most developed countries are probably the best people to approach when a reasonably long distance to the sea (or navigable water) has to be covered by the ultra-wide haulage load of a multihull. If you are not a member, it is worth joining. Of course, a reputable road transport firm will handle everything for you, providing you send them the plans before you begin building the boat. But such firms are not cheap and if you are on a limited budget their charges could make quite a difference; furthermore, inflation could mean that when your multihull is finally completed, their original estimate for the whole job has risen alarmingly.

It is generally false economy to employ a local haulier's lorry, particularly if he has never had to handle anything else but boxes, crates, sacks or loose loads. He will know little or nothing about chocking off and lashing down, and if your multihull shifts during the journey she may be badly smashed or, much worse, damage other property. A reputable firm will be covered by insurance for all such contingencies, but will your pal with his own truck? He may think he is doing you a favour; more likely he will be landing you in it up to your neck. Check and double check insurance cover for this journey, and for the launch.

Many and varied have been the processes of launching multihulls. I have already mentioned the Congo helicopter (sky-hooks are the last resort), and there is a long list of other methods. Manpower is often used, sometimes over quite long distances; it should be remembered that although a multihull looks enormous, the weight is always low: a 30-ft unrigged multihull, stripped of everything removable, will average 2000–3000 lb, easily carried by 20–30 men. On a direct 'lift' in a straight line of a mile or more. I have known several craft launched in this way. Football teams, or like-minded husky young men with a large beer consumption, can often be inveigled by temptation –

and a keg or two of ale may well be considerably cheaper than road transport. But don't expect the police to allow you to carry a multihull along a road (even although legally you may have every right to do so).

Another method which is often neglected is to make use of any local rivers, small though they may seem. A multihull does not draw much water, and although the overall beam may seem broad to monohull yachtsmen it may well be narrow enough to fit within the banks of a quite narrow river. Two points here: check the depth of water and width under the bridges all the way down to the sea, and check that no artificial barriers will be erected during your prolonged building period. I have known several multihulls launched successfully by this method on rivers which I had not known existed. My advice about transport had been sought in each case, and I had suggested checking by means of a large-scale map; the results generally saved the builders quite a bit of money – and since tris are beamier than cats, length for length, amateur catamaran builders may gain an advantage here.

Lifting should always be done by a mobile crane (25): a five-tonner for up to about 35-ft LOA cat or tri; larger cranes, *pro rata*. Hourly hire rates are surprisingly reasonable but travelling time has to be paid for, so you don't want to waste time. Have everything prepared for an immediate lift when the crane arrives. If you cannot supply the slings, tell the contractors beforehand. Oh! and remember that unless you wash your hands of all responsibility

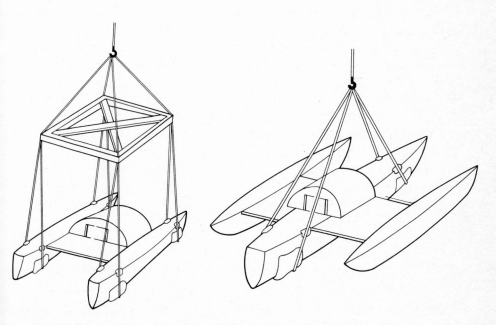

25 Catamarans should use a spreader when being hoisted by a crane; this is not usually necessary with a trimaran. Watch out for 'creep' if rope slings are used

– in which case it is better that you stay away – you are responsible for everything connected with the launching. This will include the slinging of your vessel, since the driver will know nothing at all about it. Dodge this responsibility and the contractors will have to send somebody to replace you; that somebody, like everything else you cannot do for yourself, will cost money.

Responsibilities. Sometimes I wonder if any amateur builder fully realises what he is letting himself in for when he decides to go ahead and build his very own multihull. In a lighthearted fashion, leaving himself almost completely unprotected from the vicissitudes of normal business practice, he will generally bumble his way through – just as later he will bounce and bump a navigationally and financially unsound course around the world, or whatever. What use, therefore, can advice be when beginner's luck seems to work so much better?

The answer is that the average amateur builder is seldom able to find a book, or a knowledgeable professional, who will spell out some of the major difficulties. The pro will generally give advice against the project (for obvious reasons, and I think quite rightly); a book will tell you the correct way to do whatever it is you want to learn, but will assume that the reader has already attained a certain amount of knowledge, commonsense and flexibility. For example, I have never read a learning-to-sail book yet which does its damnedest to put you off the sport by describing – as I hope I have done – all the things that can and do go wrong, and what happens after; most of them merely tell you what you should learn if you want to go a-sailing. Seamanship, however, is basically the art of knowing what can go wrong, and being prepared for every eventuality in this respect by preventing it. Most learning-to-sail books teach seamanship as a lesson on how to do things correctly – thereby implying that if you learn to do everything as the book says, then nothing can possibly go wrong. I believe this is putting the horse before the cart – quite correctly, but facing in the wrong direction!

So, in your case, you must understand that responsibility rests heavily upon your shoulders. I cannot possibly advise you within the limits of one chapter, or one book, of every catastrophe that may be imminent. The process of evaluating, costing, ordering, building and launching is very little different from the subsequent planning of the voyage, which will, in due course, enable you to fulfil your dream. In the latter role no doubt you have already decided on your rank as 'skipper', but you must not forget that your position during the laborious building period can only be that of the boss. In other words, when you finally escape to sea you can assume your rightful position as captain – but only after you have served your term as a successful 'guv'nor'.

7 Of Tris and Cats – and Other Facts

The previous chapter will not have made me very popular with multihull designers, who depend a good deal on the royalties they collect for each set of plans sold to starry-eyed, away-from-it-all amateur builders. If I have succeeded in making you think deeply, however, I will risk their displeasure. Yet the actual building is only the first of a long list of disillusionments which you will suffer unless someone takes the trouble to warn you, for if you have little or no knowledge of what to expect, you certainly will not be able to guess at the unhappy possibilities of the future. But before the doom and gloom descend again, a little cheer to brighten the horizon will not be amiss.

You may well have your dreams, and a fierce determination to fulfil them, but you may discover during the building of your multihull that as the work progresses your escapist ideas begin to fade. It is more than likely that the reason for this is that you are basically not an away-from-it-all type of escaper, and that your long grind over many months has enabled you to discover more about yourself than you could possibly have known before. Perhaps your interest in sailing has died completely, or maybe you have decided that what you really wanted was a totally different sort of boat.

Whatever your reasons, don't despair – and certainly do not give up half-way through construction. Two, or three, unconnected hulls, or even a 'shell', cannot be sold at much, if any, profit, but a completed multihull should make you a clear gain of 25 to $33\frac{1}{3}$ per cent over your total costs at the very least, and possibly as much as 150 to 200 per cent if you have turned out a first-class job. So providing you stick to your self-imposed contract, which you should have examined carefully after reading the last two chapters, you will survive any crisis, financial or otherwise, provided you complete your task. A weakness in your self-discipline, and the chances are that you will lose heavily. There is of course always the possibility that the whole yacht market will collapse while you are building – yachts, as 'luxury' goods, have always been notoriously susceptible to price variations – but in this case you will at least own something which may be valuable, perhaps even beyond price, depending on how the particular crisis develops.

So once you are committed to building you have nothing really to lose, provided you don't give up. That is the heaviest cross you will have to bear.

While I am on the subject of making a profit, I should mention the sales potential of the various types of material used in construction. I'm afraid it is a ridiculous fact that after some two decades of gradually diminishing resistance to plastic yachts, on the grounds that they require less effort to build, and are therefore cheaper than all-wood vessels, the public, having accepted them, must now pay excessively for them because the synthetic resins are made from the world's rapidly decreasing supplies of natural oil products, which are costing more and more! The moral would appear to be: don't use any more synthetics than are absolutely necessary if you want to build 'on the cheap'. The difficulty is that now yachtsmen have accepted GRP/FRP they are not very keen about other materials; ply is generally disliked, wood planking is too heavy (and much too expensive) for all but the largest multihulls, steel or stainless steel is impractical for the same reason, alloy is an expensive possibility for craft over about 30 ft (the weight factor precludes smaller multis), and ferrocement may be possible in the large sizes, but as far as I am aware nobody has yet worked out the practicalities of the size/weight ratio. So, really, the only materials which can be used by an amateur are glassed ply or the various types of all-plastic construction, while professional multihull builders use GRP/FRP almost exclusively.

If you build in ply, therefore, you cannot at present expect to get such a good price for your multihull as you could if you built in, say, foam-sandwich plastic. Nevertheless, the amateur builder may quickly discover that he cannot afford to use the higher-priced materials, in which case, like it or not, he will have to build in ply and resign himself to a smaller profit margin if he decides to sell his boat.

There are two main types of ply construction: single planking and double-diagonal planking (26); for obvious reasons, the former is cheaper, but the latter is probably slightly easier for the amateur builder because accurate

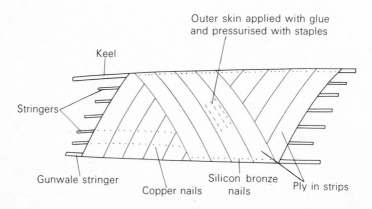

26 Double-diagonal method of ply construction

fitting of large sheets of ply is obviated. Double-diagonal planking is also almost certainly the stronger of the two, so if your budget can stand the additional cost I think this is the best method for ply construction. Yet it should not be forgotten that the majority of transoceanic multihulls to date have been single-skin ply-planked – generally with single or double chines; the curved bilge which double-diagonal planking allows is a much more recent innovation.

I am always being asked which is the better of these two types of construction. Now that I have published my multihull selection questionnaire you can answer this for yourself. If you can afford the additional cost of materials, then double-diagonal is the best; if not, then single or double-chine must be the best. Since double-chine is slightly more expensive than single-chine (and takes somewhat longer to build), the same ruling applies again. Turn back to Chapter 6 and cost up Cross 30 from the materials list; with a single mid-chine to the centre hull, and single chine floats, she is very nearly the cheapest possible 30-footer you could build. Piver's original 30-ft Nimble would cost slightly less because she did not even have chined floats, and enough Nimbles have crossed oceans to prove that single-chine construction is of more than adequate strength. So don't be misled by what is supposed to be 'good', or more seakindly, or any other esoteric factor; it can only be 'good' if you can really afford it – nothing else can possibly compete in such circumstances.

If your finances are such that you do not have to worry about such matters, there is no doubt that rounded bottoms (and there are many different shapes) are slightly more seakindly. Personally I don't think there is all that much to choose between them, but if speed is your main object then chines are definitely out. There is no need for me to advise the speed enthusiasts any further, since they are invariably well read on the technicalities of multihull design, and can talk me under the table in a few minutes. If speed is your main reason for wanting a multihull you should consult designers – or the experts in such organisations as the AYRS. I'm afraid I am not sufficiently experienced to tell you much about the subject.

I must say this, though, from my limited knowledge. When, in 1966, I entered the 33-ft Piver Stiletto racer *Startled Faun* in the Round Britain Race, we were all determined that she must show excellent windward capabilities. The skipper, Eric Willis, the crewman, Tony Smith (now designer and builder of the 25 ft 6 in *Telstar*) and myself put our heads together and altered Piver's design considerably. Among the improvements was an over-large centreplate, which certainly gave her a better performance to windward. I sat back, absolutely convinced that we would win the race.

Who could have possibly foretold that the winds during the 1966 Round Britain Race were going to remain fair for the leading yachts during virtually the whole of the 2000-mile course? Like friendly trade winds they circled around the British Isles with the fleet and made every leg a reach or a dead run. Eric and Tony told me afterwards that apart from a few short periods when they had to closehaul, *Startled Faun* never had a chance to show off her windward abilities. She finished fourth, and was one of the few in the race to go round without any trouble; the winner, Derek Kelsall's 42-ft trimaran *Toria*, suffered dagger-board breakages which would have put her out of the race if the wind had blown as it always seems to around Britain when you are cruising – against you!

The moral of this story is that all multihulls, whether for racing or for cruising, are a compromise. Develop one facet slightly too much, and something else must suffer. With *Startled Faun* we had forfeited light weight in order to gain windward performance. Racing-yacht designers and skippers are continually playing at this game of taking a little, giving a little – and hoping for the best. Then they must wait until the wind and the sea have been added to the mixture before they can possibly know whether the formula this time is right, or wrong. Yacht racing, whether mono- or multihull, is a singularly expensive pastime.

On the other hand, the development of cruising monohull yachts over the years between the two world wars and afterwards, has not been nearly so problematic, although in the 'good old days', when yachts were, by present standards, incredibly low-priced, choosing a suitable vessel for cruising, or blue-water sailing, was certainly not easy. In 1938, when I was looking for a boat suitable for solo ocean cruising, I nearly settled for a 40-ft centre-cockpit chine schooner of the *Blue Coral* class; the price, new, was £800 (oh, happy days!). I mention this not only as an example of the range of choice, but mainly because most builders of 'husky' cruisers at that time produced a vessel which was far more suitable for immediate action than present-day production models – particularly multihulls. And I am referring to designer's plans for amateur builders as well as professionally completed craft.

Forty years ago, most builders of medium-sized cruising yachts had no ambition to create such an abomination as a cruiser-racer which, when you think about it, is a compromise from the realms of fantasy. While it is quite possible for a cruiser to race (obviously against other cruisers), it is ridiculous to expect a yacht designed specifically for racing ever to supply the comfort which one expects in a cruiser. This is particularly true of multihulls. Comfort, in simple terms, means weight, but unnecessary weight in a multihull translates as reduced maximum possible speed. And I am not referring solely to the weight added by comfortable accommodation.

The notoriously weak parts of a multihull have always been the rigging – including the mast(s) and sails – and the rudder(s). Studying these items at various boat shows and elsewhere I have not been impressed by what I have seen. Rather than fitting overstrong equipment that would suit a longer waterline monohull, it seems to me that many multihull builders and designers are far too anxious to compete with monohulls by reducing all fittings to a bare minimum, to make them look 'neat' and 'yachty'.

Drop rudders, for example, are reasonably safe for local and short coastal cruises in summer, but they are unreliable otherwise. Although I prefer a transom-slung rudder, because one can get to it easily in the event of damage or fouling, there is a good deal of advantage in having underslung rudders for ocean cruising, provided the stock, and hull-entry socket and bearings in the trunk, are adequate for the heavy strains that will be imposed by breaking seas. If a rudder is underslung, it is less likely to suffer from damage of this kind than one which is transom-slung, but the fittings should be extra strong, since repairs at sea will be almost impossible, and the stock must have several inches of vertical movement in the trunk. Also, a wire or strap attached to the keel and fastened to the bottom of the stock is essential to prevent underwater fouling (27).

Transom-slung rudders should be strengthened in every possible way, bearing in mind that excessive weight in this extreme position could be dangerous in a seaway. The rudder is best slung on pintles, and even in small craft I recommend a three-point attachment to spread the load. In medium sizes and larger, when the rudder, through necessity, is becoming heavier, the load of each pintle should be spread over as wide an area as possible on the inside of the transom by four through-bolts to wide and stout hardwood pads (or, more expensively, stainless-steel strips). In addition, quarter knees should be strengthened and a rigid transom knee, through-bolted to the keel and transom, should be fitted. These precautions were devised as a result of my experience from building Piver-designed ply trimarans. I can only pass on what I have learned, and your reaction to rudders and rudder-hanging on new craft, or a multihull you are building, is entirely up to you. But do remember that rudders are very vulnerable in multis.

Another tip for transom-slung rudders is to make sure that the top of the

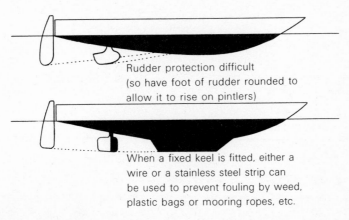

Rudder protection difficult
(so have foot of rudder rounded to
allow it to rise on pintlers)

When a fixed keel is fitted, either a
wire or a stainless steel strip can
be used to prevent fouling by weed,
plastic bags or mooring ropes, etc.

27 Rudder protection

vertical pin of the upper pintle is higher by at least two inches than those of the lower pintles. If you do have to unship your rudder in a seaway (and this applies mainly to tris, where the working area is limited), reshipping will then be made considerably easier. Also, a hole should be bored athwartships through this pin, about one inch above the gudgeon when the rudder is slung; here a brass shear-pin (a heavy-duty split-pin will do) will prevent accidental unshipping, but it will allow the rudder to rise and fall off in an emergency, such as running aground, provided the foot of the rudder is adequately rounded. Needless to say, a safety wire should always be attached to the rudder-head, otherwise you will lose it one day; don't rely on the steering-wires holding it (or the tiller, if you do not have a wheel).

It can be seen that even on such a simple subject as rudders, multihulls have many peculiarities which must be carefully considered. A balanced rudder is 'a must' to avoid excessive strains, and the construction of the blade should be (but seldom is) of prime importance. We inserted stainless-steel rods in grooves between layers of glued ply for additional strength, as shown in the sketch (28). An emergency tackle to the main or mizzen boom (depending on the rig) is a great help for reslinging an unshipped rudder, and an emergency tiller (particularly when wheel-steering is employed) is even more important. This means an extra fitting on the rudder head, above the wheel-steering quadrant, but it could prove invaluable in a moment of stress – which invariably happens when a steering wire breaks! Another

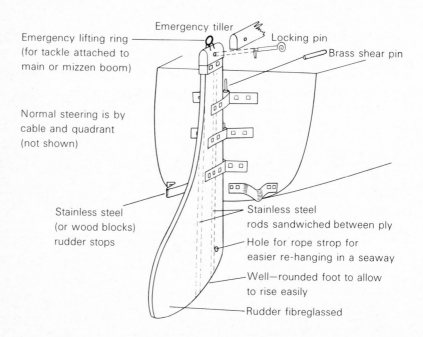

Emergency tiller
Emergency lifting ring
(for tackle attached to
main or mizzen boom)
Locking pin
Brass shear pin

Normal steering is by
cable and quadrant
(not shown)

Stainless steel
(or wood blocks)
rudder stops

Stainless steel
rods sandwiched between ply

Hole for rope strop for
easier re-hanging in a seaway

Well—rounded foot to allow
to rise easily

Rudder fibreglassed

28   These rudder precautions apply equally to cats or tris

essential for a transom-slung rudder is to fit two 'stops' on each side of the blade, just above the waterline; we made these of stainless-steel strip, and found this an excellent material as a certain amount of springiness in the steel absorbed the shock when the rudder was slammed across by a heavy sea. These 'stops' are also useful as platforms for reslinging the rudder – or even for bathing.

On the subject of wheel-steering, I think this was one of the hardest problems I had to solve when I was responsible for producing seaworthy trimarans. Catamaran builders have assured me that such troubles do not exist with two hulls, but quite frankly I don't believe it: multihull rudders are subjected to greater stresses than those of monohulls, if only because they travel faster through the water – and no doubt there are plenty of other reasons. When wires are used from the steering-wheel to the rudder I advise using the most flexible you can discover. The fairlead sheaves, between rudder and helm, should be large; we used 12-in sheaves, and would have preferred to fit even larger. The fastening of these sheaves should be by through-bolts, and never by screws. Of mechanical steering devices, including hydraulic methods, I can say nothing since I lack experience. However, I very much doubt if the average amateur builder can afford such luxuries, and if you are paying a high price for a multihull to professional builders, the responsibility lies in their hands.

Catamarans are as susceptible to rudder troubles as tris. As new designers and builders of both types appear on the scene, invariably they start at the beginning and rerun the whole gamut of errors that have been committed in the past – not only with rudders, but with everything else. Over the years it has seemed to me that the newcomers have deliberately ignored all previous experience in designing and building; I have no idea why, but it has certainly happened that way. I cannot overstress the importance of strength in every fitting on board a multihull which is used for and during sailing, yet many multihulls are still being launched with ridiculously inadequate 'yachty' fitments.

For example, I have seen beautiful stainless steel turnbuckles on multis which, quite frankly, would be more suitable for a large sailing dinghy. Why waste money on these highly expensive show-pieces when the galvanised equivalents are not only cheaper but safer. Stainless steel is notoriously fickle if subjected to twisting or racking strains – as I found out when an incorrectly-rigged, inner-forestay turnbuckle snapped under the mild load of a genoa in a force 4; I concede it was my fault that the lower section of the fitting was trapped and did not lead fair under a side load, but I was experimenting with a genoa on a tri for the first time ever and the conditions were such that I expected no trouble from temporary distortions. A galvanised turnbuckle may have bent, but it certainly would not have parted. Ultimate strength throughout all sailing vessels is achieved through 'give' and flexibility, but stainless steel cannot do either. Its sole advantage is its strength, which translates into undersize fittings, 'yachty' appearance and some slight saving of weight on a multihull. The non-rusting qualities of stainless steel depends entirely on how much you are prepared to pay for its quality, so do not be blinded by the magic of the letters 'SS'.

Similarly, an SS fitting is as strong as its fastenings, and I have seen far too many such items brass-screwed when they should have been SS-bolted. This is a common error, and I committed it myself in the early days. Again I repeat that a multihull will be subjected to far greater loads when sailing than a monohull, and that all the deck and rigging fittings must be over-strength – at least as strong as for a monohull of 5 ft longer waterline. I have often been told '... you may be right when it comes to deep-sea work, Nobby, but you don't have to bother about all this strength stuff for the family man'. Don't believe such rubbish. If there is a weak link in your multihull, the first blow will find it – as has so often happened in the past, to the general detriment of multis. You have no alternative but to rely on the integrity of the workmanship during construction, but you can and should question any fittings which have been screwed down, and you should certainly check on the size of the pad (or whatever) to which the fitting has been screwed, or bolted.

This raises a grave subject, the folly of which is continued to this day in far too many multihulls: the low height and weakness of deck rails. It is absolutely essential on the wide and spacious decks of a tri or a cat that the deck rails, if fitted, are high enough to prevent tripping over them and strong enough to withstand the combined weight of at least two heavy men being flung against them (29). I regret that seldom will you find such an installation. Let me repeat a story I told in *Trimaran Development* about *Nimble Eve*, which was not fitted with deck rails. On the eighth demonstration trip, I was attempting to sail down the River Orwell, but

> ... the breeze was negligible and the river glassy. I was standing on the starboard wing under the lee of the mainsail, about three feet from the trailing edge (an aeronautical term which is applicable to trimarans if the descriptive word 'wing' is used), when a puff from a very minor squall struck the sails. The tri accelerated immediately. I was caught off-balance. My right foot went back automatically; I was still fractionally unbalanced; my left foot went back – into space. My left hand clutched for support as I began to fall – and found the boom. The whole incident took perhaps one second.

Multihulls accelerate very suddenly, and there have been a number of occasions when people have been jerked off balance as I was. I was lucky, but others have lost their lives. In my book I went on to say:

> To those who argue convincingly about wearing a safety harness, I say this:

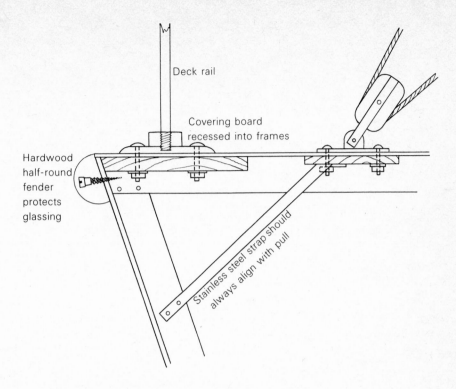

Deck rail

Covering board
recessed into frames

Hardwood
half-round
fender
protects
glassing

Stainless steel strap should
always align with pull

29   Methods of bolting deck rails, fairleads, etc. to ply decks

on a voyage around the world, in the Roaring Forties, it is conceivable that
a safety harness would be worn at all times. Given a golden summer's afternoon,
five miles offshore, on a lazy, happy cruise, I'm afraid I cannot envisage a
crew all kitted-out for desperate action. In a multihull, even during a calm,
a puff of breeze could tumble somebody overboard, and they might bump their
head on the way. Fit deck rails, and save weight on something else.

There are many varieties of dangerous deck rails on multihulls. Study the
photograph of *Three Wishes* on the pool at the London Boat Show and consider
this. A young and rather tough American came on board and castigated me
for 'the poor quality of that goddam galvanised piping round the decks'. I
asked him whether he would prefer safety or... 'Or what?' he grunted. 'Is
there an acceptable alternative?' I asked innocently. I then made him an
offer which I very much doubt if any other salesman at any boat show in
the world would make: 'Throw yourself as many times as you like against
that rail', I told him, 'and see if you can break it.' He probably weighed
around 200 lb, and he tried hard. When he had bent the top rail out of
true, without disturbing any of the stanchion seatings, I stopped him. 'Now
go on any stand in the show and see if they'll allow you a similar test', I

suggested. I never did find out if he tried, but I do know that he was impressed with the strength of my 'goddam galvanised piping'. He should have been. It was only ½-in water-pipe, but the assembly was made up on jigs as an integral whole; each stanchion had four bolts through a ¾-in × 9-in covering board under the ply decking, and which extended the full length of the gunwale. To rip the stanchions out would have meant tearing the floats apart; in other words it was physically impossible. The height of those rails was sufficient to prevent a person off-balance being toppled over; 2 ft 9 in to 3 ft is reasonable for saving people under 6 ft in height. If you are taller, fit higher rails.

Pulpits, too, should be through-bolted to a covering board, and be of adequate height and very strong. I once took a snatch-pull from a lifeboat on a Nimble's pulpit, which actually bent one of my rescuer's very tough stern stanchions. This is the sort of strength which is essential for a multihull pulpit, since the motion up forward in a seaway can be hectic and a crewman's life will depend entirely on this fitting. Never go to sea in a cruising or racing multihull without a pulpit, or pulpits.

I fitted the first sail nets between hulls on a Nimble in 1962. Originally they were intended for that purpose – to prevent sails dropping, or dragging in the water – but I soon discovered that most people regarded them more as safety nets. So although the design was unchanged, the purpose was altered. Certainly they made you feel safer when wind increased and seas steepened. Although not quite as necessary as a pulpit(s), they are invaluable in both cats and tris as an additional safety factor – particularly if children are aboard.

Again, and still up forrard, you should consider all the items which will be needed for anchoring or mooring – whether you are buying a new or a second-hand boat or building your own. This is another sadly neglected department on far too many stock multis, and the amateurs do not seem to make any attempt to solve the problems either. Yet everybody knows that when an anchor is needed, almost invariably it is needed urgently, and occasionally desperately. Equally, 'getting-the-hook' may become a major problem in a dicey situation. I wouldn't like to attempt either feat with the majority of the equipment I have seen.

The first essential is a tough and solidly bolted fairlead. This should be fitted with an invention from days of yore: a Claud Worth pawl (30). Because multihulls are reasonably lightweight, handing the anchor chain is quite possible in the smaller sizes; but 'quite possible' is made considerably easier with a Claud Worth pawl. Now although you may be advised to save weight by fitting only five or six fathoms of chain, with the rest nylon line, I doubt the advantages. Personally I believe that 15 fathoms of chain is essential before the nylon is spliced on; I like the additional weight which helps the anchor to hold, the extra bottom-chafing length, the benefit of the Claud Worth pawl, and tough metal instead of quick-wearing nylon for the main working

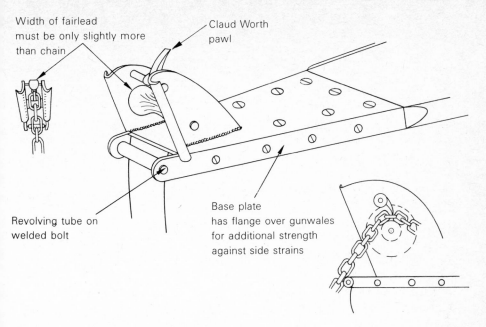

Width of fairlead
must be only slightly more
than chain

Claud Worth
pawl

Revolving tube on
welded bolt

Base plate
has flange over gunwales
for additional strength
against side strains

30   Stemhead roller and Claud Worth pawl

length (temporary anchoring is generally in shallow waters). You may be told that you can buy a gadget which hooks on to the nylon anchor cable, to slide down with weights attached; the idea is to give the negligible catenary of the lightweight line a kink, which will ensure a more horizontal pull at the anchor and thus ensure maximum holding. As a matter of fact Claud Worth invented this too, although the original idea is as old as hollowed-log canoes. I once had to send some 400 lb down my barge's anchor chain in a desperate situation, so I thoroughly approve of the basic premise, but in spite of this I still think 15 fathoms of chain is better than 5 or 6 fathoms. (Personally, I'd take a Claud Worth-type weight-carrying shackle as well.)

As important as the fairlead is a really strong Samson Post or deck bollard. The former should be fitted through a king plank, with its heel mortised into the keelson, or into a large pad seated on the keelson; the latter should be bolted to a king plank, the underside of which should be strapped to a reasonably strong part of the hull construction (the forward crossarm is generally a good place). Where's the king plank? Alas, such additional strength is seldom incorporated, but if you are building your own multihull you'll be able to build one in.

In the smaller sizes of multihull a mast dolly winch will be adequate for anchor work, but the bigger and heavier size requires a proper anchor winch or capstan. Do make sure that you can work at it on a tossing deck; I have seen some ghastly (but pretty-looking), knuckle-bashing designs, which cost the earth and in due course may well cost your boat and/or your life. I cannot choose for you, but you have been warned; do not believe everything a salesman tells you, and try to imagine yourself on a foredeck in desperate straits struggling to get your anchor, or relying on that same anchor to hold when you are pinned tight on a lee shore.

I am not concerned in this chapter, or indeed in this book, with teaching seamanship. This you must learn for yourself, as I had to, from reading an enormous quantity of books, and from bitter experience. Most of what I have had to say so far really comes under the definition of seamanship, and I have had to stress these various points because many multihull designers and builders neglect to do anything about them. The 'safety' spiel by do-gooders, who have insisted that life-rafts, ship-to-shore radios, distress signals and other aids are essential, has probably done more harm to genuine seamanship than any other single factor. 'Why bother about all those bits and pieces around the decks when we've only got to shout for a helicopter to rescue us if we get into serious difficulties?' Well, you do as you like; I prefer to be accountable for my own safety.

However, as I have written this book for multihull beginners I cannot just leave the matter like that. I must assume that you will want to know what precautions I would take with the deck fittings of a multihull.

Assuming that the designer and the builder have adequately supported the mast (which sometimes I doubt), that the various shroud or chain plates lead fair (essential if stainless steel is used), and that such important items as reefing gear, sheet winches, sheet leads, cleats, mooring bollards (at least four, large enough to make fast a thick line), fender eye-plates (often forgotten) and so on are all fastened securely, are of suitable size and positioned correctly, the next job is to ensure that you have alternatives, reserves or at least some idea of what you could do in the unfortunate event of something breaking or failing to work.

Start with the sails. The loads imposed on a multihull's sails are far greater than those on a monohull; the latter 'gives' to gusts or squalls, but the former has to stand almost upright and take nearly the full force of wind pressure, relying only on acceleration to relieve maximum strain. In these circumstances, in due course something is bound to break. To start with, supposing it is the main halliard – whether of wire or synthetic line? The answer to this emergency is that you should have steps up the mast so that you can lay aloft almost as easily and quickly as if you had ratlines.

What if the mainsail reefing gear shears, breaks, or otherwise fails to function? (I am assuming Bermudan rig.) I countered this possibility by having a set of reef points sewn into the mainsail at approximately the treble-reef position, and as far as I know I was the first to take this precaution. It has the great advantage of being cheap to install, never in the way, and yet it could quickly become a life-saver in extreme conditions.

106

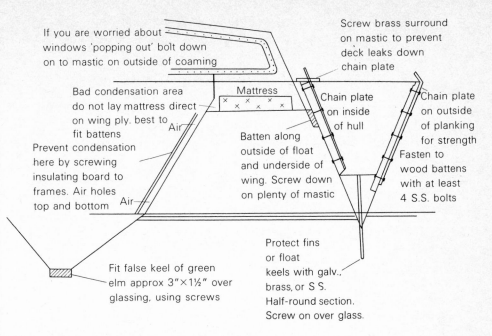

If you are worried about windows 'popping out' bolt down on to mastic on outside of coaming

Screw brass surround on mastic to prevent deck leaks down chain plate

Bad condensation area do not lay mattress direct on wing ply. best to fit battens

Prevent condensation here by screwing insulating board to frames. Air holes top and bottom

Air

Air

Mattress

Batten along outside of float and underside of wing. Screw down on plenty of mastic

Chain plate on inside of hull

Chain plate on outside of planking for strength

Fasten to wood battens with at least 4 S.S. bolts

Fit false keel of green elm approx 3"×1½" over glassing, using screws

Protect fins or float keels with galv., brass, or S S. Half-round section. Screw on over glass.

31 A few general suggestions for both tris and cats

Shrouds, backstays and forestays should always be considered carefully. If you go a-cruising in a multihull you must expect something to part sooner or later, and therefore you should ensure that there is always a temporary replacement available. Few multihulls are rigged now with a single shroud on each side of the mast – this would be disastrous – but many still have a single forestay and/or a single backstay. Always rig two backstays (one to the stern quarter of each wing or hull), and always have two forestays. If only one masthead forestay was specified by the designer, I used to rig a second to a mast-band just under the truck, and set the foresail on this wire: then, if it parted, the original masthead forestay remained intact. There is no point in rigging two forestays to one masthead and one deck fitting; separate shackling arrangements are essential.

I have lost one mast overboard, without damage fortunately, and without disastrous results; in this case the mast, together with the sails and rigging, was easily recovered and restepped the very next day. The cause of this accident was one faulty shackle which, although oversized for its job, had an externally undetectable flaw within the pin (I found both parts afterwards, lying on the deck). This shackle connected the port upper shroud to the chain plate; when it parted, the port lower shroud could not take the sudden strain and the swaged lower thimble pinged away into the sea. Some time later on another tri, the SS tang of the port upper shroud sheared the mast through-bolt, which meant that all the upper diamonds and upper shrouds collapsed;

the lower shrouds held this time, however, and I managed to get her into harbour. If she had been rigged with masthead shrouds, the job would have been much easier. On another occasion, in force 7, unreefed, *Nimble Eve* snapped the deck eyebolt to which the masthead forestay was attached. The inner forestay held until temporary repairs could be made. I concede that all these accidents occurred during the early testing days, but I still think it is better to be safe than sorry. A multihull is hard on all her sailing gear, so in my view it is seamanlike always to have at least one card up your sleeve.

Another common fault in either professionally or amateur-built ply multi-hulls is an almost complete disregard of ventilation – and I am not thinking about crew comfort. Trimarans suffer most in this respect, but catamarans cannot be excluded, particularly when the bows and sterns of the hulls are sealed off with 'collision' bulkheads. It is essential that every hidden corner of a ply vessel be ventilated, particularly the insides of box-spar crossarms, and yet in almost every multihull I have inspected virtually nothing has been done to prevent rot in the ply or the timber. Furthermore, I have seen many amateur-built multis with foamed-polystyrene pumped into the bows and stern 'for additional buoyancy'. How ridiculous can you get?

Timber and ply must breathe, the latter at least on one side. Obviously if the outside of your multihull is covered with glassfibre it cannot breathe there – so you must take precautions on the inside. Firstly, all the interior must have a good soaking of anti-fungoid solution – all the interior includes deckheads throughout the floats (often neglected) and the insides of box-spars. Then all these surfaces should be hand-painted with a first-class marine primer, even if they will never be seen again; this primer should also contain an anti-fungoid solution. All bilges should then be painted with the special material supplied by most top-line manufacturers for this sole purpose; all other paintwork will then continue as on any other yacht.

Ventilation plans may well vary, and I can only quote my own methods. As with all fast-moving objects, the movement of air inside a multihull is forward when under way, consequently the arrangement for ventilation should be reversible, depending on whether the boat is lying at anchor or sailing. The sketch (32) shows only a trimaran, because this is the most difficult to ventilate, but the same plan can be followed for a cat. When anchored, the forward cowl vents should face forward and the after-cowl vents face aft; when under way, the forward vents should face aft and the after vents should face forward. But what about rain driving into the forward vents when she is lying at anchor, you may ask. In my experience occasional summer showers send very little, if any, water into the floats. This may be because of the position of the cowls, which are protected from near-vertical rain by their shape and from horizontal driving rain by the length and shape of the floats or hulls. However, if you intend to leave the boat for a long period, say in winter, turn all four cowls to face aft – there will still be a slow circulation of air. You could of course fit water-draining cowls at least on the foredecks, but these would tend to be cumbersome in this position and not so easily removable when required. With my system, if you run into heavy headseas it only takes a minute or two to remove the cowls and screw in the waterproof plugs (33); the stern cowls seldom, if ever, need this attention. If water-draining cowls are fitted in the two forward positions they must be of the removable type, with a screw-plug to fit in the flange; do not rely on these cowls to keep water out of the forward compartments in heavy seas.

Inspection hatches to otherwise inaccessible parts of the floats or hulls are essential – although this applies more to the former than the latter. In ply-built craft, never fill these areas with foamed polystyrene and then forget

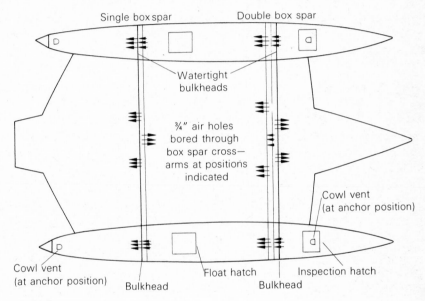

32 Floats and crossarms ventilation plan

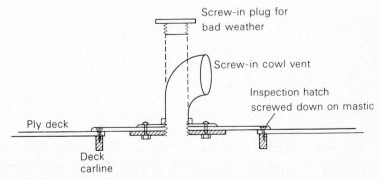

33 Cowl vent installation on forward inspection hatch (see also jacket photograph)

about them. If you must add emergency buoyancy, fill the spaces with granulated polystyrene in plastic bags, leaving an air gap at the top so that your ventilation system can continue to function throughout the rest of the ship; the plastic bags should all be removed at least once a year to check the bilges, and for signs of fungus, rot, etc. Alternative to granulated polystyrene could be table-tennis balls (stowed in plastic bags for easy removal), small plastic bottles, cans or globes. But all of these will prove more difficult to stow and to remove than my original suggestion.

As an example of what can happen to an unventilated section of ply, the Piver-designed, 64-ft × 32-ft Empress class tri *Triptych*, built in England in 1965 by the now-defunct Multihull Services Ltd, was nearly lost at sea off New Caledonia one dark and stormy night when she suddenly began making water fast in the bilges of the port float. This happened some seven years after she was launched, and after she had crossed the Atlantic, chartered in the West Indies and finally fetched up in Auckland, New Zealand, on an extended world cruise. The interior of one float of *Empress* is much roomier than a monohull of the same overall length, and *Triptych* had been designed for charter work. The result was a luxurious interior, with insufficient attention to air circulation in the non-passenger regions, which included the port float bilges. The result of this was the disintegration of two sections of ply planking: '. . . two holes, one big enough to climb through, the other big enough to poke your head through. Dry rot!' wrote Malcolm Pullman in the New Zealand yachting magazine *Sea Spray*.

Tests with tobacco smoke, whilst at anchor and during sailing trials, proved that the smell was expelled by both my ejection cowls in Nimble, Lodestar and Victress within one minute of a pipe-smoker puffing heavily into just one intake cowl. This was a crude test, and it failed to prove that bilge ventilation was adequate, but certainly tobacco smoke could be detected faintly in the bilges and in due course it dissipated; so at least some air circulated in this otherwise forgotten area. In all three cases the smell was almost immediately detectable in the saloon, which meant that the crossarms received a good draught of air.

Another item which is neglected on most stock multihulls is a false keel(s). Whether a tri or a cat is built of GRP or glassed ply, and whether or not the precaution of quadrupling the cloth around the keel(s) has been taken, it is a fact that glassfibre does not like abrasion. And what can be more abrasive than a boat settling on or rising from a mud, sand, stone, rock or coral bottom? A simple precaution is to screw a 1-in thick by (preferably) 2- or 3-in wide false keel(s) of green elm along the length of keels which are remotely likely to come into contact with the sea bottom. This should be inspected annually (more frequently in tropical waters) and discarded at the first sign of worm borings or excessive chafe. It is cheap, easily replaceable, and will save the plastic from damage. If, following abrasion, worm penetrated into the glass-protected keel(s) of your multihull, you would soon have as much trouble as *Triptych* had with dry rot.

In this chapter I have covered those items which I have learned through experience are peculiar to multihull safety; hundreds of other points, applicable to yachts of any type, can be discovered by reading as many books as you can beg, borrow or preferably buy. You can never read too much about 'the way of a ship upon the sea'; all too often yachtsmen don't read enough. Even a good sailing novel will enable you to work your mind at the problems, and possibly the mistakes, made by the author. Every aspect of seamanship should always be in your mind, so that even if you crash your car into a ditch you will immediately begin to think of a seamanlike method of getting it out. Yachtsmen for the most part appear to be only as seamanlike as the depth of their pockets and the laws of land-based legislators persuade them to be; for survival at sea, neither of these factors is particularly reliable. Only by continually thinking about seamanship can a yachtsman ever hope to develop a seamanlike approach to sailing, or indeed to any problems at all.

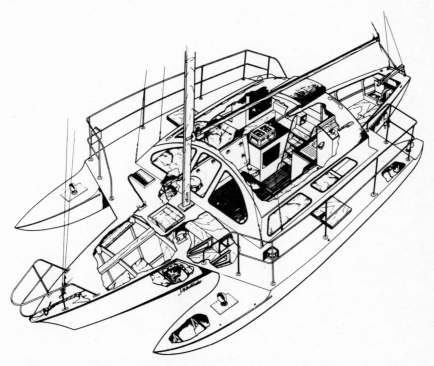

34　This is the standard Nimble (30 ft × 18 ft × 2 ft) which I sold between the years 1962–6. I include this drawing because it shows features which I still believe are essential, although many multihulls lack most of them. Notice in particular the strong high deck rails and pulpit, cowl ventilators, unobstructed navigation lights and the outboard in a well in the cockpit; note also the simple anchor stow and anchor chain stowage box, the transparent forehatch and the interior steering.

8 The Blue-Water Game

I am of the opinion that it is impossible to cry 'Wolf!' too often when blue water voyages in multihulls (or indeed in monohulls) are contemplated.

I have already written about the pre-building (or pre-buying) dreams of the away-from-it-all escaper, and I have attempted a table which should have warned such people that building or buying a multi is only a small portion of the financial troubles that will beset them in due course – whether they intend to escape by the day, the week or the year. But although many deep-water voyages have failed through money troubles, this is only one facet; the multitudinous surfaces of such a jewel must be studied thoroughly before its final value can be appreciated.

In the very first place, the Blue Water Game in multihulls seems to start with anybody who has purchased a multihull – even if their original intention was simply for local sailing. This seldom seemed to happen in the past with monohulls, and I can only conclude that the condition of mind which in the past I have called the Tricycle Complex (equally applicable to two hulls) is responsible. A person may be unable to balance on a two-wheel bicycle (it does happen occasionally), but can quickly gain confidence by riding a tricycle. Yet is this form of transport any safer than using two wheels on crowded roads? The answer, obviously, is no – in fact it could be argued that a tricycle is fractionally less safe. But the person who has discovered a certain freedom of movement, having been previously restricted to public transport or walking, will argue emphatically that three wheels must be safer than two, because of the stability. It should not be necessary for me to elaborate this analogy further.

It can be seen therefore that once a person has sailed nearly upright for a season or two in his multi, and survived two or three blows in comparative comfort, he (and perhaps his wife) will begin to think: why shouldn't I take a few months off and have a good holiday for a change? Why not indeed, but how much of his decision can be attributed to the Tricycle Complex? The answer, I think, is all too often too much. Cats and tris, like tricycles, make the Blue Water Game look too easy, and herein lies their greatest fault. This undoubtedly is why, in proportion, so many more multis have crossed oceans than monohulls – and also why multis have managed to accumulate such a bad press. It is not news any longer if a monohull gets into difficulties, but just as an accident involving a tricyclist would automatically be news-worthy so do multihull accidents attract the attention of the media.

A multihull is not safer than a monohull, and conversely a monohull is not safer than a multihull – no matter what the supporters of either may say. It is argued that a multihull is safer because no matter what happens – even a capsize – it will always keep afloat; monohullists frequently claim that their vessels are safer because even if they capsize they will always right themselves. These ridiculous arguments have been going on for a couple of decades, and I suspect similar rows occurred when, for example, somebody had the temerity to launch the first iron ship: 'Iron, sir! Every demned fool knows that iron sinks in water' (but please, sir, so do wooden ships).

From all this it can be seen that although I am personally in favour of multihulls (and tris in particular) for ocean cruising, I am not supporting their use on specific grounds of safety or otherwise. It just so happens that I prefer the advantages of a multihull more than the advantages of a monohull, and I am prepared to accept the disadvantages of a multihull more than I accept the disadvantages of a monohull.

Yet I must confess that my enthusiastic approach to trimarans in the early days undoubtedly was partly responsible for arousing the Tricycle Complex in many people, for this is what I had to say in a brochure describing the yachts I was selling:

> 'Transocean tested trimarans.' This key has opened the gateway to adventure for so many – young, middle-aged or old, it makes no difference, our customers range from teenagers to septuagenarians. Thoughts of blue seas, fresh trades, rainbowed spray, taut sheets, coral islands … escape … adventure. There is no age limit for dreamers. But now those dreams can become reality, and the cost is not high. In these pages are described yachts which are equally suitable for ditch-crawling, coastwise cruising, or deep-water sailing, and the prices are remarkably low. Examine the specification, check the cost of the tri-maran which interests you and note exactly what you are getting for your money; compare the price and specification with any similar-sized monohull (or multi-hull). Then delay no longer … Open the gateway to adventure!

Well, now that I am not committed I am prepared to alter the quotation to 'Transoceanic tested multihulls'; otherwise, although my prose is a little florid, I see no need to change the dream element. 'We all have our dreams', wrote Ralph Stock, who sailed halfway round the world in his Colin Archer *Dream Ship* as some compensation for what he had suffered in World War I. 'Without them we should be clods. It is in our dreams that we accomplish the impossible…' It can be said that multihulls have inspired dreamers to attempt the impossible to a much greater extent than have monohulls, for reasons already stated in Chapter 5 and because of the Tricycle Complex.

The Blue-Water Game is probably as ancient as the first log that drifted

away from shore with a man straddling it, although sometimes I wonder
if the proto-Polynesians were not the original inventors. We don't actually
know how the first men took to water, or who they were, so perhaps they
were not quite so dim-witted as we have been led to believe. The urge to
adventure, to explore, to escape, is a primary one, developed no doubt by the
need to survive. In the early days survival would always have taken prece-
dence; nowadays it would seem that these basic urges have been reversed. This
is how I put it in *The Lure of the Sea*:

> As civilisation enfolds us more and more in its cloying, politically-inspired
> wrapper of womb-to-grave protection, only the safety valve of individual freedom
> can relieve the mounting pressure of routine drudgery and endless frustration.
> In the quest for Utopia we are, as slaves, forced to descend into a hellish abyss
> of mediocrity – but not, I think, to everlasting damnation. For it can be said
> that as long as an escape route is possible, then there is hope; and when hope
> springs eternal in the breasts of some, then the majority can dream of the day
> when they, too, will escape.
>
> On this world only one area remains which is still reasonably free of inter-
> ference: it is, of course, the sea, which covers over 70 per cent of the surface
> of our planet. The air you are allowed to breathe but not to fly in freely, for
> man is determined that man will never really fly like the birds. The earth – be
> it the good earth, or rock, sand or swamp – is an area of impossible taboos
> which are broken daily by every person throughout the world as he or she strives
> to survive; you are allowed there only by the gracious consent of the politicians
> who control the taboos. So freedom on land is non-existent, although freedom
> on the high seas is still possible.
>
> Take warning! There have been many attempts to intimidate this last freedom:
> three-mile limits have been extended to twelve miles, fifty, two hundred ... vast
> areas of ocean have been sealed off in the sacred name of science and big bangs,
> piracy by governments has occurred on many occasions, and alert do-gooders
> constantly try to impose restrictions which may have escaped political notice.
>
> Of course, not everybody goes to sea in small boats in order to escape taboos.
> Some do it because it's there, because they like the sea, for personal publicity
> and money, or to prove themselves to themselves (whatever that might mean).
> Some do it to prove a particular type of craft, or to get to another part of
> the world; some do it in the interests of science, or because they have found
> that they are ineffectual at anything else, or because it offers a somewhat different
> social life to one they would otherwise follow. Whatever the reason it can still
> be summed up as escape; somehow you cannot imagine going to sea in a small
> boat as anything but escaping.
>
> Irrevocably tied to escape are the words 'from responsibilities'. The awful
> truth is that the responsibilities of escape are far, far greater than learning to
> live with taboos. Nobody knows what percentage of blue-water sailormen have
> failed – sometimes even to leave their home port. My guess is that for every
> person who accomplishes his dream, ten fail. It is a dismal thought.
>
> The fault lies in ignorance. Dreams may be gloriously satisfying, and they

15, 16 (*below*) For those who like to experiment with rig, I recommend
and 17 serious consideration of the old-fashioned squaresails
(**17**). Otherwise the simple Bermudan ketch (**15**), as she
was when John and David Glennie launched her in New
Zealand in 1964, may develop a rash of complications
(**16**) after seven years of transpacific cruising.

17 Lord St David's 25-ft 6-in Telstar *Triplet* displays her experimental square topsail off the white cliffs of Dover.

18 *(left)*
and **19**

If you have taken the trouble to cost up the
Cross 30 (**18**) and the Wharram Tangaroa
34 (**19**) from the materials' lists on pages 86
to 88, you will want to know what the craft
look like.
I think the space in which the tri was built
shows exactly what an enthusiast can
achieve, although I do not recommend
building in the open – not even in sunny
California.

20 The Lodestar *Three Wishes* on the pool at the 1965 London Boat Show (see pages 75 and 122). Note the height of the pulpit and deck rails, and in particular the steps up the mast. (You can't see them? Yet I was repeatedly told that this invaluable method for easy laying aloft was too ugly to fit on a yacht.)

undoubtedly help to pass the time between conception and reality, but in far too many cases the dream lasts throughout the long process of evolution, and there is nothing to fall back on at the moment of truth.

There are two great destroyers of deep-water voyagers: money and disillusionment. The former because escapists and dreamers just will not consider the project as a business venture; the latter because they seldom realise exactly what they are letting themselves in for. Adventure in business is known as calculated risk; disillusionment can be avoided by knowing the subject and a fair proportion of the answers.

Even a fierce determination to fulfil your dream will not guarantee success if you are fighting against impossible odds. Surprisingly, the worst odds are not necessarily shortage of money, lack of perseverance, or even the overwhelming forces of nature; bitter experience has shown me that other people are very often the greatest enemy: from builders to helpers, from crew to wives. Ah wives! What losses unimaginative men have suffered because all too often they assumed too much about their spouses. I will not bother to repeat what I have already written on the subject in *The Lure*; it is up to you to read it if you want to know more. Never take a wife for granted when cruising in a small boat – that is all I am prepared to say here.

A crew, too, can be frustratingly difficult, no matter how well you get on with them ashore. Remember that they, too, have their dreams – which is why they are coming with you – but seldom will their ideas of what they are about to receive coincide with yours; since none of the variegated hopes can remotely parallel the cold hard facts about a voyage, it follows that crew troubles will almost certainly overwhelm the skipper/owner unless he has taken pre-departure precautions. These, too, are listed in *The Lure*, but if I am asked for one clear-cut piece of advice about skipper/crew relationship on cruising yachts I invariably reply, 'Make quite sure that the crew have read the same books about sailing as the skipper – no more and no less.' Then I add, cynically, 'Assuming that the skipper realises his delicate position and always ensures he is one book ahead of the crew.' It is on this point that the amateur builder gains slightly on his stock-purchase counterpart, for he has already served his time in the capacity of 'guv'nor', and the takeover as skipper is correspondingly somewhat easier. There can only be one captain in charge of a ship; it is up to you to learn the responsibilities of this unique and lonely position which can never be entirely democratic.

Of adventure itself, I can do no better than quote from a famous American sailing book of the mid-thirties by Lt Warwick M. Tompkins, FRGS,USNR, who sailed the Schooner *Wander Bird* around the Horn, and told the story in *Fifty South to Fifty South*. 'There is in America a virtually religious belief that we are an adventurous and sporting people', he wrote. 'Americans like adventure. Regard the gaudy, burdened newstands! Americans like their adventure to meet them on a familiar corner, neatly packaged at a dime a bundle; they embrace it avidly when it is cheap, comfortable, safe and quite vicarious.'

Whatever your country or your beliefs, never be persuaded by such enticements to escape to sea as a simple way of climbing out of the rut. Better by far to introvert with your dreams and adventure vicariously – in comfort, at low cost, and as safely as is possible in our chaotic world. Tompkins wrote his book before television brought live adventure into the home, when survival is made to look so easy through clever editing and cutting; a more modern method of attracting the unwary! Yet I should add that Tompkins' outburst was because he had advertised for a crew to man his 87 ft × 18 ft 6 in ketch, and out of an estimated 300,000 Americans who knew about his proposed voyage, only 30 were interested enough to write for particulars; of these, just three sailed with the ship. It could be argued that things were different forty years ago, but my point in mentioning this incident is that the prospect of adventure invariably produces unforeseen results, so that each and every case differs. Therefore it is impossible to set down any hard-and-fast rules on the general subject of adventuring at sea.

Advice is nearly always sought in the pre-building or pre-purchase period, but I have found that for the most part such help as I have been able to give is largely wasted. What Blue-Water Game entrants are generally seeking is pre-voyage acclaim – and pre-voyage financial support, without strings, is often at the back of their minds too. Failing success in this branch, they will often believe that a post-voyage book will solve all their money problems. Take it from me, it has all been done too often before. Even if you are fortunate enough to find a sponsor, cash will be strictly rationed and contracts rigidly enforced. You would be as controlled as you were before you left the rut – with the disadvantage that you have probably had to sell up the one stake which gave you security in your country: your house.

This leads me to a point which is seldom considered by the inexperienced escaper: what happens after you have 'enjoyed' your adventure? If you have sold your house, to what do you return when you are almost certainly at your lowest ebb, financially, psychologically and physically (apart from your sea-legs!)? I mentioned in a previous chapter the moment of truth when you ask yourself whether or not to build; returning home after a long association with Old Man Neptune will invite catastrophic disillusionment which could well become the most momentous truth you will ever discover, unless you pre-consider this final move in the Blue-Water Game.

Of course, most of these miseries-to-come can be avoided if you have sufficient money to cover them all, although it is an interesting fact that hardly any modern yachtsmen ever has – no matter how wealthy he may seem. There is a ridiculous fault in yachtsmen which persuades virtually everyone who enters the Game to spend very nearly all his capital on the boat, and to hell with the future. So the five-thousand man will spend nearly five thousand, and the fifty-thousand man will spend nearly fifty thousand. The safest procedure is to lay out only half your capital – no matter how large or how small – on the boat, and retain the balance to pay for your voyage – and for your eventual homecoming. Regardless of how wealthy you are, or how poor, put a raincheck aside in a bank, or some equally safe place, and never touch it. This is the very last card up your sleeve and I only hope you will never find yourself in such a hopeless position that you will have to use it. On one occasion in my life, after I had spent even this sparse reserve, I experienced the appalling limbo of the vast emptiness which exists outside that same rut from which so many try to escape; I would not wish such a fate on anybody. So take this last-ditch financial precaution now, while you can afford it. You will never regret it.

The sunny hopes of the dreamer generally begin to cloud over (not for the first time, I'll wager) when he spends his initiation period afloat in his multihull. The vicissitudes he has suffered during the building (whether professional or amateur) may have been acceptable, but now, he thinks, this is it: this is the enjoyment I have paid so much, worked so hard and waited so long to attain. Only very occasionally is this first trial a success; generally it verges on disaster – and I am not referring only to deep-water cruising enthusiasts who should know better, but all too often do not.

The interiors of yachts are seldom, if ever, satisfactory for the habits and requirements of individual owners. Stock boats have stock accommodation fittings, but, alas, the buyers continue to spoil this nice and tidy arrangement. Unless you are rich, you cannot afford to alter standard accommodation; unless you are experienced, the chances are that your money will merely assist you to move out of the frying pan and into the fire. You may think you have designed a better interior for your multi, but I expect you will regret it in due course – and you will still have to live in it.

This is the important point to consider. Whatever your requirements you should be able to adapt yourself to the average stock interior of the craft you have chosen. You may believe that by spending money to adapt the interior to your requirements you will be doing the right thing, but in fact you will still have to adapt yourself to accept whatever you have designed or requested. So why waste the money in the first place? You do not normally have the interior of a house or a car changed, so why a yacht?

On the other hand, the average stock interior of a multihull lacks a number of necessities which you can quite easily add, without all the hoo-ha and unnecessary expenditure implied in the previous two paragraphs. Here is my list of requirements for any but the smallest of multihulls. Since I wouldn't sail for pleasure in any boat unless I had full headroom – I am a six-footer – I am referring to multihulls over about 26-ft LOA.

1   *Heating*. Thin-skinned boats 'sweat' even more easily than old-fashioned,

solid-planked monohulls. Not that the latter were entirely free from condensation, but the designers in those days were more lavish with the interior panelling, and often fitted a coal-burning fire for additional comfort. Take heed! Do not despise the lessons learned by the monohullists.

A small fire and a chimney are essential in a multihull which sails within the temperate zone. Since it can become damned cold at night even in the tropics, I would go as far to state that a fire and a chimney are an asset in a multihull at all times. Never rely on the many fancy convenience heaters (kerosene, butane, electric, etc.) – they are useless because they actually increase condensation. There are a number of suitable anthracite, or other smokeless solid-fuel stoves on the market, but my own preference for small to medium-sized multis is a tiny charcoal-burning fire, totally enclosed, with a $1\frac{1}{2}$-in bore chimney. This ridiculously small gadget can be lit easily and quickly with alcohol, and within a very few minutes even an icy cabin is warming up, with much of the dampness being thrust up the shotgun-like chimney, and consequently less condensation forming on the insides of the hulls and coachroof.

Charcoal is light in weight, economical in its burning and surprisingly low-priced. It also has the advantage that in times of financial stress you could make your own. Clearly it is ideal for small multis when load tonnage (see pages 55–6) is an important consideration. In larger craft, the heavier smokeless fuels can be used in correspondingly bigger stoves with wider-bore chimneys.

2 *Panelling or lining.* Condensation in a multihull is a much greater problem than is generally realised, and it certainly deserves more attention than has been given to it by the majority of designers and builders. The reason why it is such a problem is quite simply because there is so much more interior surface area in a multi than there is in a monohull; also the window area is considerably larger. Even a child at school knows that glass is a wonderful surface for the condensation of moisture; ply and plastic must be nearly as good. Yet, seemingly, few multihull designers or builders have ever considered this simple fact.

At the other end of the thermometer we have another problem, also ignored by designer/builder teams who are supposed to consider the comfort of their customers. The large area of coachroof and/or decking of a multihull is undoubtedly a wonderful sunbathing platform, but on a hot day it can be stifling down below. And what about the sun's rays streaming through all those large windows?

Ideally, the whole interior of a multihull above the bilges should be lined. Regrettably, in the small/medium sizes at any rate, this is not practical, since the LT must be considered. So you should concentrate on those areas where human contact is likely, the sleeping accommodation being the most important. For example, in trimarans I soon discovered that the bunks built into the wings were such wonderful condensation traps that we had to bore holes in the undersides to let the water escape! A simple and cheap way out of this problem was to line the bottom and sides with $\frac{3}{4}$-in sheet polystyrene, which weighed next to nothing and made a near-perfect insulation. But although this was a cheap solution, I had disobeyed my own ruling of never sealing ply on both sides, so I had to raise the mattress on boards to allow a current of air to pass under it. This additional expense had to be added to the total cost of the boat.

It is, of course, the price of such essentials which precludes their installation in a standard production model. If you don't know how essential they are, you are hardly likely to ask for them to be built in. What is worse, after the multi is launched you will be loath to spend yet more money on such work, and so you will sail her and accept her often miserably damp, and occasionally oven-hot, interior as an unfortunate fact of yachting life.

Line the whole of the underside of the coachroof, I say, and you will at least have done something towards reducing interior heat on a hot day. Painted hardboard is suitable, but there are many alternatives on the market – some lighter, some heavier. The gap should be filled with good insulation material, of which there is a great variety; if you lack money, even crumpled newspapers are better than nothing. The panels should be screwed for easy removal, and each section between the coachroof carlines should have a few holes bored for air circulation. Side panels between hull frames can be treated similarly, although here I prefer the panels to be of soft insulation board rather than hardboard (the smooth surface of which could still sweat, in spite of the insulation material behind it). Ventilation holes in vertical panels should be along the top and bottom, and the insulation material behind the panel should never be tight-packed, but loose enough to allow a flow of air. Don't use absorbent insulation like newspapers here!

Ideally, double-glazing would solve all the window problems, but as few people could afford the expense, and few medium-sized multihulls could stand the additional weight, more practical steps should be taken. Curtains will help to some extent to cut down temperature rise and slow down the condensation rate. With vertical windows, there is some gain if the curtains are fastened close to the window by upper and lower rails or wires; for the inward-sloping windows common to most multis this is a 'must'. However, even with the stove and other insulation installed, the windows will always produce their quota of condensation if the weather is cold enough. So it is essential to fit all windows that can cause damage or dampness by dripping with an alloy or plastic guttering, and an appropriate non-splash container to receive the accumulation. Take it from me, if you see an unprotected window above a bunk in a multihull, you are looking at a torture instrument equal to any devised by the Chinese or the Spanish Inquisition: rheumatics by condensation!

3 *Ventilation.* I have already discussed the ventilation of the interior of the hulls (or floats), but the method I outlined will not make any difference to accommodation ventilation – which should be additional.

The most obvious beginning is to get rid of all the galley smells and condensation, and I consider this area alone warrants two or three separate systems:

(a) There should always be at least a skylight or a window which can be opened – preferably the former, since the leeward flap can be selected.

(b) There should always be an overhead extractor, or venturi-type ventilator – preferably immediately over the cooking stove, in which case a hood should be fitted to contain, as far as possible, the ever-rising heat, smells, steam, etc.

(c) Heat escaping does not necessarily imply that the poor cook is being cooled; therefore a clean-air intake is also essential. Look after a good cook, and you will never regret the expense!

For the rest of the vessel, adequate opening skylights should be provided. I rather fancy the plastic dome type which can be tilted in any direction, mainly because they are so much lighter than the conventional old-fashioned roof types (which are seldom installed now). A cheap method for the amateur builder is something similar to the forehatch I invented for Nimble (35). The clear plastic is strong enough to take a man's weight and yet the whole assembly is easy to build and light in weight. If the opening-aft method is unsuitable, a central pivot can be easily arranged. Don't forget to fit suitably-sized bolts for all such openings – to prevent entry and as a precaution against lifting by high winds or deck-invading seas.

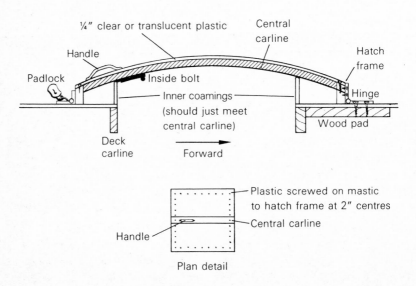

35   A low-priced forehatch or skylight

Forward-opening portholes or windows are a mistake as they will always leak; in my opinion the same ruling applies to side-opening windows too. A multihull at speed slashes up a good deal of spray and the penetration is sometimes unbelievable. It is far better to fit one or two largish water-draining cowl vents on the coachroof top, with a trunk or plastic pipe to feed the ventilation to individual bunks, etc. than it is to have too many opening windows. And while you're about it you may as well send a branch of this type of ventilation down into the bilges – just to be on the safe side (and don't forget to bore holes through any webs or bulkheads which may block free circulation of air).

I must stress that there are a good many other precautions I would take if I was going to join the Blue-Water Game in a multihull, but this book is intended only for multihull tyros. I recommend most strongly that you read as many books as you can about the experiences of people who have actually cruised deep-water – whether in monohulls or multihulls makes little difference. I wish only to put you on the right track by mentioning those points which are generally avoided or, through scarcity of multihull literature, very few people seem to think about. The bulk of seamanship lessons can be learned from any type of yacht.

As a matter of fact I was in some doubt as to whether I should mention such a sport as the Blue-Water Game in a book written specifically for beginners. To me, it seems daft! Yet as I have already pointed out, too many enthusiasts develop the Tricycle Complex too quickly, and even if I had dodged the issue here I am sure it would have made no difference to their secret dreams: they'd have gone anyway! So I have accepted the inevitable and acted accordingly.

Most of what I have had to say in this chapter so far is equally as applicable to the local potterer as it is to the transoceanic adventurer. All too often, I'm afraid, the ditch-crawler believes that because he never strays far from home he is safe from all the hazards experienced by the death-or-glory boys. Such a believer is, of course, the sort of person who has given multihulls a bad name in the past – again, probably the result of the Tricycle Complex. *Those who always sail close to the land are in more continual danger than those who sail across oceans.* This is a truism which, unfortunately, is not always appreciated.

The weekend potterer will probably ignore this chapter because of the title, and yet he will be setting forth into more danger than the fellow I am trying to advise. I suppose it is fair enough to take in small doses the unnecessary discomfort he is bound to suffer, but is he right to set sail in a multihull which is badly equipped and more likely than not inadequately victualled? Don't make the mistake of believing that you will always get back to your moorings on schedule; every yacht that leaves harbour should have sufficient hard rations and water on board to last the crew for at least a fortnight. You never know – but you will certainly find out if you lose your mast, the engine won't start, the wind is offshore, and you've only brought sandwiches and a vacuum flask for the day...

By badly equipped, I mean lacking any of the necessary fitments I have been describing in this and previous chapters. You own a boat that is capable of entering the Blue-Water Game, but for heaven's sake don't expect it to perform miracles when you get into difficulties. The Lodestar *Three Wishes*, on show at the 1965 London Boat Show, was sailed single-handed across the North Sea to Sweden immediately afterwards – in January! But very few glittering boat show multihulls can immediately perform like this. Only you, as owner/skipper, can ensure your own safety, and it is fatal to rely too much on overworked rescue services.

For example, another flaw which can be found all too often in stock multi-hulls is lack of suitable pumps. You may be told that since a multihull cannot sink, a pump is superfluous; you may even believe that as you have no intention of sailing out of sight of land, and since pumps are expensive and multihulls cannot sink, and because you have spent all your pump money on a more expensive ship-to-shore radio (for safety – and no doubt for prestige), in dire distress you could always ring up to be rescued. I wouldn't count on it if I were you! Regard the situation exactly as if you were setting out on a circumnavigation: fit powerful, non-jamming pumps in both, or all three hulls, and then pray they will prove to be a complete waste of money.

While I'm on the subject it is advisable for me to point out two further faults which are all too often found in wooden multihulls:

(a) When you take over a new boat, personally inspect every inch of all the bilges – shavings, sawdust, dirt, etc. in these areas can prove fatal in a crisis.

(b) Ensure that all bilges are connected in each hull, and that all limber holes are clear of obstruction; builders often seem unwilling to cut limbers through ply or glassfibre webs athwart hull bilges, or else they bore them ridiculously high. One gallon of bilgewater weighs ten pounds! A series of low dams in one hull can increase the load to a dangerous amount.

Then again, there is this business of 'self-draining' cockpits, which generally speaking means a couple of one-inch holes. This is so blatantly ridiculous that I wonder the farce is maintained – unless the real purpose is to clear rainwater. It is true that a wave is unlikely to swamp the cockpit of either a cat or a tri, but 'unlikely' does not mean never. Catamarans, having much larger cockpits than tris, could very easily be overwhelmed by a pooping wave; the answer is to fit a large grid (teak, if you want something fancy) which will immediately dump most of a flood back where it came from. Trimaran cockpit drainage schemes depend largely on the size and position of the area, but they must always be arranged so that inundating waves are returned into the sea as expeditiously as possible. In this respect the local cruising man is at more risk than the Blue-Water Game adherent, since shallow waters produce short, steep seas – just the job for invading unsuspecting cockpits!

I believe it is much better to think about all multihulls as potential entrants for the Blue-Water Game than to divide them into coastal cruisers, cruiser-racers, offshore cruisers and deep-water cruisers (plus racers, but I am not concerned so much about these expensive toys). The points I have made so far are applicable to all types, and if a multihull is reckoned unsafe for deep water, then I wouldn't like to use her at all. I am quite sure that it is a mistake to build cabin multihulls for 'day' sailing, or 'summer' cruising; a new title, 'joy-boats', is as puerile as it sounds. There's precious little joy in being at sea in a small boat once the sun goes in, the wind increases and the seas rise; this is when it is very comforting to know that your multihull has proved that she can take it even if you can't!

What else can I say? I don't want to continue with the doom and gloom, and it shouldn't really be necessary – except that the Tricycle Complex continues insidiously to provoke foolhardiness in far too many tyro tri- and cata-mariners. I defend the right of every adventurous person to commit suicide in whatever manner he or she chooses, but I abhor the legislation that such people invoke as a result of their idiocy. A very good rule to remember comes from the days of wooden ships and iron men: 'It ain't the ships, it's the men in 'em.' How exactly right this old saw has proved to be in the case of multihulls!

You may think that I have overstressed the necessity of comfort in this chapter. Never make the mistake of 'roughing it' when participating in any adventure, least of all at sea. The time will inevitably come when you will have to rely on your ability to take the rough with the smooth; your survival then will depend on your physical and psychological condition immediately previous to the worsening situation. It is your duty, either as skipper or crew, to be prepared for the worst; when the trouble finally arrives you must be in tip-top condition to tackle it. You will not achieve this state in uncomfortable accommodation, and your chances will diminish even more rapidly if you have been living in perpetual dampness.

Even the bunks in multihulls are all too often badly planned – or rather they are inserted more as a sales gimmick than a sailing necessity. Double bunks, previously sparse to non-existent in all but the largest monohulls, are now spread around the large interiors of multihulls to use up the space. These might prove attractive to newlyweds, but they are not at all suitable for ensuring relaxed sleep. The motion within a multihull may be minimal – insufficient to spill a drink standing on the cabin table – but a small, narrow bunk is preferable in any size of seagoing vessel to the body-rolling space in a double bed. One double bunk is fair enough if that is what your spouse demands, but far too many multihulls have used the space without much thought for those who have to use it. 'Sleeps six' sounds fine – until you discover that it only really means three bunks; even a division by a wooden bunk board, angled so that the occupants sleep nose-to-tail, can hardly be regarded as satisfactory. Certainly I would not like to use this arrangement for weeks at a time while crossing an ocean.

The cramming of sleeping accommodation into multihulls as a selling factor naturally does not take into account the LT (see pages 55–6), nor the cooking or eating facilities (36). All too often you will find a multi recorded, say, as 'sleeping ten', when the size of the cooker, the space for the cook and the dimensions of the sink and flat-top surrounds would preclude preparing hot meals for more than half this quantity. After all, the average housewife seldom, if ever, has to cater for ten persons at home in her large and comfortable kitchen; so why expect her to tackle the job in a ridiculously small space in a wave-tossed multihull? Furthermore, in one particular 'sleeps ten' (in five double bunks) multi, the cabin table could seat only four persons! Even assuming that a cook could be found willing enough to prepare for two-and-a-half sittings, at half a gallon of water per head per day tankage for just two weeks at sea would amount to 700 lb. Since the LT of this multihull was in the region of 2500 lb, and ten people and two weeks' water alone would weigh very nearly this much, it can be seen that the whole conception was misleading, to put it mildly. Yet many of these particular plans, and completed craft, were sold to unsuspecting enthusiasts around the world.

So to return to the earlier part of this chapter, where I suggested that the first trials in your new multihull could easily verge on disaster, it will

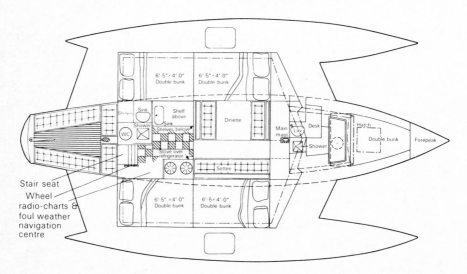

36 A typical example of overcrowding in a multihull, with double bunks
    and negligible cooking and eating facilities

be seen that provided you think, as precisely as you can, about each point I have raised, making whatever sensible inferences you wish, you should avoid many of the misconceptions which have misled tyros in the past. And if you have understood the reason why I have included weekend potterers in a chapter about deep-water cruising, then you are well on the correct way to knowing about the dangers of the Tricycle Complex. Assimilate and infer – I can give no better advice.

To conclude, I can only say that I believe more and more people will continue to escape to sea in their own multihulls in order to get away, at least for a time, from the dreadful political bickerings which hang like thunder-clouds over nearly every country in the world. Take heed of what I have said, but do not hesitate in your ambition. Whether the oil crisis is solved or not will make little difference to those who intend to enter the Blue-Water Game. Although there are many difficulties to overcome, and although the task is great and the stakes are high, of one asset you can always be assured: at least the wind is free!

9 Bad Weather and Good Times

If you are seeking confidence, or some pearls of positive wisdom about handling multihulls in bad weather, you will not find much of either in this chapter. So many different designs of trimarans and catamarans have proved by example that they are capable of riding out extreme weather conditions at sea that further assurance or reassurance from me would be superfluous. You have been solely responsible for your choice of boat; now you must be equally responsible for ensuring that you, your crew and your vessel are ready in all respects for the sea. The object of this book is to prime your thinking, not to lay down hard and fast rules.

To be realistic, I don't think that enough is known about multihulls anyway for me to be too specific concerning bad-weather seamanship. Some may say this, some that – and all methods work to some extent. This is not a new malady; the handling of monohulls in extreme conditions is still argued about just as intensely as when I was a kid, particularly when something happens to a well-known yacht or a prominent yachtsman. You will, for example, continue to find staunch supporters of John Voss's sea-anchoring theory and practice, now over 70 years old – although Voss was by no means the first to use the gadget when he sailed his 38-ft × 5-ft Indian war canoe nearly round the world in 1901–4.

Needless to say, the sea-anchor argument has filtered into multihull seaman-ship, and although the majority of experienced skippers seem to be against using this method of preventing a vessel from moving through the water in extreme conditions, others, equally experienced, have tried it and have after-wards approved. More popular for controlled running before gales is the old trick of towing heavy warps or lines from either quarter, or a looped warp from both quarters; this has been tried many times and found satisfactory. One point is made quite clearly by most deep-water multihullists: never run directly ahead of breaking seas, but always angle across the slopes; in the early days Jim Wharram and Arthur Piver (to quote but two) quickly dis-covered the advantage of this after their respective multis had nose-dived steeply into a trough ahead and had been brought up all standing. It is interesting to note that Bernard Moitessier and others advocate angling for monohulls as well.

There is not even a safe rule about heaving-to or lying ahull. Multihulls differ so much in their handling characteristics that you must discover for yourself which is the best for your particular design. Do not despise monohull seamanship in this respect; monohull yachtsmen have been experimenting in small craft for very much longer than modern cat and tri sailors, and the lessons learned by them should be assimilated even if they are not used. You cannot expect to be capable of experimenting with your multihull in adverse conditions unless you have learned about all the possible methods of surviving a storm at sea.

For example, having read most of the books listed in Appendix I, I cannot recollect anybody mentioning the one item which I would regard as an essential card-up-sleeve last resort: oil. If ever there was a life-saver in extreme weather, this is it. In the old days of floating lead mines and straight keels it was an essential part of the vessel, since seas breaking over the decks had to be tamed, but although this is unlikely to happen to lightweight multis I would still forfeit the weight penalty and carry a couple of gallons of fish oil, with some small canvas bags stuffed with oakum to spread the balm on troubled waters. You may never need the stuff but by golly if you do you will be as grateful for it as you may be for that gold coin reserve I hope you have tucked away for a rainy day. Competent seamanship always implies an unfailing production of cards from up the sleeve, or ideas from a suitably trained mind; only the incompetent scream 'Help!' before they've given themselves a chance to exhaust all the possibilities which no doubt are scattered in disarray around their boat and in their minds.

The biggest danger facing you in bad weather is your Tricycle Complex. Here I must repeat a story I told against myself in *Trimaran Development*, which will enable you to avoid the same mistake.

On one occasion I had to deliver a Lodestar from Great Yarmouth to Ipswich in mid-winter. I had one moderately experienced crewman with me. We left in the late afternoon, and the force 4 westerly wind allowed us to lay a course straight down the Norfolk/Suffolk coastline, about two miles offshore. As darkness came, the chill wind whistled around the open-sided wheelhouse, so we put up the terylene curtains. Soon, the warmth from the saloon fire crept into the wheelhouse, and we smoked and chatted and brewed hot drinks in comfort very nearly equal to the bridge of the *Queen Mary*. Four hours passed.

I became aware of a flurry on deck, and I peered through the windscreen to see what was happening. In the dim radiance of the port and starboard navigation lights, the seas looked very much the same as before – or did they? Were we going any faster? I felt the foresheet, and then the mainsheet strain. Then my senses were alerted.

I opened the lee curtain. A cacophony of noise beat inwards. I scrambled on deck. The roar of our progress and the battering of the force 7 gale was a shattering reminder that I had been incredibly lax – and very lucky. After that I kept the lee curtain open. The comfortable warmth was soon dissipated, and we no longer lounged in contented idleness. Suddenly, but not surprisingly, I relearned the truth that you can never afford to relax when at sea.

Even with open-cockpit multihulls, a far greater sense of security is felt than in an average monohull cockpit. This may be because it is seldom necessary to dress up in oilskins and other foul-weather gear unless it is actually raining, whereas the poor old monohullist has to prepare for the worst long before it arrives, in all but the hottest summer weather. This advantage (on the one hand) is so obviously true that time and time again it is quoted by enthusiasts and salesmen; what you are not told is the disadvantage, which I have now brought to your attention.

Personally, I regard the multihull wheelhouse, either open-sided or totally enclosed, as a very positive advantage – provided you learn, as I did, from my one experience of slackness. Not only is this shelter invaluable for saving you from penetrating and insidious fatigue brought about by rain and cold, but it is also a wonderful protection from the direct rays of the sun, which can also become energy-consuming if you have too much of it. Never despise comfort for the helmsman; on the other hand, never over-indulge yourself with the comfort provided.

Another advantage of a cat or tri wheelhouse is that it is situated above the hulls. I have already mentioned how, in the early days, most multihullists were sufficiently surprised by the noise produced by the hulls rushing through water to pass comment on it; now you will learn that the least noisy position aboard is in the wheelhouse. Continuous noise, as well as wet and cold and too much direct sunshine, can induce a numb resignation which can become just as enervating.

And not only noise; the motion of a multihull when conditions worsen tends to be sick-provoking, particularly for ex-monohullists who have learned from previous boats to accustom their stomachs to the see-saw pitch, the lurch to leeward and the ever-present gyrating roll. Multihulls don't roll, particularly when on a dead run (the worse direction for bad rolling in monos), but they produce an action which is really a combination of everything a monohull does – only over a shorter distance, and much more rapidly. 'Anything you can do I can do quicker; I can do anything quicker than you' would seem to be a suitable song for multihulls to boast to monohulls. It is of course this continuous rapid movement which enables you to walk about the decks in reasonable equilibrium at all times, and keeps that motion-testing, three-quarters-filled mug from slopping its contents on the cabin table. It took me some time to accustom myself to the seakeeping action of a trimaran, but in spite of having been seasick on several occasions I prefer the steadiness of the multis to the extreme movement of the monos.

Nevertheless, the movement on and in a multihull at its extremities can be extremely violent, and for this reason the galley should always be kept as near amidships as is practical. In fact, as far as possible keep everything out of the 'ends' – particularly weight. Neither cats nor tris react kindly in a seaway if there is weight in any of the bows. Although most tri plans show sleeping accommodation in the forepeak of the centre hull, in my opinion the designer should be made to spend one night at sea in a gale in this wretched position for every tri built to his design. Admittedly some are not as violent as others, but the sickening hanging-in-space/crushing 'G' action and reaction is generally not very sleep-provoking.

On deck, the motion in the bow pulpit of a trimaran when beating into bad seas is an experience never to be forgotten. I think this must have been where Art Piver began whooping and hollering, for that is exactly what one feels like doing. Exhilarating hardly describes the sheer joy of it. But you've got to hang on tightly, otherwise you'll be catapulted over the stern – if the mainmast fails to stop you! This is when you will appreciate my advice about a well-secured and very strong pulpit. I've handed jibs on long bowsprits that have dipped me waist-deep, but I've never sailed on anything that beats the thrill of a pulpit-ride on a tri. It should be remembered that almost invariably this is a dry position, except in very bad conditions indeed: even then, you should never take solid water aboard – if you do, you're overloaded forrard.

There seems to be a distinct difference between cats and tris when the subject of reefing comes up. I can only repeat what I have written before about my tri experiences and leave it to cat fanciers to make their own rules. However, from what I have read in books and articles it appears to me that early reefing is more necessary in cats than in tris. Don't take this as a general rule, since it is no more than an observation.

I have sailed a Piver Nimble, unreefed, in winds which have been coast-guard-confirmed as force 8 and 9 – that is to say, between 34 and 47 knots, or 39–55 mph. As I explained in the chapter about capsizes, when the wind-speed exceeds 40 mph statistically you are entering the capsize danger sector unless you reef, so my several exploits during this testing period should not be taken to mean that I do not recommend reefing early. Nevertheless, I believe that a good deal of uncomfortable coastal cruising has been suffered because too many people have become so nervous about capsizing. The difficulty is that different designs of tris and cats have such varied mast heights and working sail areas that it is quite impossible to come up with a ruling which will make any sense. But my own experiences indicate that a Piver single-chine tri prefers a press of sail in short, steep seas; if reefed in the same conditions, she 'dies' – that is, the feeling of 'flying' is suddenly reduced to wave-slashing, common-or-garden sailing. So I am of the opinion that a light-weight trimaran (you couldn't get away with it if overloaded) sails better in a bad seaway when unreefed because she is literally beginning to fly, i.e. her wings are supplying some lift to offset the smashing effect of wave action.

129

I feel sure that if designers would only exploit this unique feature we could sail even faster and in greater comfort; maybe hydrofoils are the answer, but I doubt it.

To return to more normal reefing problems, the 'barrier' figure of 40 mph will undoubtedly seem much too high for most multihullists. This is force 8 (39–46 mph): a fresh gale. If, however, you have followed my advice about oversize reefing gear, (and adequately strong rigging) there is no problem about doing the job now – even at this late stage. And what is more, you can handle it in comfort by heaving-to, which most multihulls do easily. (This is when you will appreciate those tough deck rails I discussed earlier.) On the other hand, if you are a cautious type – and there is nothing to be ashamed of in this, since it is the basis of good seamanship – you will probably begin to think about pulling a reef down when the wind reaches force 5 (19–24 mph). Well, why not? Better to be safe than sorry, so try it out. You will find that the balance between main and foresail is rather critical, but it varies so much between different multihulls that you will have to find out for yourself how your particular design reacts. Better by far to do this in force 5 than force 8! A fair guide is not to reduce the headsail(s) in proportion to the mainsail, but to leave rather more sail area forward of the mast than you would in a monohull. At the same time, be wary of reducing sail too much: multihulls do need the firm thrust of their wind motors, otherwise they will not perform if you have to tack or turn sharply.

The delicate art of helmsmanship comes into its own when you tack a multihull in a bad seaway. This is probably the one and only occasion when a monohull has the advantage, simply because sheer weight must carry more way. Faced with a strong wind and a barrier of advancing waves, any light-weight multihull will tend to become temperamental and react accordingly. It is up to you to be ready with whichever ploys are necessary to ensure immediate response from your vessel. I take for granted your intention of becoming a conscientious skipper, so I trust that you will have worked hard during the early days of sailing your boat by experimenting throughout the wind range, at least up to force 8. Of one saving grace you can be certain: all multihulls, if they get into irons, will immediately begin a sternboard, so apply full rudder in the opposite direction to the way you want to go, and very quickly you will be back on course and heading in the right direction.

All too often the Tricycle Complex ensures that a nut-case will manage to miss stays in some impossible position at the worst possible moment – unreefed, in a narrow channel, with a flood or ebb tide racing against 'hurricane-force winds' (to quote what the newspapers will say about it afterwards – actually probably no more than force 7). Our hero misses stays, makes a sternboard, remembers to reverse his helm, pays off on the correct tack – and his tri or cat promptly capsizes. Why? *Because any sailing vessel will be knocked flat if the sails are presented broadside to the wind without way on the vessel.*

My sailing barge, *John & Mary*, measured 81 ft × 18 ft and carried some 3000 square feet of working canvas. She was flat-bottomed, and drew only 3 ft 3 in aft; her masts, rigging and sails weighed over 5 tons. Built in 1897, she could carry over 100 tons of cargo, and had done so until I bought her in 1946. I sailed her 'light' for eleven years, until 1957. It would be thought that such a vessel, unballasted, would be extremely cranky in high winds – and therefore easily capsizable. The highest wind I met with all plain sail was a half-hour squall which reached 48 mph (according to anemometer records at a nearby airfield on the east Lincolnshire coast). Close-hauled, *J. & M.* very nearly submerged her mighty bows (freeboard 8 ft at the stem), and lifted her port chine some 3 ft clear of the racing seas. *But she showed no signs of imminent capsize.* The only occasions when Thames barges have capsized – and they are very few – were almost always when they had lost way (generally whilst 'winding' or tacking) and were struck by a heavy squall. Whereupon they just fell over on their side, and that was that. The extremely heavy gear and tackles necessary to control these giants meant that the skipper, with only one crewman, was almost helpless in such a situation: between them, they could not possibly pay-out the mainsheet and vangs, and brail the mainsail and ruck the topsail in time – and even if they could, the chances were that a ferocious squall would still overwhelm her through the sheer windage of all the heavy spars and complex rigging, before the inertia of about 100 tons displacement could be overcome and she could begin to move through the water again.

And so it is with multihulls – with the proviso that our nut-case could so easily have prevented an ignominious capsize if he had slackened his sheets, and then overhauled them as his vessel paid-off on the right tack. In this way, ea-a-a-s-s-sing her into motion, he would have displayed his seamanship and helmsmanship, and not just his total dependence on the Tricycle Complex.

All this can be summed up in one simple rule: when sailing a multihull in winds of force 5 or above, or in any area which is apparently partially or fully protected from wind by hills or tall trees but where squall flurries are likely, never lose way, or if you do immediately slacken all sheets and bear away to take the wind as much as possible on the quarter.

Having followed my advice to read as many books as you can, you will of course, already be aware that in squally weather you react in the opposite manner to monohulls: they luff; you bear away. But you are not generally told what to do after you have followed this important rule, AND THE SQUALL CONTINUES TO INCREASE – or perhaps firms up into a gale. It doesn't always happen, but it can. The answer is not to waste a second: REEF THE MAIN NOW. The great advantage of all multihulls is that they are easily controlled before the wind and they don't roll, so you will find the process of reefing quite simple. But never do anything, apart from heaving-to or lying ahull, which may result in your multi losing way, and certainly never luff to squalls or bad seas unless you are very experienced indeed.

Most, if not all, multihulls heave-to very easily, but you should experiment with your design in varying winds in order to find out precisely what she can and cannot do. In Piver designs I found that all I had to do was tack, and leave the foresail aback. Immediately the tri stopped sailing, although the bows would swing a little downwind until the drive from the mainsail held them up. In a few seconds the foresail and mainsail would be balanced, and in any blow the tri would drive ahead almost directly into wind at a speed of around 1–2 knots. How this sailing-into-wind miracle worked I am unable to explain technically, but I can assure theorists that it did happen – always. But heaving-to in this manner is not necessarily the best method, as the following story, taken from *Trimaran Development*, indicates. My skipper for four years, Mike Fowler, was certainly experienced enough at handling Piver designs in local waters, but when he sailed a 40-ft × 22-ft Victress, *Zhu-Dum*, to Malta in May 1969:

As we neared Finisterre, the north-east wind veered south and began to increase. I reduced sail to mizzen and foresail, and this eased our motion somewhat; but the effort was still very much as though one was driving a powerboat into a short steep chop – a continuous rush and plunge which made it impossible to sleep, sit, cook, or in fact do anything in comfort.

The wind was by now force 7, gusting 8, but as I had been dead reckoning for two days I decided that I must continue to press to windward for as long as we could stand it in order to clear Finisterre. It went on for fifteen long hours, wind and sea getting steadily worse. On several occasions I backed the foresail in an attempt to ease the motion, finishing up in a hove-to position, but as with all Piver designs Victress continued to head-reach at 2½–3 knots, which was too fast for the prevailing conditions.

I realised I must do something to slow her down. Conditions below were appalling, and I was also beginning to worry about the possibility of structural damage from the violent pounding. The foresail in use was the smallest we had, but somehow the area had to be reduced: I decided to use the good old barge method of tying a knot in the head.

I jammed myself in the pulpit, and Richard eased the halliard while I gathered the sail. Suddenly I realised that the motion of *Zhu-Dum* had altered radically. Instead of having to hang on to prevent myself from being catapulted overboard, I found that I could now sit perfectly comfortably on the lower rail of the pulpit. It seemed almost as though the seas had quietened down, although in fact they and the gale were as bad as ever. The tri's motion was reduced to nothing more than gentle swoops.

It dawned on me then what I had done. Without the pressure of her foresail, *Zhu-Dum* was being forced further into the wind by the mizzen until it lost its drive; then the bows would fall away a little and the mizzen would fill and force them up into wind again. She lay now like a monstrous gull: her tremendous buoyancy kept her decks free from spray, while below there was practically no sensation of being afloat at all! The three of us looked at each other for a full minute, and then we all grinned. 'Put the kettle on, Richard', I said, 'while I stow this bloody jib.'

It did not take us very long to prepare a three-course meal, and we sat down together and ate in comfort, with all civilised appointments. Everything stayed where it was put, even the wine glasses – although we soon transferred the contents of the latter to a safer place, just in case!

I had in the meantime obtained DF fixes, and found that we were some 30 miles offshore and well clear of the Bay. That night it was only a question of keeping a lookout for ships from the comfort of the wheelhouse – a sort of glorified anchor watch in warmth and dryness – while outside the gale raged, and the high seas hissed and foamed around us. On board it was as though we were moored in a rather uneasy harbour – no worse than that!

By 1100 next morning, the wind went round to the north-west and moderated. Before getting sail on her, I checked our position again by fixes. We had made 10 miles to windward in 17 hours, and this under mizzen alone. I call that windward work in comfort!

This sort of experience indicates the importance of thoroughly knowing your boat. Why suffer hours or days of misery, when quite simply you could do this or that and live in comfort? Why, indeed – but all too many multihullists accept implicitly what they are told and never bother to experiment until they are nearly overwhelmed by their first storm at sea.

The pure racing boys have tended to make multihull sailing appear difficult, suitable only for the very experienced. In some respects this is a good thing, although I know of cases when the Tricycle Complex has converted previously-dedicated monohull racing men into multi enthusiasts – with disastrous results. Equally, sponsoring has been the curse behind many a cat or tri which has hit the headlines in the wrong way; wealth does not necessarily buy the best, and although sponsors may believe they are 'on to a good thing, publicitywise', the chances are that they are merely suffering from a touch of the old Tricycle Complex. Wise multihullists will ignore the toings and froings of such people, and will hug the secret of their own sea comfort with silent laughter. Fortunately we no longer have to rely so much on publicity, good or bad. Let the headlines scream 'Disaster' and 'Drama' as they will; you and I know what multihulls can accomplish – once the Tricycle Complex has been sorted out in one's mind.

This is as good a time as any in this book for me to clear the decks for somebody who has had much more than average experience of sailing both trimarans and catamarans. Surprisingly, few people have built, owned and sailed both, but Phil Patterson had the good fortune to be in at the beginning

133

of tris in Britain. He was the chap, you will remember, who sold me the plans which ultimately became *Nimble Eve* – so he was ahead of me in this aspect of tri experience. He sailed Piver's original *Nimble* in 1961, and built and sailed several different designs of tris during the next five years. In 1966 he made a transatlantic voyage from Fort Chimo, Ungava Bay, N.E. Canada to Ardrossan, Scotland, in a Nimble, and during 1970–3 he chartered his 42-ft cat, *Iconoclast*, making some long coastal voyages which included a non-stop trip to Gibraltar. In 1974, he raced his design, *Heavenly Twins*, a 26-ft cruising catamaran, in the Round Britain, finishing 37th. So who better to judge between two or three hulls?

I have never known a multihull to equal a reasonable monohull when it comes to tacking. The best cats and tris will go about surely, but in strong winds you must always be prepared to hold the jib aback. I have known some designs – and I am thinking now of one cat and one tri – which refused to tack in strong winds, even when suitably reefed. However these were exceptional examples. It is in the nature of the beast, having high windage, light weight and little in the water, that she will tend to be skittish, so before tacking you must not pinch her up and then expect her to tack with little way. Rather she must be sailed around fairly fast. Also some have their own idiosyncrasies. One cat ketch I know requires her mizzen sheet released; on a particular tri you apply a little helm, then a bit more, and finally, almost in the eye of the wind, full helm. On others you just put the helm down. Nor, as a general rule, do they like being sailed under mainsail alone. Normally you must have both main and jib set to retain full control, although some, particularly those with the mast stepped well aft, may well handle satisfactorily under foresail only.

I sail a multihull much as a monohull, although it is a little more difficult on a multihull to tell when to reef or change down. A mono tells you it's time when her gunwale is awash; in a multi you get a feeling that sailing over-canvassed is going to cost you dear in rigging and sails!

Because it is so easy, even in foul weather, to move about on a multi, I believe they are safer than monohulls, particularly in the smaller sizes – say under 30 ft. Crew fatigue is generally less, as it is so much easier to handle the sails. The fact that you are not so tired, and have a big safe area from which to hand the jib, means that you are not only capable of doing the correct thing, but you are still sufficiently alert to make the correct decision. A gale at sea can be a very numbing experience. I have noticed time and again how, when finally making port after a spell of hard weather, my experiences have been nowhere near as hairy as the monohull boys.

Hove-to in a gale off Bloody Foreland in 17–20 ft waves (trough to crest – a monohull surviving the same gale claimed they were 40 ft!) in one of my 26-ft Heavenly Twins cruising catamarans, I found that periodically a gust would blow the bows off and, if unlucky, a breaking sea would catch her broadside on, creating a lot of foam and spray on deck and down the ventilator. So I tried streaming from the weather bow a 300-ft heavy nylon line with a rubber tyre on the end. It worked like a charm. We rode all the seas at about 40°, with not a splash on board. The storm jib was aback, the main deep-reefed, and the helm alee. It was so comfortable that we had a four-course meal, and each a flannel bath.

On another occasion in the same boat, single-handed off Portland Bill in rapidly deteriorating weather, I tacked so that the jib was aback and the boat hove-to. Deep reef the main, then release the jib sheet and let go the halliard, clip on safety harness, and go forward to hand and stow the jib. The mainsheet is hard in and the helm left free. The cat is moving at about 2 knots between 50°–70° off the wind, so with the leeway we are making almost square drift. Everything is quiet enough, and if a collision seems likely, I can quickly spin the wheel and pay off down wind. My Aldis signal lamp is ready for instant use. Sudden gales such as this are usually soon over, so provided I keep well away from shore, the boat will be quite safe. I could have used either the working jib or the storm jib rather than the main, and certainly I would have done so had I wanted to sail down wind. I do not think I would have handled the situation any differently had I been in either a tri or a monohull.

For my type of cruising – drying harbours, tidal creeks and the occasional long-distance cruise – I find cats are best. However, others with the same requirements may well choose either a tri or a monohull. If you have tried all three types, then at least your decision on which type suits you is based on more than just prejudice.

Nobody actually enjoys storms at sea in any type of vessel, but I think it is reasonable to say that one feels somewhat safer, and a good deal more comfortable, on board a multihull – provided the skipper has done his home-work and knows what he is about. When you read the books I have listed in Appendix I, you will find that the greatest complaint against multihulls – the possibility of capsize – is seldom, if ever, mentioned. This is indicative of the enormous difference in thinking between those who actually sail multi-hulls, and those who are convinced that they know best, even when they are ignorant of the facts.

Such accounts of good living in multihulls during periods of bad weather that have been published over the years seem to infuriate monohullists. When my book *Trimarans* was first published in 1969, one yachting magazine reviewer was sufficiently incredulous to comment, 'Sir, you must be joking!', to the following extract:

A yachtsman who was crossing the Bay of Biscay in a Lodestar told me that he hove-to for three days in force 9–10 conditions, a gale in which seventeen French and Portuguese fishing vessels were lost; although he lost his rudder from the violent battering, he claimed that he had gained 60 miles to windward, and '... most of the time we lounged about in deckchairs and enjoyed the sunshine'.

Replying to my answer, in which I quoted other similar facts, the reviewer wrote, '. . . call me stubborn, but I just cannot believe that one would sit around in a deckchair, or that any sailing vessel would make such distance to windward'. Well, I could quote any number of cases to prove that sailing-to-windward-when-hove-to has been an accomplished fact for well over a decade. The best example of enjoying life in a deckchair on board a trimaran can be found in the book *Trimaran Against the Trades*, when Granny Emie Cole, aged 92, knitted contentedly in this fashion during a voyage from East Africa to New Zealand, '... in fair weather, flat calm, and really bad weather'. I do not intend to imply from these statements that multihullists automatically live a life of ease and comfort during storms at sea, but I have printed my critic's condemnation in order to show that opposition to multihulls has been, and still is, based almost entirely on monohull experience. Single hulls in gales are hell, but provided multihulls have been strongly built, carefully rigged, and the many precautions and extras I have mentioned incorporated, I am convinced that they are not only easier on the crew than a monohull in bad conditions, but they are also safer. I know this is so with trimarans, but as I cannot speak with experienced authority about catamarans, I asked Roland Prout who, with his brother Francis, started it all on the eastern side of the Atlantic, to let me have his views. Here they are:

> Since the days when David Lewis took his family around the world in the catamaran *Rehu Moana*, a great deal of experience has been gained and many lessons learned about cats in rough weather and in the open sea. Dozens of ocean crossings have been made in various designs, and from the first-hand accounts of many adventurous sailors we now have a pretty good idea of the capabilities of cruising catamarans in most conditions. The net result of these accounts and experiences seems to be that, given a boat of good design and construction, a catamaran of say 35 ft and upwards is capable of sailing safely over the oceans of the world and is able to take care of herself and crew at least as well as, and in some ways better than, her monohulled sisters.
>
> I am now talking about a cruising catamaran which is solid and stable enough not to be capable of being capsized in winds up to force 6–7, even should the crew be inexperienced enough to keep all sail up and be inattentive to the sheets in such conditions. I would consider our Snowgoose 34 as being just such a boat, meeting the minimum requirements for safety of this kind. This is not to say that a lighter and more heavily canvassed catamaran cannot quite safely be sailed in open water in rough weather when in the hands of an experienced and alert crew.
>
> When we judge a boat's capacity to survive strong winds and rough seas, we must consider one or two situations. If one is out in the ocean, and well away from land when severe weather is encountered, one is able to reduce sail to a minimum and either run before the storm or simply heave-to or, as is often done in cats in storm conditions, let the boat lie ahull, close up hatches and doors and go below to read or sleep. One seldom has these choices in a situation near land, and it may be necessary to keep up sufficient canvas to sail out of

the danger of land or shallows, often in seas which are far less comfortable than those encountered far out in the ocean. It is in these situations that a boat needs to be capable, tough and heavy enough to carry her sail in order to make progress to windward. I believe that a well-designed cat is more capable than most boats and is easier on the crew when coping with strong and rough conditions. A catamaran of good design can run down large waves and is able to surf down steep slopes at high speeds. I have often surfed at 16–18 knots down steep seas with the greatest feeling of safety and with complete control. Broaching in such conditions is not the frightening and dangerous experience it would be in a monohull. A cat is also light enough to lift and ride up over breaking following seas and I have not heard of anyone having heavy water over the cockpit. In fact, even the Swales, who sailed their well-loaded *Annalese* from Australia across the southern ocean, encountering many gales, said that at no time did they get the cockpit swamped. Also Colin Swale told me that he did not find it necessary to tow any warps or drogues in order to check the forward surfing rushes they often experienced. This could become necessary if one wished to run stern on to the seas and leave the boat to herself with tiller either lashed or under self-steering vane. A bridle made by attaching a line from each hull seems to be the best way to stream a drogue aft. I also believe a cat would ride a severe storm very comfortably to a well-weighted drogue streamed aft from one hull, allowing the boat to take the oncoming seas at an angle between the stern of one hull and the opposite bow.

We have had many reports of cats riding out a storm lying ahull. Most boats and especially catamarans assume a beam-to-seas attitude, and all who have had experience of riding out a storm in this way agree it is both safe and comfortable. The cat will slide sideways in heavily-breaking beam seas and there seems no danger of a capsize through sea action. This is not true of a keel yacht, where a heavy-breaking beam sea will roll the hull down, with the keel gripped by solid water to assist in the knockdown; should the seas be large enough, the yacht will then roll down the slope of the wave and turn right over as has often been described – the Smeetons' experience being one example of this. A catamaran clings to the side of the wave like a fly on a wall and is lifted bodily in the foaming crest and carried along sideways as the wave passes under the boat. I believe it is in these circumstances that a catamaran has some advantage over a trimaran in that a fully buoyant hull is supporting the boat on the down slope with no fear of being driven under, and the crest slams into the windward side of the lee hull under the bridge deck, lifting and dragging it sideways down the wave. We experienced this action during a sail back from Holland in a Snowgoose during a north-east force 8 gale on the beam. In this instance we carried very little sail, but the beam seas were so steep and large that they would certainly have been quite dangerous to a keel yacht of our length, yet the Snowgoose rode them well without giving the crew undue anxiety. On about two occasions a beam sea broke right over the cabin top and the cat was taken sideways with the force as described above.

Although I am sure that smaller catamarans can safely travel the oceans, I would put the minimum size for completely acceptable safety at almost

34 ft, or about three tons. I do not believe a cat of this size and weight is likely to be capsized in normal gale or severe gale conditions at sea by wave action alone.

Smaller, lighter catamarans should have some form of masthead buoyancy and a means of righting themselves in event of a capsize if they are to be sailed far out to sea where no help is available. Of course the dangers are just as great close to shore around our coasts where most people do their sailing, but help or a safe harbour is often within reach, and a cat could save itself and the crew by beaching if the coast allowed.

To sum up, I believe a catamaran when well designed is as safe and sea-worthy as any other form of boat of its own size, with certain advantages in its favour. Ordinary seamanship applies when dealing with heavy weather as with any other type, so experience and knowing the characteristics of your own boat are the most important factors for safety. Not least of the safety factors, and one which can be of great comfort in extreme heavy weather conditions, is that a multihull can easily be made unsinkable and is therefore the best form of life raft available.

So there it is. I will not go as far as to submit that going to sea in multihulls is all fun and games, but I do feel sure in my own mind, from the many reports I have read, that provided you follow the advice I have offered, and that you possess a modicum of common sense, there is no reason why you should not emulate the feats of those who have preceded you in slicing feathery wakes across the oceans of the world in multihulls. I quote from my experiences of many desperate adventures in the air in my book, *What Were They Like to Fly?*:

> The actual moment of battle is nothing more than action: when pumping adrenalin has ousted sickly anticipation and bowel-loosening fear. But the moment of truth comes first: the gnawing doubt of what will happen; this inner personal battle against the unknown is the hardest fight of all. In retrospect, almost any adventure is glamorous...

The 'good times', which follow 'bad weather' in the title of this chapter, will become the happiness you seek in your old age. In retrospect, after you have survived storm and tempest...

It is imprudent to wish for more.

10 Future Hopes and Fears

I said at the beginning of this book that knowledge of the historical facts about multihulls is of much greater importance for the newcomer into this branch of yachting than information about the development of monohulls is to the tyro in that sector. I also mentioned at the end of Chapter 1 that somehow the image of an ancient South Seas paradise has lingered in modern multihulls as an aura of hope for dreamers who dwell in our unstable western society. In spite of all the heated arguments for and against this modern version of the escapist idea, the multihull has not only survived but has steadily gained a rhapsody of supporters. '... *when hope springs eternal in the breasts of some, then the majority can dream of the day when they, too, will escape.*'

Sailing multihulls were resurrected a tick of time ago, mainly because they were thought to be faster than monohulls. Within less than no time their true value was appreciated, and they became again what they had been originally: vessels for transporting people and goods in safety across open waters. Because they are faster than monohulls, however, no doubt we shall continue to hear much more about the publicity-oriented multihull racers. Of the quiet comings and goings of the many cruising multihulls which are criss-crossing the oceans of the world, we hear very little. And why should the very few who have rediscovered the joy of self-reliance want to attract attention to themselves when it is their prime aim to escape from the rat-race of western society? It may be impossible to break entirely from the world of commercialism, but I hope I have shown that temporary escape is a practical possibility in a multihull, and I can only pray that this route will not be abused by those who are incapable of self-sufficiency.

If I have disappointed those who expected to receive within these pages exact tuition on how to sail a multihull, I cannot honestly say that I am sorry. Either you can sail a boat or you have not yet tried. If you are capable of sailing a monohull you can handle a multihull, and the rest is experience; if you cannot sail, then it is about time you tried – in a multihull. Whether you teach yourself, or pay to be instructed, is entirely up to you; I can only repeat that I taught myself, without ever reading a book on the subject, when I was thirteen – but life for youngsters was not so safety-regulated in 1932 as it is now. Naturally I prefer the old system to the new.

If I have indulged in too much prattle about deep-water cruising it is mainly because this has always been the most popular subject among potential multihullists. I also submit that currently worsening world conditions are likely to encourage many more blue-water escapists than ever before. Since the prices of yachts, new or second-hand, have soared to such ridiculous levels – far beyond the reach of the average dreamer – home-building a boat is their only hope. Some have pinned their hopes on ferro-concrete, and some on wood, steel, GRP/FRP or ply monohulls, but more and more amateur builders are turning to less complicated multihulls for the realisation of their dreams – just as a century ago so many of the first transoceanic yachtsmen invariably sailed in very small boats because they could not afford the price of larger vessels. Even *Nonpareil* was only 25-ft LOA, and there was a surprising number of open or semi-open boats of less than 20 ft which crossed the Atlantic in the latter part of the nineteenth century.

Already, the nations of the world are beginning to squabble about who owns the oceans and the mineral-rich ocean floors. The Americans no doubt have had time to become accustomed to the oil rigs off their shores, but British and European yachtsmen are only just now learning what happens when commercialism takes over a sea bed. Rigs sprout in the North Sea like mushrooms used to grow in mist-hazed, dewy meadows, but regrettably the former are as tasteless as the cultivated replacements of the latter. Such is the way of what used to be called the Romance of Commerce, and I have no doubt that the situation will continue to worsen – particularly with the enforced control of freedom-loving yachtsmen.

Let's face it: time is running out for all those who strive to maintain individualism in one form or another. Better by far to accept the absolute control from mighty combines – owned either by the state, or by business moguls. Didn't the Polynesians, and all the other 'nesians, achieve so much more with their lives once western civilisation showed them the correct way? If the politicians are to be believed, why should anybody want to opt out when obviously they will be so much better off if they remain in. So if you must go, you shouldn't delay: now or never may be more confining than you realise.

For the rest – those who still believe that they will be able to continue their seasonable sport – I can only say that I hope their optimism is not misguided. Since the prices of new yachts continue to soar, and everything connected with yachting becomes more and more impossibly expensive, I cannot see how the current trend can last much longer. What will happen then is anyone's guess, but as this book is a primer I will not attempt to tackle the subject in depth.

Having drawn your attention to imminent possibilities which may affect your thinking, I must now consider the future of cats and tris, and supply at least some food for you to assimilate. I will take the points one by one.

1　Construction

I have already explained the price factors involved in the various types of construction. Although personally I do not like plastics, I concede that since it is popular this is obviously the material to go for if you are buying a stock multi, and if you can afford it. Since the price is so high, I recommend that you have your cat or tri built under Lloyd's supervision. No matter where your multihull is constructed this is always possible, and if Lloyd's turn down your builder you will know that there was a very good reason for their decision. A Lloyd's classification not only ensures a superior second-hand value, but it is an additional safety factor which should not be lightly disregarded. If you are spending a large sum on a multihull, Lloyd's fee will hardly be noticeable. Don't be parsimonious and spoil the future of your ship! So, no matter where you live, or in which country your multihull will be built, write for initial information to: The Secretary, Lloyd's Register of Shipping, 71 Fenchurch Street, London, England. They will, of course, classify any type of yacht, built of any material, providing that both conform to their high standards. It is even possible for a reasonably skilled amateur to build to Lloyd's, provided he has found good premises for the job and that the temperature can be rigidly controlled. But generally speaking this is impracticable, and I do not recommend it unless your standards are very high. I'm afraid a Lloyd's surveyor would send an average amateur builder into mental stasis when the complications of all his requirements were revealed; equally an average happy-go-lucky amateur is not likely to charm the deep-rooted professionalism of a Lloyd's surveyor. There is no point in being ambitious beyond your capabilities.

Amateur builders, as I have said before, will, for the most part, have to depend on ply planking. In spite of the fact that most designs in this material now follow the double-diagonal form of construction, it should be remembered that the cheaper method of single planking – generally on single or double chines – has proved adequate for the majority of the transoceanic crossings made by multihulls to date. Therefore, in view of rising prices I will not be surprised if many impoverished builders decide that the somewhat stronger double-diagonal, and the more seakindly rounded bottoms will have to be sacrificed for the lower-priced and humble forerunner of all the more fancy methods which are available now. 'Chines for cheapness' could well be added to my list of alliterations.

I forecast, therefore, that amateur builders will increase in numbers, and that they will revert to ply construction rather than the more expensive plastics. Whether they will go as far back as simple V-bottoms, I do not know – but be assured that there will be no danger involved if this recession does occur. As I have said before, chines are as seaworthy as any other hull shape.

2 Cost

Because the world is in such a mess, it is doubtful if the development of large ocean-racing multihulls will continue. They are extremely expensive to build and even more pricey to race and maintain. I doubt very much whether the public are particularly interested in such sponsored giants, and so I expect them to die quietly in due course. I only hope they do, for if anything happens to a cat or a tri in such circumstances (as occurred in the 1968 Singlehanded Transatlantic Race), dissension inevitably rips asunder the whole peaceful world of multihulls and threatens to violate their freedom. The giant racing multihulls are as useless to the world of yachting as all the highly expensive vessels which have tried to win the America's Cup. Prestige participation in such events seldom produces anything of use to anybody – which is why the old 'J' class racers are as dead as dinosaurs, and the 12-metre replacements will probably go the same way.

On the other hand, I hope that the somewhat smaller sizes of multihulls will continue to prove that you don't have to spend a fortune in order to beat large monohulls. Discounting such giants as the cat, *British Oxygen*, tris in the 1974 Round Britain Race did exactly this: the 35-ft tri, *Three Legs of Mann* (37), came in ahead of the 80-ft monohull *Burton Cutter* (5th and 6th). The 1972 Singlehanded Transatlantic produced similar results: the 46-ft tri, *Three Cheers*, beat the 65-ft monohull, *Strongbow* (5th and 7th). These are just two of the many examples which prove that you don't have to spend vast sums on special, one-off giants if you want to beat highly expensive

37 When multihulls such as the 35-ft tri *Three Legs of Mann* can beat the giant monohulls, represented here by the 80 ft *Burton Cutter*, why bother to race in expensive monsters?

monohulls – although one must concede that until all the big 'uns are killed by their own vast expenditure you will not stand much chance of actually winning a race in which they are competing. Then it remains only of academic interest that, for example, the 1972 Singlehanded Transatlantic was won by the smaller giant tri, *Pen Duick IV*, 70 ft, which beat the larger giant monohull, *Vendredi 13*, 128 ft. I sincerely hope this trend will terminate in the very near future, and I suspect that it will.

Public interest in such contests has undoubtedly increased since the 40-ft C/S/K cat *Waikiki Surf* unofficially competed in the 1955 Trans-Pac, and the 46-ft C/S/K cat *Aikane* unofficially won the 1957 race. However, the gradual awakening of general interest in the battle which developed between single and multi racing hulls scarcely warranted the sudden upsurge of expenditure by sponsors who previously had been only distantly involved in advertising themselves in this manner, and preferred (if they had money to spare) to restrict their expenditure to supporting well-organised adventures or nationally popular sports. Well, they certainly spent a good deal during the brief period of maximum interest, but it would seem that they are now regretting their commitments. In the future I doubt if much money will be available from such sponsors, so responsibilities of finance will revert again to the individual, or possibly to syndicates.

This means that the 1976 Transatlantic Race may well be the swansong for commercially-sponsored entries, although I think that the event itself will continue. Money, therefore, will be considerably more restricted, which will undoubtedly reduce the size of the craft entered to more sensible proportions. Then the promoters will probably be forced to introduce a maximum-size rule.

I have mentioned all this in connection with future costs because, as a result of this type of promotion, far too much has been made of the racing capabilities of expensive multihulls and too little of the low-priced cruising possibilities of the cheaper models. Only Arthur Piver and James Wharram seriously considered this in the past, and I was sorry that Art began to develop expensive tastes when he introduced his Pi range in 1964. With a lessening of competitive racing pressures, I believe it would be in the interest of present-day designers to revert to the more simple methods and much cheaper ideas of these two early creators. That is my idea of how to tackle the future of multihulls, but I am dubious about whether it will actually happen. The *nouveaux riches* almost always want to display their newly-acquired wealth, and therefore they seek only maximum expenditure. If this trend continues, you, the impoverished, will just have to build your own dreamboat.

3 Rig

I was hopeful that part of the large sums of money which have been spent on racing multihulls, as described in the previous section, would at least have been spent on developing more suitable rigs. Regrettably, virtually nothing has been accomplished in this field. Multihulls have run the gamut of various types of Chinese rig since Eric de Bisschop sailed *Kaimiloa* back to France in 1937, and apart from one or two idiosyncrasies over the years the majority of designers have unimaginatively stuck to the Bermudan concept. They have part-, fully- or leech-battened the main, and fitted revolving masts, and done their best to make the sails as efficient as possible, but the Bermudan rig, surely, is at best an inefficient method of propelling a vessel which occasionally is capable of sailing nearly as fast as the wind (as far as I know, only ice yachts can sail faster). And, furthermore, Bermudan sails and Bermudan masts are very expensive!

All of which is why I thought that when John Walker invented *Planesail* in the mid-sixties the idea would catch on quickly. What could be more simple than using a set of aerofoils which require neither complicated rigging nor involved halliards? They are as aerodynamically perfect for close-hauled work as Bermudan sails are inefficient. Provided a compromise flow/camber section could be established, the mast stepped securely, the stowage of the aerofoils in storm conditions simplified and the control system made as foolproof as possible, I feel certain that this method of wind propulsion – or something similar – is the rig of the future for multihulls (38). Unfortunately, yachtsmen are so conservative that nobody has yet taken the risk of attempting to beat existing multihulls by installing a new rig: to become a double-pariah is asking too much! So *Planesail* staggered on for a few years, and then faded away. But this idea, or something like it, undoubtedly will be back.

Jim Wharram, at least, has experimented through a whole range of sail plans for his cats and tris, and one or two other multihull designers have done their best to discover more suitable rigs for cruising. But the racing boys have stuck to Bermudan, so the predominant rig is currently unchanged.

Lord St David wrote to me a couple of years ago about square-sails – which I favour. After all, a multihull is a perfect platform for a rig of this type, since one has both the adequate beam and non-rolling characteristics which monohulls lack. Although he was only experimenting with a deck awning, hoisted on a yard above the forestay of his 26 ft 6 in Telstar trimaran, *Triplet*, he reported:

> I find this square-sail is most useful as a topsail, set right up to the masthead where it catches the last breath of a dying evening wind above the heads of the jibs [this was in Yugoslavia]. It also sets well on a reach. We once carried it in force 3, with only a genoa, and it was very effective and controllable. I want a proper square-sail some day. It will be slightly narrower and longer in the drop. Our present sail is 15 ft × 9 ft; I want one 14 ft 6 in × 12 ft.

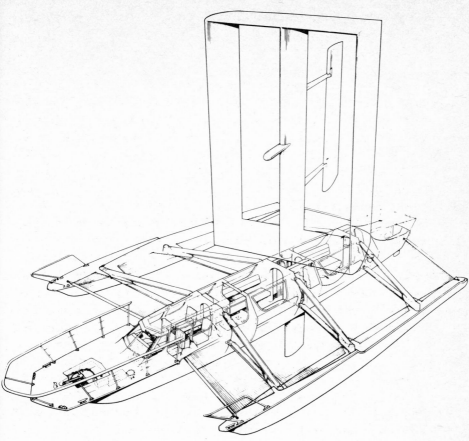

38　Multihull of the future?

I cannot help feeling that this is the thin edge of what could become a very
thick wedge, which may in the end force Bermudan enthusiasts to think of
better rigs – for cruising that is, not racing. On the other hand, who knows?
A squaresail-rigged racing multihull must obviously have the advantage over
inefficient triangular sails on every point of sailing except close-hauled, and
if the sheets and braces etc. are correctly rigged I can see no reason why
five to four points off the wind should not be possible. For ocean racing,
one does not need to get closer, if as close as this. For those who may be
interested in developing this idea, I recommend reading the three books
written by Conor O'Brien, who circumnavigated eastabout in his 42 ft ×
12 ft × 6 ft 9 in square-rigged ketch *Saoirse* in 1923–5: *The Small Ocean-going
Yacht* (1931), *On Going to Sea in Yachts* (1933), *The Practical Man's Cruiser*
(1940), all published by the Oxford University Press. There are many other
books on the subject, but these three are written by a man who put his ideas
into practice by sailing round the world, and they are well worth the trouble

of borrowing from a library. Don't be put off by their age; naturally you will not be able to find up-to-date text books on the subject. Incidentally, they should be read in date order; otherwise some of the points raised may not be clear.

To sum up this section, I think that experimental minds will soon begin to condemn the Bermudan rig. I cannot foresee what will replace the old but I hope it will be more efficient, much cheaper, and not involve unnecessarily tall, long-leverage masts. This, surely would be a step in the right direction for capsize-worriers.

4 Government interference

If I am right about the increasing interest in multihull blue-water cruising, then the future must reveal one of two possibilities, because freedom of the individual is anathema to far too many in positions of authority, no matter how much they may protest otherwise. I have before me an article written by Donald Hamilton, and published in the American yachting magazine, *Boating*: 'THEY are stealing our freedom in the name of safety!' states the headline: 'Under the banner of the Federal Boat Safety Act of 1971, bureaucratic safety freaks are threatening to make enjoyment of the water a thing of the past.' Of course, there is nothing new about this sort of attack by 'safety freaks': New Zealand tried to impose impossible controls on yachtsmen in the late fifties, and Australia attempted similar restrictions when do-gooders decried multihulls as 'floating deathtraps' in the mid-sixties. In Britain, we have been on the brink for many years, and I fully expect the clamp to come down in the near future – unless an entirely new organisation for the protection of those who wish to cruise offshore, or do their own thing in small boats, manages quickly to acquire some teeth, but this seems unlikely.

It is all very well for existing associations, clubs and what-have-you to claim that they represent all yachtsmen, and that they are doing a first-class job in protecting them. What such established organisations fail to see in the wood which surrounds them, is that an occasional tree needs a very different kind of protection – nurturing. Security- and safety-consciousness may sound appealing to those who shun true adventure, but the resulting mediocrity can only be assessed in every respect as depressingly average, and rapidly worsening. In every aspect, not just individual survival. Allow the adventurous free rein, and in due course all will inherit a wind (whether fair or foul, it must be to our common advantage). Prevent the individual from following the route of his own choosing, and as has so often been proved we are blasted by storms of such terrifying ferocity that they are virtually uncontrollable. What has already happened in the world is indicative of the furies to come if individual freedom is restricted further.

146

21 (*above*) and **22**   A rare picture of Jim Wharram's *Tangaroa* (**21**), in which he crossed the Atlantic in 1956–7. He built *Rongo* (**22**) in Trinidad, sailed her to New York and then across the Atlantic to Wales in 1959. This was the first double crossing of any ocean by the same crew in different multihulls. However, in 1961–2 Jim and Ruth Merseberger made a double crossing in *Rongo* and thereby achieved this 'first' as well.

23 For many years most catamaran designers ignored the hulls-only accommodation principle which was instigated by Eric de Bisschop and continued by Jim Wharram. Now I notice that there is a tendency to return to the sleeker and possibly safer, early beginnings. Here is one of the latest designs by Prouts: the cruiser-racer Wildgoose class.

24 There are so many multihulls which have crossed oceans, or broken one record or another, that representation here has proved very difficult particularly because my collection of such photographs is far from comprehensive (so please help me if you can). Here then is just one of the many hundreds that have sailed transocean: Charles Dennis's 31 ft 6 in × 13 ft 6 in Iroquois class, *Snoopy*. See Appendix III.

Size and unadulterated luxury can sometimes be made to pay
for its enormous capital expenditure by chartering. This
beautiful creation in alloy by MacLear and Harris, the
62 ft $\times$ 21 ft 3 in $\times$ 3 ft 8 in catamaran *Stranger*, charters
regularly in the Caribbean – as do so many giant multihulls.

26 and **26a** Trimarans, too, do well chartering, and the larger sizes with accommodation in the floats are probably more suitable than cats because of the complete privacy of each stateroom. Here is the starboard float double-berth in the Nicol, 45 ft × 24 ft × 2 ft 6 in Voyager class, *Trespasser*.

26 (*above*) The cabin looking forward.

26a (*right*) Looking aft towards the private, shower, heads, etc.

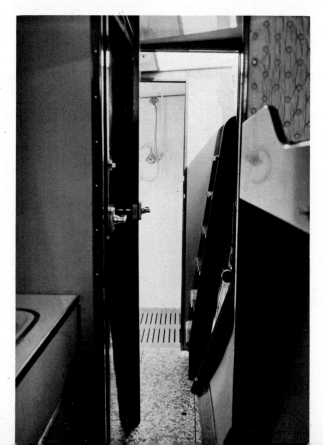

So the possibilities for the future are twofold: either the establishments of developed countries will impose more and more restrictions (ostensibly for reasons of 'safety') on deep-sea voyaging in small boats in an attempt to eliminate the unsettling effect they may consider it has on the masses of their respective populations, or life will go on just as it has in the past, which will mean that more and more will opt out, at least for a time.

It will be seen, therefore, that there is every possibility that the ancient history of the development of Oceania may be repeated in reverse – and once again in multihulls. So perhaps there may also be a chance for the formation of an entirely new non-political organisation for the protection of Blue-Water Explorers (or some such title); it could operate on somewhat similar lines to the international organisation for the exchange of medical and scientific information which most politicians dislike but are forced to accept. Whether such an organisation, shared by both developed and developing countries, would be capable of maintaining the freedom of the seas for the individual is for you to judge and to react to as you see fit. However, I submit the idea as a new concept, far removed from all the current machinations of international yachting; multihulls have been, and no doubt will continue to be, used in many pursuits which have no connection at all with sport, and I expect possible new developments along the lines indicated in the next section.

5   Scientific Uses

I have described how *Copula* became the first post-World War II catamaran to sail across an ocean, and how she was used as a floating laboratory for scientific research. During the past fifteen years I have been approached by several scientific bodies, generally American, with questions relating to the possibilities of using a large trimaran for similar purposes. Generally speaking I have had to say that a catamaran would be more suitable for their requirements because of its better load-carrying ability, but some tris have been used when all-up weight was minimal. I will not bother to go into all the arguments for and against the use of multihulls as opposed to monohulls for scientific research; suffice it to say that the shallow draught, the amplitude of deck and accommodation space and the overall seakindliness, were some of the acceptable features for the scientists involved.

Equally, great interest has been aroused in recent years in an individual's physiological and psychological approach to survival. Such esoteric experiments as those of the German Hannes Lindemann, who crossed the Atlantic in a 17 ft 1 in Klepper canoe in 1957, taking 71 days, and the Frenchman Alain Bombard who did the same thing in a 15-ft inflatable dinghy in 1952, without food or water, taking 65 days, were the beginnings of what has now become a subject involving international participation – particularly in view of space research requirements. (The individual is an important being, if only his assets could be more generally appreciated.)

So there is a good chance that the stature of cats and tris may increase if more scientists decide to use them for oceanographic and other researches at sea. And remember this too: such sailing vessels, which can be handled easily by small crews, may well become a necessity as natural oil slowly but surely turns into liquid gold. Taking this aspect into further consideration, there are many other ways in which multihulls could easily become commercially viable in the not-too-distant future.

6   Commercial uses

I have not previously mentioned such money-making pursuits as chartering, or other commercial enterprises with multihulls, because I did not want to confuse the beginner during the early stages of selection, etc. It may surprise those who think of multihulls only within the context of the sport of yachting that quite a fair percentage of owners buy either cats or tris – generally the larger sizes – because they intend to charter, or otherwise use their vessels for commercial profit. Of all the trimarans I ordered for clients, nearly 30 per cent were used in this fashion at some time, and of these about half were built with chartering actually in view. The sizes ranged from 24-footers for day charter, to the enormous Piver-designed 65-footer, *Triptych*, mentioned in Chapter 7, which operated successfully in the Caribbean for several years. One of the earliest 'giant' charterers out there was also for a customer of mine: the 45-ft Piver Medallion class *Spearhead*, which began work after crossing the Atlantic from Britain in 1962. In the same year a catamaran, which was larger in overall length than my two tris put together, was launched for the specific purpose of chartering: 150 ft × 38 ft × 5 ft of 407 tons, powered by twin 270 hp diesels (which gave her a speed of 12 knots), the gaff-rigged schooner *Tropic Rover* cost £170,000 in 1962; she slept 21 in single cabins, with 18 double staterooms and 2 double Admiral's cabins where '... you can enjoy the seagoing luxury of a private head and shower, as well as a view of the sea around you such as that gazed upon by Lord Nelson from his private quarters on *Victory*'. This was undoubtedly a return to the luxury which the Victorians tried to attain at the latter end of the nineteenth century; *Tropic Rover* even had an underwater viewing room with a six-foot-long picture window inset in her bilges, so that charterers could gaze into the clear waters under her keels. With a total, all-cabins-filled turnover of 14,000 US dollars per ten-day cruise, plus extras, she must have paid well.

These larger sizes of multihulls (not giant racers) undoubtedly have considerable commercial potential for the future, particularly when the present high cost of fuel is taken into account. If they are designed and built by experienced multihull craftsmen, there is no doubt that the low usage of fuel, necessary only to make handling in port easier, will considerably offset the high cost of construction. Suitable not only for chartering, but for ferry work and for fishing (particularly in shallow waters) and no doubt many other projects, the multihull has, I believe, a great future in this sphere.

7　Port facilities

Finally, to return to the sport of yachting as it is now, I am often asked if multihulls will continue to survive in view of the high prices asked, and the restrictions imposed, by the majority of yacht marinas and other crowded anchorages. The simple answer is that if a marina charges a multihull more than $1\frac{1}{2}$ times as much as it charges a monohull of the same length for lying alongside, or berthing, then you should take your custom elsewhere. An average catamaran of over 35-ft LOA is no wider than, say, a Colin Archer or a motor-fishing vessel conversion of the same length (39). A trimaran, unfortunately, will be half as wide again as these equivalents, and so in all fairness should pay half as much again, but for the most part crowded yachting anchorages have been reaping a rich harvest from a fictitious assumption that all multihulls take up more space than monohulls. (I don't suppose they

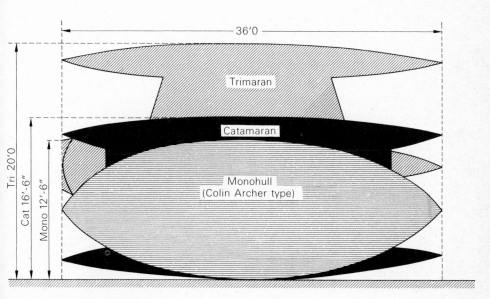

39　Marina berthing charges. It can be seen from these examples of average beams on 36 ft-LOA that the cat should pay only $33\frac{1}{2}$ per cent more than the mono, and the tri 25 per cent more than the cat. Assuming the rate is £4 per foot, the charges *should* be as follows (instead of figure in brackets): mono £144; cat £192 (£216); tri £230 (£288)

would charge half price if you happened to own an old plank-on-edge yacht, say 35 ft × 6 ft?) If you have been stung in the past, then you have only yourself or your association to blame. Personally, I wouldn't go near the places.

A multihull gains over a monohull in that you can often take her where monohulls fear to go. If you insist on being corralled, sheeplike, in an expensive marina, that is your business, but do not decry the design on these grounds. If you must keep to the herd, stick to a catamaran and refuse to pay any more than the additional percentage I have suggested. Or buy a folding-wing trimaran, such as the one designed by John Westell (Plate 11). But do not expect multis to vanish from the sea simply because marinas dictate terms; in my view, the marinas are more likely to collapse first.

I have tried to write a book about multihulls in general, and not about specific designs. In the bibliography, you will find brief remarks about those books I have managed to obtain on the subject, many of which are concerned with performance and designers. These you should read if you require further data. The reason why I have not gone into detail about multihull handling techniques will then become apparent: in brief, agreement is not yet sufficiently established for me to lay down hard and fast rules, and certainly the sailing characteristics of the many designs available of both cats and tris vary considerably. Therefore you should read what you can, experiment with your own vessel, and formulate your own brand of multihull seamanship. In due course perhaps you will decide to put pen to paper and give us all the benefit of your experience.

In approaching the subject on general terms, I deliberately avoided, as far as possible, reference to either cat or tri designers (except in an historical context) or their successful products. My object – whether intentional or otherwise – was to leave the thoughts of my readers uncluttered by suggestion. This is why, for the most part, I have used obsolete or obsolescent designs as examples. The only real exception is the self-righting trimaran *Trinity*, but since the prototype has yet to be built (at the time of writing), this is really a project of the future rather than the present.

In spite of what you may read, or hear said, against multihulls in general or a specific design in particular there have been surprisingly few really bad multis launched since the end of the Second World War. It is reasonably safe to assume that if more than a dozen of one particular design have been launched, then the craft cannot be all that bad. On the other hand it should be borne in mind that an indifferent design can often be improved by an experienced multihull builder, but it can also be turned into a dangerous menace by builders who have little or no knowledge of either cats or tris.

I must be very careful what I say, but I know of some yacht builders, highly skilled at their trade, who attempted to 'improve' the construction of a well-known design of multihull. The resulting loss in LT was ignored, and the subsequent overloading very nearly ended disastrously; financially, the results were no consolation to anybody. Even as I write this, I have before me an advertisement in a current yachting magazine offering an obviously already grossly overloaded second-hand multihull for more than four times its original cost. I sincerely hope that nobody buys it for the ocean cruising which the advertisement suggests it is fully capable of tackling. Always be alert for this kind of 'luxury' vessel – particularly if it is a trimaran.

You should have learned from these pages to approach the buying of new or used multihulls with considerable caution, so perhaps I am overstressing the subject. Yet I have seen such mistakes made so often that sometimes I wonder if anybody has ever heard of the old proverb about a fool and his money being soon parted. I am not so much upset if such a fool drowns himself, but I resent strongly the subsequent bad publicity: 'ANOTHER Multihull Disaster!' the headlines will scream, and we'll be back to square one yet again.

It is now nearly fifteen years since I saw *Nimble Eve* lowered into the River Yare in a downpour of rain. I am glad she died as she did, for from the moment I saw the builders enclose for ever the box-spar crossarms I worried constantly about the rot that might be forming within them. Suppose she was still afloat: why, even you may be tempted to buy her! What would be her price now? I paid £1500; you could easily be asked £5000 – perhaps more. And who knows what her condition would be like now? Would a surveyor know that in my ignorance I had not even had the ply within those crossarms painted with an anti-fungoid chemical? Would he know about all the dozens of built-in faults which I subsequently removed in later craft, one by one? I'm afraid he wouldn't, and so I am glad she died. But there remains a fair number of multihulls from the early days, and many of them are similarly bung-full of troubles. I cannot do more than warn you.

I am often asked about the life expectancy of ply and plastic multihulls. In the early days I stated that in my opinion a ply trimaran, covered externally with glass, should last for 25 years, or longer. I have inspected several tris (you will appreciate that since I am best experienced with three hulls, I am not often asked to look at cats, but these remarks are applicable to all multihulls), aged 10 years or over, and although they were withstanding the ravages of time and the effect of the average yachtsman's poor maintenance very well, I had to reconsider my early statement. Provided a ply multi is properly maintained, it should certainly last 20 years or more, but with the lackadaisical maintenance of the average yachtsman, who tends to leave the small details until things go really wrong, I think 10–15 years would be more like the limit. A ply multihull must be looked after with care and intelligence; if you don't like this sort of discipline, then buy plastic; certainly this form of construction should be safe for over 25 years – although I would not be too sure if all, or most, of this life were in the tropics. Sun and synthetics do not live very happily together, but it would be best if you consulted a qualified surveyor, or Lloyd's, about this.

Because I have always worried about the bad effects that poor quality used multihulls could have on the yachting public anywhere in the world, I asked Patrick Boyd, director of the multihull division of Camper and Nicholsons (Yacht Agency) Ltd,* and author of *Catamarans in Closeup*, to answer a few questions.

Do multis age more than monos?
> No, they don't; a poor multihull will age just as fast as a poor mono. Unfortunately, at this moment there are quite a lot of early plywood multihulls with or without glass sheathing, which were badly made in the first place, i.e. most of the Bobcats, home-made Wharrams, Pivers, etc. which have come to the end of their natural life.

Is there any appreciable ageing difference between cats and tris?
> No, if both are well made and of similar materials.

Do glass-ply multis age more than all-plastic etc.?
> Yes, mainly because with age, the knocks and abrasions and groundings seem invariably to cause breakdown between skin and ply, which when left undetected and unrepaired, allows rot and delamination to take a quick grip.

Do amateur-built multis show their origins?
> Yes, almost always. Occasionally, very occasionally, it is better than the factory product.

Is there ever any apparent evidence of strain as a result of either hard sailing or of ocean cruising? (i.e. evidence that an amateur surveyor could spot easily)
> Yes, mainly at the junctions under the wings or bridge deck, which quickly give evidence of wringing; internally, cracks on the deckhead, particularly in the way of bulkheads; these may even go as far as the deck, completely wringing off the partition.

Do multis suffer more than monos from long laying-up while awaiting sale? (i.e. one cannot conveniently cover a multi with a canvas or plastic tilt like a mono. Is this a snag?)
> Yes, I suppose so, for reasons stated, but in my experience few multihulls hang fire in selling.

Have you any evidence of the inevitability of delamination in glassed-ply multis; if so, in approximately how many years can one expect trouble?
> Ten years and onwards unless lovingly cared for.

Similarly with various types of all-plastic construction; do they give trouble? after tropical cruising? or in temperate climate cruising? what sort of trouble?
> Not so far as I know. Balsa or foam sandwich seems best from an insulation point of view, but is a bit accident prone from knocks, grounding or sitting on pebbles.

How much do second-hand prices vary between professionally and amateur built multis, if they are of the same age?

* Address: 16 Regency Street, London, England.

No fixed rule; badly built boats won't sell, whoever built them.

On the whole, are customers for second-hand multis beginners? ex-mono? or ex-multi? or are they as average as the usual second-hand mono buyers?

I put beginners off multihulls unless they have been to a multihull school or crewed extensively on one. Most customers are ex-small multihull, but occasionally ex-monohull. What is certain is that multihulls are getting wider and wider acceptance and it is high time somebody like yourself got back into building decent cruising trimarans again.

From Pat's answers you will see the same warnings that I have been giving, and I hope that as a result you will be extremely careful when or if you consider buying a used cat or tri. From my own experience, I have not seen signs of wringing strains in any of the older trimarans I have inspected, but this is probably because I have mainly dealt with those which have been constructed by my builders at Great Yarmouth, and I think our many modifications had taken care of most of these types of snags. For example, the inward/outward sideways flexing of the floats in the early days actually tore the sheathing along the connection between the underside of the wings and the float gunwales; this I cured by not glassing into the joints, but protecting them throughout their length with 2 in × 2 in half-rounds, screwed into a mastic compound which allowed the flexing of the wings and hulls without leaking in water. It was a simple but effective remedy, and there were many others. But I cannot go on for ever.

This has not been an easy book to write because, although I wanted to pass on to the multihull beginner as much simple information as I could, I did not want to repeat too much from my previous writings, nor did I want to become involved in the complications of discussing designs. I hope I have succeeded to the extent that you will now voluntarily seek such information for yourself, and in the end make your own decisions. As I said in a footnote in the introduction, I called this book a primer because it is for 'one who primes, especially to ignite an explosive compound'; you will soon learn, as you come to love and understand multihulls, why others will begin to think of you as a sort of walking firework.

So saying, having lit the blue touch-paper, I will retire to a safe distance and leave you alone to enjoy the resulting pyrotechnics.

Appendix I   Multihull Bibliography

A large number of pamphlets, technical papers, articles, booklets, etc., have been published about catamarans, trimarans and multihulls in general since the Second World War, and magazines devoted entirely to the subject have come and gone in several countries throughout the world. Fortunately for enthusiasts the book trade, after a tardy start, is now beginning to look after their interests, and a great deal of what was once difficult to obtain is now available in readable form within hardbacks. Some of the books listed are out of print, but all of them should be obtainable from your local library. For this edition, I have concentrated mainly on publications in the English language, but I welcome information about multihull books published in any country, and certainly I would appreciate your corrections to any errors or omissions I may have made in this present compilation. For those books I have read, I have added some brief remarks to guide your selection.

Of all the clubs, associations and societies devoted to multihulls, I will mention only one – partly because I could not possibly list them all, but mainly because the Amateur Yacht Research Society was probably the first, and is certainly the most famous of them all. Their long series of paperback publications, the majority of which are about multihulls (dating back to No. 1 *Catamarans*, in the mid-fifties), are still available at surprisingly low prices, considering the invaluable data and illustrations which they contain. Membership is no more than a hour's wages for a skilled man, for which sum current publications alone, plus the many other privileges, make joining well worthwhile. Write to: AYRS, Hermitage, Newbury, Berkshire, England.

Catamarans (publications in date order)

1   *The Voyage of the Kaimiloa* by Eric de Bisschop.
    Bell, London, 1940.
    Considering that this was the first transoceanic voyage by a catamaran to be made in modern times, it is surprising that so little is known about the adventure. In every respect it was a remarkable feat, and our lack of knowledge is undoubtedly caused by the advent of the Second World War. Unfortunately de Bisschop has almost nothing to say in this book

about the design and construction of his vessel. What happened to her after her historic, three-ocean crossings? Can anybody supply me with news, photos or plans of her?

2 *The Crossing of the Copula* by Jean Filloux.
Collins, London, 1955.
Well worth reading if you are interested in the early struggles and vicissitudes suffered by those who dared to go to sea in multihulls. A remarkable 'first'.

3 *Catamarans* by John Fisher.
Adlard Coles Ltd, London, 1959, 1962.
A first-class little book, but mostly about dinghy-type cats. Cruising multihulls are mentioned only briefly.

4 *Modern Sailing Catamarans* by Robert B. Harris.
USA, 1960; Kaye, London, 1961.
A useful book by an American naval architect who later became famous for his multihull designs. Well illustrated, and worth reading.

5 *Building and Sailing Catamarans* by Percy W. Blandford.
Foyle, London, 1963.

6 *Dreamers of the Day* by D. Lewis.
Gollancz, London, 1964.

7 *Daughters of the Wind* by D. Lewis.
Gollancz, London, 1967.

8 *Children of Three Oceans* by D. Lewis.
Collins, London, 1969.
All three books are by the remarkable Dr David Lewis, and well worth studying for every snippet of information you can squeeze out of them. The first is about the initial testing voyage in *Rehu Moana* from England to Iceland and return; the second covers his entry in the 1964 Single-handed Transatlantic Race (the first solo ocean crossing in a catamaran), and then the voyage to New Zealand, via the Magellan Straits, with his family aboard; the third completes the description of this first circumnavigation by a catamaran, when they sailed back to England in 1967.

9 *Sailing and Racing Catamarans* by Edward F. Cotter.
Chilton, USA, 1963; Hodder & Stoughton, London, 1964.
A mid-period book on the subject, which is now obsolescent. Mostly it

covers dinghy types, racing and day-cruising. There are some interesting photos of these, plus a few of the early cruising cats and tris.

10 *Cook on a Cool Cat* by Merton Naydler.
Temple Press, London, 1965.
Another version of *Rehu Moana*'s voyage to Iceland – this time by the all-important cook. Worth reading in conjunction with Lewis's *Dreamers of the Day*.

11 *People of the Sea* by James Wharram.
Sun and Health, England, 1965.
I wish I could say that I enjoyed this book, since Jim, like Art Piver, instigated the low-priced, ocean-cruising multihull: Wharram cats, and Piver tris. I'm afraid, however, that there is very little in this book for those who seek to learn catamaran seamanship – which is undoubtedly why Jim went to these specialist publishers.

12 *Catamaran Racing* by Reg White and Bob Fisher.
Cassell, London, 1968; John de Graff, USA, 1969.
Almost entirely about dinghy-type racing cats, but there is one chapter on the subject of racing cruisers and another about early cat development.

13 *Project Cheers* by Tom Follett, Dick Newick and Jim Morris.
Adlard Coles Ltd, London, 1969.
The story of the proa, *Cheers*, and her success in the 1968 OSTAR. Good reading for the ocean-racing fraternity.

14 *Two Girls, Two Catamarans* by James Wharram.
Abelard-Schuman, London, 1969.

15 *Catamarans Offshore* by Rudy Choy.
Macmillan, USA, 1970.
I was very disappointed with this book. It states unequivocally that Brown, his wife Rachel, Kumalae and Choy created the catamaran world: 'Every catamaran afloat today anywhere in the world is related directly or spiritually to *Manu Kai*.' This premise appears to be the basis of Choy's philosophy, and record claims by C/S/K listed in an appendix further confirm this god-like attitude, since they are made without reference to any other record-breakers, e.g., C/S/K's Italian-built *Dushka* is quoted as being the first cat to sail transatlantic (1963). Perhaps he meant the first C/S/K cat – but he doesn't say so. Seemingly Piver was not the only hot-gospeller in multihull business!

16 *Catamarans in Close-up* by Patrick Boyd.
Ian Allan, London, 1972.
I recommend this to all tyros who are thinking about going into catamarans – whether they are beginners or ex-monohullists. A very good
general guide to the subject, with excellent illustrations.

17 *Cruising Catamarans.* Edited by John Morwood.
AYRS, England, 1972.
A 372-page collection of articles written by AYRS members over the
years, and published for the first time in one volume. Although it is
copiously illustrated, and contains a fund of information, I do not recommend it for beginners who lack a knowledge of basic seamanship, and
the technicalities of multihull designing. Buy it, yes, while you can! But
don't try to assimilate it all at once; and don't believe all you read, since
a lot of it is now out of date.

18 *Catamaran Sailing to Win* by Chris Wilson and Max Press.
Kaye and Ward, London, 1973; A. S. Barnes, USA, 1973.
Almost entirely devoted to Little America's Cup races and C-class cats,
this is a good book for the dinghy racing man.

19 *Children of Cape Horn* by Rosie Swale.
Elek, London, 1974.
The first rounding of Cape Horn by a catamaran – from a woman's point
of view. Personally, I would have preferred to read her husband's account
of what appears to have been a cosy cat cruise with kids, but I suppose
Colin was otherwise occupied in his capacity as captain while Rosie
ravishingly recorded the daily routine.

20 *5000 Miles in a Catamaran* by Ralph Stephenson.
Hale, London, 1974.
An interesting story of a conversion from monohull sailing to catamarans.
Good reading for those who hover on the brink of making the change.

21 *Catamarans for Cruising* by Jim Andrews.
Hollis and Carter, London, 1974.
I recommend all multihull enthusiasts to read this book, tri as well as
cat-fanciers, whether beginners or experienced. In these pages you will
find answers to many of the questions which no doubt you would have
liked to ask me, immediately after reading this multihull primer. You
can then make up your own mind whether my answers would be similar,
or very different, from Jim Andrews' recommendations.

Trimarans (publications in date order)

1 *Transatlantic Trimaran* (1961) ⎱   by Arthur Piver
2 *Transpacific Trimaran* (1963) ⎬ Published in America
3 *Trimaran Third Book* (1965) ⎰   by the author.
   These three books cover Art's Atlantic crossing in the first Nimble, his Pacific crossing in a Lodestar, and the development of his racer, *Bird*. All are illustrated with photos, plans and line drawings. As they were the first tri books to be published, they are now somewhat out of date and only of historical interest.

4 *Barrier Reef by Trimaran* by John Gunn.
   Collins, London, 1966; USA, 1966.
   An interesting account of a cruise in a home built Lodestar around the Great Barrier Reef of Australia. I corresponded with John during the building of this craft. A very readable book, but it does not have much to say about trimaran building and handling problems.

5 *Trimaran Against the Trades* by Jean Cole.
   Reed, New Zealand, 1968; USA, 1968.
   Lt-Cmdr Cole purchased the first set of Victress plans sold in England, built his tri in East Africa and sailed her across the Indian Ocean to New Zealand. A woman's angle about tris – not forgetting the experiences of 92-year-old Granny Emie!

6 *Trimarans – an Introduction* by D. H. Clarke.
   Adlard Coles Ltd, London, 1969, 1972, 1975.
   As the title implies, my intention was to write a book for beginners. Reviewer R. du Plessis, in AYRS *Multihull Safety Study No. 1* wrote: 'Finding out about multihulls must have cost me the price of a day-sailer in boating magazines. And now at long last here in this book I have found much of that widely scattered material brought together in a straightforward, comprehensive and eminently readable form.'

7 *Racing and Cruising Trimarans* by Robert B. Harris.
   Scribner, USA, 1970; Nautical Publishing, England, 1971.
   Written by a naval architect, one would expect this book to be directed more to designing and performance. It reveals a professional designer's approach to the subject.

8 *Trimaran Solo* by Nigel Tetley.
   Nautical Publishing, England, 1970.

This account of Nigel's circumnavigation in *Victress* is one of the best trimaran cruise stories to date. All prospective transoceanic tri-mariners should read it, and note in particular the advanced planning (both actual and mental), and subsequent fortitude.

9 *The Strange Voyage of Donald Crowhurst* by Nicholas Tomalin and Ron Hall. Hodder and Stoughton, London, 1970.
In my opinion, every yachtsman, and certainly every tri-mariner, should read this expert analysis of what can happen to a singlehander when planning is rushed and things go wrong. There is not a great deal about trimarans, but there is an awful lot about the human mind, which should enable you to realise that running away to sea in your own boat does not necessarily solve all your problems. Tomalin and Hall have covered the subject in great detail.

10 *Yachtsman in Red China* by David J. Steele.
John de Graff, USA, 1970.
Not entirely a trimaran book, but the author tells how he built a Piver Nugget (24-ft LOA) and a Herald (32 ft 6 in LOA) in war-torn Saigon, only to lose her, and his freedom, to the Chinese. First-class adventure stuff.

11 *Magnificent Ordeal* by Lt-Col. Edward A. Walsh.
Carlton, USA, 1970.
The problems of having a trimaran built overseas, in this case Japan, are revealed in this book. Equally, there is some hectic material about surviving typhoons and other storms. The American magazine *TRImaraner* reported: 'For those who like trimarans and travel, we recommend this book as a worthwhile experience in vicarious living.'

12 *Journey with Caravel* by Fred Carlisle.
John de Graff, USA, 1971.
A double crossing of the Atlantic in a Piver Pi-40 by the author, his wife and two daughters. A good account of an inexperienced escapist learning the hard way.

13 *Searunner Construction* by Jim Brown.
Almar Enterprise, USA, 1972.
This book started out as a construction manual for Brown-designed tris, but finished up as a general guide to tri-mariners on just about everything. I have not read it, but the magazine *TRImaraner* sums up its value thus: 'For anyone interested in building or just owning a trimaran, this is the best eight bucks worth you'll ever find.'

14 *Trimaran Development* by D. H. Clarke.
Adlard Coles Ltd, London, 1972.
Brian Burns, editor of the American quarterly magazine *TRImaraner*,
reviewed: 'Clarke brings a typical British thoroughness to the writing
of this book. I think its chief value to you, as a trimaran sailor, will be
its descriptions and analyses of capsizes, as well as numerous accidents,
with ideas on how they might have been avoided. An excellent book – one
I consider an absolute must.'

15 *Love for Sail* by Mark Hassall and Jim Brown.
Almar Enterprise, USA, 1974.
I have not read this book, but it has been described as 'the best tri cruising
book to date'. It is really the result of many cassette tapes which were
recorded by Hassall and his family during a three year, almost-tied-the-
knot, circumnavigation in their tri *Talofiafaoe*, during which they survived
two hurricanes and two near-hurricanes. The tapes were edited by Jim
Brown with his additional comments. (Jim, incidentally, started his multihull conversion in a Piver Nugget, before he became a designer in his
own right.)

16 *Hell and High Water* by Thomas Thompson.
Deutsch, London, 1975.
I recommend this book to every multihullist who has starry-eyed visions
of getting-away-from-it-all. Here is an almost perfect example of a builder/
skipper who preferred to put his faith in God rather than in multihull
seamanship, and a crew who, in spite of desperate odds after their
trimaran capsized, survived 72 days adrift by applying seamanlike rules,
rather than leave such matters in the hands of the Almighty. Note in
particular how this 31-footer was grossly overloaded.

Multihulls

1 *Twin Ships* by Alexander C. Brown.
Mariner's Museum, Virginia, 1939.
A 90-page booklet about the history of multihulls.

2 *The International Book of Catamarans and Trimarans* by Edward F. Cotter.
Crown, USA, 1966; Kaye and Ward, London, 1967.
The tri part of this book is minimal, containing two brief accounts of
bad-weather sailing, one of building a Lodestar, and one of a cruise. The
cat section contains similar accounts by various individuals. Not very
informative.

3 *Multihull Sailboats* by Edward F. Cotter.
Crown, USA, 1963, 1966, 1971.
A fair book on the subject, but in my opinion much too generalised. There
is very little really that you can get your teeth into, but the copious
illustrations are interesting.

4 *Polynesian Concept* by Christian Ebsen.
Prentice-Hall, USA, 1972.
The story of the Multihull Transpacific Yacht Race.

5 *The Evolution of Modern Sailboat Design* by Meade Gougeon and Ty Knoy.
Winchester Press, USA, 1974.

6 *Multihull Seamanship* by Michael McMullen.
Nautical Publishing, England, 1976.
Although this book is well worth studying, I found that I was not always
in agreement with the author's conclusions. To be fair, it is written
primarily for the racing enthusiast, so as my interest is mainly cruising my
disagreements are understandable. However, McMullen does emphasise
as much as I do the major rule for troublefree sailing in multihulls:
GOOD SEAMANSHIP.

Some multihull publications in other languages

1 *Le Catamaran, ce méconnu* (The Underrated Catamaran) by Paul R.
Bruneau.
Paris, 1955.

2 *Parusniye Katamarani* (Sailing Catamaran) by Yurii S. Kryushkov.
Published in Leningrad, Russia: Part I, 300 pages, 1963; Part II, 275
pages, 1967.

3 *Catamaraner och andra flerskrovsbatar* (Catamarans and other multihulls) by
Heinz-Jurgen Sass.
Stockholm, Sweden, 1970.

Note: This is a start, but there must be other such books published in various
languages, particularly about personal cruises or experiences. So if you can
add anything to my lists, do let me know.

I must warn you though that I only have the English, and often I wonder
if I have enough of it to answer all the enquiries I receive about multihulls
and send thank-you letters to information suppliers from just about every

country in the world. To date I have maintained my principle of answering all correspondence by return of post, but after the publication of this book I must revise this practice, and I think this is as good a time as any to let you know.

Postal rates have increased alarmingly since *Trimarans* was first published in 1969. So I'm afraid you will not receive an answer from me unless you enclose a stamped-addressed envelope. Enquiries from overseas should include sufficient International Reply Coupons for overseas airmail reply (stamps from the country of the sender are useless – I mention this because I receive so many); if there are insufficient IRCs, I'm afraid I shall have to reply by surface mail, and this will take weeks. For those who live in countries where IRCs are unobtainable, please send the same value of loose stamps as appear on your envelope.

With these points in mind, I will always be pleased to answer general enquiries about multihulls, but not such specific questions as: 'Is a so-and-so better than a such-and-such?' Opinions about designs are up to you, and I will not take over your responsibilities. Also, I'm afraid I will not help spur-of-the-moment callers, either on the telephone or at my house; they are invariably the biggest time-wasters of all. So if you really need help, just write to the following address and I will do my best; you can at least be assured of a reply by return of post.

> D. H. CLARKE,
> 'GABLES',
> WOOLVERSTONE,
> IPSWICH IP9 1BA,
> SUFFOLK,
> ENGLAND.

Footnote. As this book goes to press, I will be on my way to Toronto to act as Moderator at the First World Multihull Symposium. Organised by Canadian Multihull Services (Toronto Island Airport, Toronto, Ontario M5V 1A1) and Multihulls Magazine (91 Newbury Ave, North Quincy, Mass., 02171, USA), I am as hopeful as the many hundreds of multihullists who have decided to attend that the twelve top-line designers on the panel will provide a veritable mine of 'Brains Trust' information.

Appendix II   Multihull Designers

My original intention had been to include a complete list of every designer and builder of multihull cabin cruisers and ocean racers in the world. Alas, after some checking I found that this would not be a very sensible path to follow. During the twelve-month period that this book has taken to prepare (1974–5), many little-known, and several well-known multihull yards have been driven to the wall and eliminated. This unhappy state of affairs is not confined to multis, of course, since every trade similarly suffers in a recession. In due course no doubt things will improve and the law of the jungle will prevail – that is, the weakest will have succumbed and the strongest will survive. Unfortunately the strongest are not necessarily those who produce the best goods, and so we shall have to wait and see what happens in the natural course of evolution.

I concede, however, that in a book such as this you need to have some addresses to which you can write, and so I am including the world's better-known multihull designers in Britain, America and Canada, and the Antipodes. As an indication of their experience, I have tried to keep this list to those designers who have had more than 25 cabin multihulls built from their plans, either by professionals or amateurs. Since a number of famous designers also run their own boatyards, I have added their names whenever possible, and because some of them may not be familiar, I have indicated whether the designer is mainly interested in cats or tris, or either (multis).

To those designers whom I may inadvertently have missed, I apologise; please send me details, including the number of craft built from your plans, and I will enter your name in the next edition. From designers in non-speaking English countries, I welcome details; it is possible that this book may be translated into your language, in which case the sooner I hear from you the better.

Britain

A. J. S. Sandwich Yacht Construction Ltd (Tony Smith: tris)
Sandwich Marina,
Sandwich, Kent

Aristocat Marine Ltd (Robin Chaworth-Musters: multis)
Avon Works,
Bridge Street,
Christchurch, Dorset

Bayside Marine (Derek Kelsall: multis)
Sandwich Marina,
Sandwich, Kent

Bobcats Ltd (Bill O'Brien: cats)
Slaters Paddock,
Totton, Hants

Tom Lack Catamarans Ltd (Tom Lack: cats)
Avon Works,
Bridge Street,
Christchurch, Dorset

Erick J. Manners (multis)
34 Riverside,
Martham, Great Yarmouth, Norfolk

G. Prout & Sons Ltd (cats)
The Point,
Canvey Island, Essex

P.T. Yachts Ltd (Phil Patterson: multis)
Foss Quay,
Millbrook, Plymouth, Devon

Sailcraft Ltd (Rod Macalpine-Downie: multis)
Waterside,
Brightlingsea, Essex

Simpson-Wild Marine Partnership (tris)
19 Kings Road East,
Swanage, Dorset

Solaris Marine Ltd (Terry Compton: cats)
Hazel Road,
Woolston, Southampton, Hants

James Wharram (multis)
The Longhouse,
Milford Haven Docks, Pembs., South Wales

America and Canada

Almar Enterprise (Jim Brown: tris)
241 West 35th St, Suite K,
National City, California 92050

Vence Buhler (multis)
9376 River Road,
Delta, British Columbia, Canada

Cross Trimarans (multis)
4326 Ashton Street,
San Diego, California 92110

C/S/K Catamarans
2815 Newport Boulevard,
Newport Beach, California 92660

Joseph C. Dobler (multis)
801, 8th Street,
Manhattan Beach, California 90266

Bruce Ewing (cats)
5040 Golden Arrow Drive,
Palos Verdes, California 90274

Robert B. Harris Ltd (multis)
Three Coal Harbour Wharf,
North Foot of Cardera, Vancouver, B.C., Canada

Harris and Heacock (multis)
199 West Shore Road,
Great Neck, N.Y. 11024

Edward B. Horstman (tris)
P.O. Box 286,
Venice, California 90291

Kantola Yacht Designs (multis)
7200 Bark Avenue,
San Jose, California

MacLear and Harris (multis)
11 E. 44th Street,
New York, N.Y. 10017

Lenman Industries Inc. (L. Susman: tris)
P.O. Box 689, 1010 S.E. 12th Court,
Cape Coral, Florida 33904

Louis Macouillard (tris)
1 Aladdin Terrace,
San Francisco, California 94133

Richard C. Newick (multis)
R.F.D. Vineyard Haven,
Massachusetts 02568

Victor Newman (tris)
Chesterton Shores,
West Hill, Ontario, Canada

Myers Catamarans International (Hugo Myers: multis)
3719 Oakdale Court,
Huntsville, Alabama 35810

Pi-Craft (Arthur Piver: tris)
P.O. Box 449,
Mill Valley, California 94941

Bernie Rodriguez (tris)
R.D.2 Box 375,
Highland, N.Y. 12528

Searings Trimarans (Skip Johnson: tris)
1056 East Front Street,
Ventura, California 93001

Lauren Williams Trimarans
P.O. Box 137,
Mill Valley, California 94941

Australia and New Zealand

Lock Crowther (tris)
P.O. Box 35,
Turramurra, New South Wales 2074

Frank Pelin (multis)
P.O. Box 30-062,
Takapuna North, N.Z.

Jim Young Plans (cats)
P.O. Box 30,004
Auckland, N.Z.

A Warning

There are in the world about fifty or sixty regular professional builders of cruising and racing multihulls sleeping two or more persons. Some are very experienced, most are enthusiastically anxious to please, a few are fortune hunters or band-wagon climbers. Higher-than-average prices do not necessarily indicate better-than-usual craftsmanship. If you want to have a multihull built for you, and you do not take my advice about building to a Lloyd's classification, then your best bet is to check on how many multihulls a builder has launched – and preferably contact some of the owners and see what they have to say. Never, unless you are very rich, go to a monohull builder who has given you an attractive quotation: this is likely to turn into the most expensive mistake you ever made. Another point: only those who are sufficiently experienced in the many trades and aspects of boatbuilding, and can spare the time to supervise the construction of their craft from the beginning, should contemplate going overseas to wherever wages are low; almost always, cheap wages mean a cheap boat in more ways than one; don't risk it unless you are very knowledgeable – and preferably can speak the language.

Amateur builders should stick to established designers, and not risk the whizz-kids who come and go like demented grasshoppers. And never buy plans on the cheap, especially those of a well-known designer ('I couldn't spare the time to build her, old man, but you can have them for half price'); although they may have been excellent plans when they were first sold, most designers are continually modifying and otherwise bringing their designs up to date, so why try to save a few miserable pennies at the beginning of an expensive task in time and money? This is built-in obsolescence with a vengeance! Equally, never alter plans in any way without consulting the designer; I could tell you stories – but not here. For the same reason, never design your own multihull (even if you have studied the subject, as an amateur of course); if you must design and build, then begin with something small, and not a super-large cat or tri – bighead!

Remember that in spite of my warnings many will choose to go their own way, and the used boat market will continue to contain a selection of obsolete and obsolescent 'cheap', 'foreign', 'amateur' and similarly describable abortions which inevitably will become the journalist's 'yot dramas' of tomorrow. Why risk it? Yet some of you will. You must be potty if you do.

Appendix III Sample Transatlantic Voyage by Catamaran

Because I hold the view 'tris for transocean, cats for coastal', I do not want to be considered so biased that I will not publish the other fellow's point of view. As luck would have it, while I was researching my previous book (*An Evolution of Singlehanders*), a cata-mariner who was planning a transatlantic voyage wrote to me enquiring about speed records between Britain and the West Indies, via the Azores. This is an unusual route to take, so I could not find any particular record in the westabout direction, but the direct result was that Charles and Susan Dennis and I began to correspond. I think that the whole adventure is worth printing since it is well up to date, it gives an idea of what good planning can achieve and it shows that modern cats are just as capable of crossing oceans as tris (which I have never doubted); also my correspondence enabled me to ask the sort of questions I expect you would like to have asked.

First, Charles Dennis's sailing experience:

Born 1947. Started sailing dinghies, 1957; crewing offshore, 1962. I learned sailing and seamanship mainly through the Island Cruising Club, Devon, but I also took the Yachtmaster (Ocean) course at Hull Nautical College. I first skippered offshore in 1971.

Before buying *Snoopy*, we owned a 20-ft Manners trimaran in which we did a little coastal sailing. Since buying *Snoopy* early in 1973 we cruised 2400 miles, including the Crystal Trophy race and sailing round the Fastnet course. In 1974 we cruised 1300 miles before setting off across the Atlantic.

Now for the story of the voyage:

In 1972 we decided to buy a boat with the idea of ocean cruising. There were many boats to consider, but we chose the Iroquois as the fastest and most comfortable in our price range. Nevertheless, once we had the boat it took time before we could afford to venture across the seas, so the summers of 1973 and 1974 were spent in practice and preparation. We cruised between Fastnet and Orkney and raced the Crystal Trophy and Fair Isle events. Our travels included a visit to Whitby – only 11,000 miles to Tonga!

By the end of July 1974, the bank manager gave his approval so we started the final preparation. We resigned from our jobs, Susan an auxiliary nurse and Charles an engineer with a paint firm in our home town of Hull. Eric

Hammond and Catherine (Kate) Martin joined the complement, Eric a fisherman from Wales and Kate a new university graduate. The next few weeks saw us busy organising equipment, stores and medical supplies. A long weekend was used to sail down to Cowes, Isle of Wight.

In Cowes we met yachtsmen who had made similar cruises and who advised us on routing. After studying the pilot charts, which show average winds and currents, we chose the unusual route, sailing almost direct via the Azores. This route passes through large zones of light winds and is only suitable for boats which perform reasonably well in these conditions. We never logged less than 70 miles in any day, even in the calmest weather. Areas of calm are small, and by utilising every catspaw one can usually find a wind, however light. We were pleased with our passage times, taking 13 days from Cowes to the Azores and 19 days from the Azores to Antigua. The shortest routes are 1460 miles and 2130 miles respectively, so our average speed based on the great circle distance was 112 miles per day.

On Sunday, 29 September 1974 we set sail, encouraged by cheering and waving from friends we were leaving behind. The date was intended to be after the equinoctial gales and before the winter weather, planning to reach the Caribbean soon after the hurricane season. Before sailing, the outlook had been checked with the Meteorological Office at Bracknell.

The start was slow, a beat against a light wind for the first three days, logging 90 miles per day. It was soon clear that we were not heading south quickly enough to avoid advancing unsettled weather. Whilst we were becalmed a gale warning was broadcast. A depression which had been forming when we set off had deepened and accelerated. We dreamed of magnificent dishes at the Baie des Anges restaurant and we only just resisted the temptation to motor into L'Abevrach! Luckily the centre of the low passed to the south giving a fresh free wind for a few days, and we made 140 miles per day. Abeam of Ushant the Atlantic bares its fangs and the sea was too rough to drive on at full speed without discomfort.

On the fourth day dolphins accompanied us. A group of twenty had no difficulty in swimming circles round the boat although we were making seven knots! They criss-crossed in front of the bows and leapt from the water in formations of up to four, keeping up their playful antics for two hours. Much film was spent on them but eventually we tired of watching and they tired of performing without an audience. This was to happen several times during the voyage.

The following day a Mother Carey's Chicken flew over. It was rare for a day to pass without anything to be seen but sea and sky, although sometimes there was only a beer can. Ships passed within sight every other day or so.

This was one of the few days that the spinnaker could be set. Usually the wind was too fine on the bow or too strong. Today the wind reached force 5 and *Snoopy* surfed up to 15 knots on large waves. Eventually the ride became too hairy and reluctantly we handed it. The following morning a fish, a braille, was washed up on the foredeck. Although we trailed a line for many hours, we only caught the fish that jumped aboard!

On a dark calm night when only 250 miles from the Azores, a whale paid a surprise visit. Kate, on watch alone, screamed: 'There's a thing!' This brought us all on deck in a great hurry in various stages of undress, expecting a sea-serpent. A dark mass with three metres of length showing above the water was swimming about a metre from the boat. We did not shine a light to examine it in case this should antagonise or attract it. After a couple of minutes it dived and seemed to pass under the boat. Lightning lit the sky and we rested uneasily that night.

There is a whaling station at Faial in the Azores. When cliff-top lookouts see a whale blowing they sound an alarm and fishermen hurry to the whaling station. A motor launch tows them out to the area in rowing dorys, they chase the whale and harpoon it by hand in the traditional way. On leaving the Azores we passed a quarter of a mile from a school of some fifteen sperm whales. Some were jumping almost clear of the water and beating the surface with their tails. They seemed to be daring the hunters to give chase.

The wind was light on the last three days of the first leg to the Azores, the weather one might expect in this area which on average has high barometric pressure. We made 90 miles per day. At last the sun shone, the water was warm and we enjoyed a swim and a good wash all over. Sea water was always used for washing to save fresh water. Although we carried 65 gallons of water, topping up at the Azores, only 45 gallons were used on the whole trip, an average of less than three pints per person a day.

Eric 'Hawkeye' first spotted the islands. We approached Pico and Faial at sunrise on 11 October. The 2100-metre-high island of Pico was a fairytale picture, pointing up into the clouds. As we entered the Baia da Horta, Faial, we met four large tunny-fish coming out, jumping slowly and majestically in formation. By 0920 GMT (0820 local time) *Snoopy* was moored alongside at Horta.

The four-day stop was all too short for we yearned to spend a month cruising the Azores. Pierre at the Café Sport speaks excellent English (and other languages) and could not have been more helpful. Everywhere we were received with great hospitality and friendliness. Horta is a good place for eating out but should not be relied on for buying provisions.

Eventually we tore ourselves away. There would have been no benefit in having a weather forecast before leaving, as Horta is not a sheltered harbour, and in a gale a well-found yacht is safer at sea. From the start the wind increased and the barometer fell. The plumb-line course was a dead beat. Although we could have sailed south away from the centre of the depression, we plugged westwards on the port tack knowing that we would soon reach north-westerly winds and be able to lay the course. By the second day the wind was force 6 and the sea had built up frighteningly. We drove on thankful to have a strong and weatherly boat.

That night the wind reached force 7 with stronger gusts and the ride became uncomfortable. By now we had a good offing from the islands and so lay ahull for three hours in order to get some sleep. This instantly transformed the comfort down below, and *Snoopy* lay quietly and peacefully, bobbing up and down on the great waves like a cork. She made less than half a knot of leeway and almost half that speed forwards. If it had been a race we could have kept going, but for the sake of cruising comfort and peace of mind we preferred to take it gently. The only damage was a broken watch strap!

By dawn the wind moderated and we got under way again. The barometer rose as quickly as it had fallen and a strong ridge of high pressure passed over quickly. The wind blew from SSE and remained between this direction and ESE for the rest of the voyage. Apparently the stable high pressure area normally associated with the Azores had settled to the east of us. There was no need to strike a southerly course towards the trades, as we were confident that the direct route would carry good winds as far as the Horse Latitudes. The strength was between 2 and 5 as far as 25°N, the latitude at which we had expected to reach the trade winds. During this period *Snoopy* averaged 150 miles per day, the best day being 160 miles.

The self steering was a boon in these steady winds. It is a simple and in-expensive horizontal axis vane which worked perfectly for the whole trip. This system is most effective on a well-balanced boat. Our watchkeeping system required one person on watch and another on standby. The watchkeeper usually spent his time lazing around in the cabin or cockpit, having a good look around every fifteen minutes. It was rare that his standby needed to be awoken, although fairly frequent sail changes were needed to keep up speed.

On the sixth day out from Horta the weather became bright again and we washed the laundry in sea water. A shark swam around and dissuaded us from swimming. Apparently they are more dangerous well offshore where they are likely to be hungrier. We sailed through clumps of yellow Sargasso weed and found they contained tiny crabs, shrimps and barnacles – meagre fare for the bigger fish.

On 21 October, a few days before the date considered as the end of the hurricane season, we entered the area where tropical storms occur. Although we sometimes imagined warning signs, there was no storm. Apparently the Americans have been rain-seeding off the West African coast to reduce the frequency of hurricanes.

On a peaceful night nine days out Eric was on watch, standing on the fore-deck enjoying the ride. Suddenly something slapped him in the face and he almost died of fright! When he had recovered he found a twenty-cm-long flying fish at his feet. We had seen these skimming over the water and even had tiny ones come aboard, but this was the only large one that was caught. Unfor-tunately the weather was rough next morning and no one ate it. On the same day a yellow and brown butterfly fluttered by.

A couple of days later a great fish passed by a quarter of a mile away, jumping and gyrating three metres out of the water. Was it a marlin?

Happily the weather and ship were stable for Charlie's birthday. This was a day of unparalleled gluttony. There was freshly baked toast for breakfast and fresh scones with jam at lunchtime. The brown bread bought in Cowes had lasted as far as Horta but on the second leg we baked our own. On the dinner menu there was *chili con carne* washed down with our last bottle of Pico wine.

This was followed by birthday cake, a voluptuous chocolate confection with imitation cream filling, chocolate icing, and topped with a marzipan model of a catamaran!

We found that our diet was as varied as at home. The popular dishes were oriental in style with Chinese vegetables, popadoms and so on. We also relished various grills with chips and French-fried onions so we were delighted that the English vegetables kept for the whole voyage.

Charles had hoped for a trade wind for his birthday but sadly he got light airs. We had arrived too early in the season for the trades. At 25°N we found the Horse Latitudes and only sailed 80 miles per day for a few days. We made a southerly alteration of course to cross the light wind belt quickly, but even when close to Antigua we made only 120 miles per day.

The day before our landfall dawned with clear weather and little swell so that we took good sun sights. The sights were reduced using 'Hughes Tables', a method which allows quick calculation by addition and subtraction without interpolation.

On the same day we started a new $8\frac{1}{2}$-lb propane cylinder for the first time since Horta. The electric power also lasted well and only one battery was used for the whole trip. We economised by using Eric's attractive dolphin-supported paraffin light when reading after dark. During the voyage we read and re-read many novels, sea stories and Snoopy cartoon books. On some nights we read by moonlight. The sailing was so undemanding that time was moving slowly. Kate helped Sue make a long dress, possibly because we had room to carry non-essential items and space to spread ourselves out and relax in.

That night the Virgin Islands radio broadcast flood warnings. An hour or two later came the heaviest rainfall we had ever experienced. The visibility was nil and we thundered towards an imagined treacherous lee shore. By dawn (3 November) the rain eased off a little and soon after we obtained a reasonable fix from radio beacons on Antigua and Guadeloupe, a neighbouring island to the south. Antigua came into sight between rain showers and by 1715 GMT (1315 local time) we were moored alongside Nelson's Dockyard, English Harbour. It took time to adjust to civilisation in this unique yachting community housed in renovated dockyard buildings. Soon the rain stopped and the sun shone hot again. That first cold beer was bliss!

A nice, tidy voyage, but don't be misled into believing that it is always as easy as this! Now for the questions and answers.

1 *Why a catamaran?*
    The features we were looking for in our boat are as follows:
(a) *Seaworthiness*. We were looking for a production boat of well-proven design, that could be driven hard. Six other Iroquois have crossed the Atlantic, and the class has a good record in the rugged Round Britain race.
(b) *Speed*. We needed to make quick ocean crossings as we have only limited funds to support ourselves when we are not earning.
(c) *Comfort*. Comfort requirements were:

(i) Comfort for four people to make 21-day (approx.) passages.
(ii) Comfort for my wife and me to live aboard for a couple of years.
(iii) Enough luxury to take two or more guests on one- and two-week charters, and as many as possible on day charters.

The Iroquois was the only boat we found that would fulfil the requirements within our price range, and we are very pleased indeed with her. We have been pretty busy doing day charter work, and from July onwards we hope to do more one week or longer charters,

We would set out on the same voyage in the same boat without any hesitation. In six or twelve months' time we will be setting out to cross the Pacific. I would love to do it in a trimaran, provided it met the requirements. We wouldn't like to do it in a monohull, as we have got used to sailing upright! Also, we prefer an unsinkable boat.

2 *What did you like least?*
(a) The noise, particularly in rough weather.
(b) The drop-plates banging about in their slots.
(c) Big waves occasionally slamming hard under the bridge deck.

3 *Were you worried about capsizing?*
I do not know whether cats have a worse safety record than tris or monos for transocean crossings, but we were never worried about the capsizing risk as we took precautions.

4 *What worried you most?*
Possibility of structural or rigging damage caused by slamming into big seas.

5 *Did you load carefully?*
We were very conscious of weight, as *Snoopy*'s design displacement, complete with gear, stores and crew, is only two tons. If the boat is loaded heavily, the slamming under the bridge deck is much worse. The heavier boat does not give nor accelerate under wave impacts, and hence absorbs much more force when a wave strikes. We chose all equipment for lightness and took only essentials. When fully loaded, *Snoopy* still floated above her marks. We carried 65 gallons of water, and topped up our tanks at the Azores, but on the whole trip we used only 45 gallons, less than three pints per person per day.

We did not notice any loss of performance due to the heavy loading, but we did slam under the bridge deck more. We now regularly day charter with up to nine adult guests aboard, plus Susan and me as crew. Although the sea can be pretty rough when the trades are at their strongest, we do not have any problems.

Appendix IV Booms are Obsolete

I was not entirely correct in assuming in Chapter 10 that very little has been done to improve the rigs of multihulls. Frank R. MacLear of MacLear & Harris Inc. sent me a paper with the above title which he presented to the Chesapeake Sailing Yacht Symposium on 19 January 1974. Many yachts have since been rigged by this unique method which no doubt will become increasingly popular – particularly with singlehanders.

Based on principles which were moderately popular in the past, such as the Wyckham-Martin foresail-furling and Ljungstrom mainsail-rolling systems (both pre-W.W.II), the MacLear Rig consists of a vertical revolvable stay for the luff of the mainsail and rotating forestays very similar to the Wyckham-Martin invention, but greatly improved by modern technology. The best rig for the system is cutter, with two forestays. As can be seen from the illustrations which Frank has very kindly allowed me to use, the headsails and mainsail are all sheeted to the backstays, which eliminates foredeck hazards in bad weather. With sheet and furling winches electrically powered (with manual backup in the event of power failure), all the hard work of pully-hauly has been removed at a stroke – and with it, most of the dangers of man overboard.

There is no doubt that the MacLear Rig works well, but unfortunately it has only made the boom redundant – the tall Bermudan mast remains. I still think that multihulls should have a rig of their very own – more suited to them than to the requirements of monohulls.

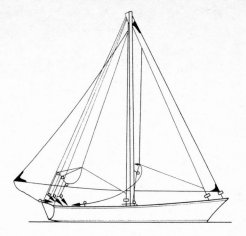

40a   The MacLear Rig. A complete rig with three roller furling stays, two
for headsails and one for the main. The clew of the giant jib projects
aft of the boat in the sail plan but moves forward as the sail is filled and
curved by the wind

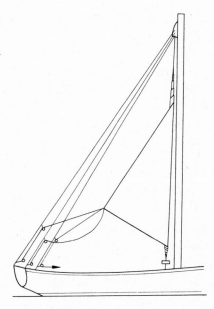

40b   The MacLear Rig. Roller furling mainsail winding up. This roller furling
mainsail is shown winding up on its jackstay just aft and parallel to the
mast. The three backstays are shown separated for clarity's sake. In
practice the leeward sheet and possibly the centreline sheet would be
taut but the weather sheet would always be slack. As the sail is rolled
up it is necessary to lower the blocks on the permanent backstays and
this is accomplished by backstay sliders that are supported by lifts

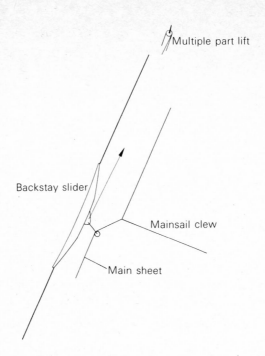

Multiple part lift

Backstay slider

Mainsail clew

Main sheet

40c   The MacLear Rig: Backstay slider

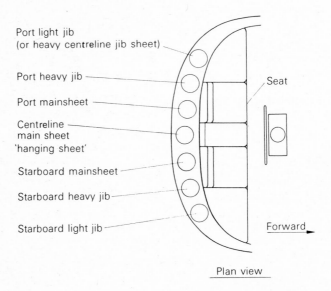

Port light jib
(or heavy centreline jib sheet)

Port heavy jib

Port mainsheet

Centreline
main sheet
'hanging sheet'

Starboard mainsheet

Starboard heavy jib

Starboard light jib

Seat

Forward

Plan view

40d   The MacLear Rig: The 'crescent winch pedestal' on the back of the
helmsman's three seats. When going to windward the mainsail requires
two sheets, the hanging sheet on the centreline and a leeward sheet.
In heavy weather windward work the jib also requires its hanging sheet
and a leeward sheet

Appendix V   Multihull Records

Surprisingly, in view of the incredible voyages accomplished by small boats of every type and size since the year dot, and certainly since the first yachts began to cross the Atlantic from the middle of the nineteenth century, no really serious attempt has been made to compile a comprehensive list of all these many records in chronological order. It is true that Humphrey Barton gave us *Atlantic Adventurers* (Adlard Coles, 1953 and 1962), which is the only accurate reference for this ocean; Jean Merrien's *Lonely Voyagers* (Hutchinson, 1954), Charles A. Borden's *Sea Quest* (Hale, 1968), and Don Holm's *The Circumnavigator* (Prentice-Hall, 1974), gave a lot of facts but insufficient for accurate conclusions to be made.

It was about this time that I began to think somebody ought to get down to the task of collating all the small boat records before it was too late. Big business was beginning to infiltrate into what had for so long been almost entirely an amateur sport, and with the lure of money came inevitable commercial propaganda – at first half-truths, and sometimes blatant false-hoods. This bludgeoning of records was not difficult because so much of the truth was virtually unknown.

This is why I came to write *An Evolution of Singlehanders* (Stanford Maritime, 1975), which for the first time in yachting history lists such records chrono-logically. It was an appalling task, made possible only by the unstinted (and unpaid) efforts of my many worldwide correspondents.

And now here for the first time I list the multihull records – not all of them by any means, but at least a start. The rest is up to you. If I am in error, or if you have a claim or know about a record-breaking voyage, then please write and let me know. Most multihull history has occurred within living memory, so there is no reason why we should not between us produce comprehensive lists about every aspect of our sport.

OWNER/CREW	NATION-ALITY	NAME OF MULTI	DIMENSIONS			HULLS	RIG	ROUTE	DATES	
			LOA	BEAM	DRGHT					
John Mikes George Miller Jerry Mallene	USA PR PR	*Nonpareil* (tri)	25′	11′ 6″	1′	Rubber	2-mast gaff schooner	W–E	1868	2·
Eric de Bisschop Joseph Tatibouet	F F	*Kaimiloa* (cat)	38′	17′	3′	Wood	2-mast junk- rigged schooner	E–W	1937–8	3·
André Sadrin Didier Petit Nick Scherer	F F F	*Ananda* (tri)	42′ 10″	22′ 1″	4′	Wood	Semi-junk- rigged Ketch with foresail	E–W	1946	4·
Raoul Christiaen Josette (wife) (three crew)	F F	*Copula* (cat)	46′ 8″	17′ 9″	5′	Steel	Semi-junk- rigged ketch with foresail	E–W	1950–1	4·
Woody Brown Rudy Choy (three crew)	USA USA	*Waikiki Surf* (cat)	40′	13′	2′	Ply	Bermudan cutter	W–E E–W	1955	6·
James Wharram Ruth Merseberger Jutta Schultze- Rhonof	GB GER GER	*Tangaroa* (cat) *Rongo* (cat)	23′ 6″ 40′	11′ 17′ 6″	1′ 1′ 3″	Wood Wood	Both ketches with fully- battened main and mizzen	E–W W–E	1956–7 1959	2· 2·
Arthur Piver George Benello Bill Goodman	USA USA USA	*Nimble* (tri)	30′	18′	2′	Ply	Bermudan sloop	W–E	1960	5·
James Wharram Ruth Merseberger	GB GER	*Rongo* (cat)	40′	17′ 6″	1′ 3″	Wood	Ketch with fully battened main and mizzen	E–W W–E	1961 1962	4· 3·
Arthur Piver John Daigneault	USA USA	*Lodestar* (tri)	35′	20′	2′ 6″	Ply	Bermudan ketch	E–W	1961–2	6·
Alex Grimes Roy Garside	GB GB	*Trinui* (tri)	30′	18′	2′	Ply	Bermudan sloop	E–W	1962–3	
David Landgraf	USA	*Golden Fleece* (tri)	24′	14′	1′ 6″	Ply	Bermudan sloop	E–W	1963	
David Lewis	GB	*Rehu Moana* (cat)	40′	17′	3′	Ply	Bermudan cutter	E–W	1964	3·
Derek Kelsall	GB	*Folatre* (tri)	35′	20′	2′ 6″	Ply	Bermudan ketch	E–W	1964	4·
Bernard Rhodes	GB	*Klis* (tri)	22′	14′	1′ 9″	Ply	Bermudan sloop	E–W	1967	5·
Tom Corkhill	AUS	*Clipper I* (tri)	25′	17′	1′ 6″	Ply	Bermudan sloop	E–W	1966–7	
Eric Tabarly (two crew)	F	*Pen Duick IV* (tri)	67′	35′	9′	Alloy	Bermudan ketch	E–W	1968	1C (1
Eric Tabarly (two crew)	F	*Pen Duick IV* (tri)	67′	35′	9′	Alloy	Bermudan ketch	E–W	1969	1C (1
Ingeborg von Heister	GER	*Ultima Ratio* (tri)	35′	20′	2′ 6″	Ply	Bermudan ketch	E–W W–E	1969 1970	3·
Alain Colas	F	*Pen Duick IV* (tri)	70′	35′	9′	Alloy	Bermudan ketch	E–W	1972	6· (7
Nick Keig	GB	*Three Legs Of Man* (tri)	35′	21′	2′ 3″	Ply	Bermudan sloop	N–S	1975	1ξ (1

Clarification: It should be noted that the fastest-ever crossing of the Atlantic by sailing vessels are: (1) 1860
only slightly slower, seemed a more appropriate comparison for this list. (2) 1916 W–E: *Lancing* (2764 tons),
averaged only 11·5 knots: 1854, *Red Jacket* (2434 tons) Sandy Hook–Bell Buoy, Liverpool, in 12 days, or an ave

DETAILS

rk to Southampton. First recorded transoceanic trimaran. 3 hulls of inflated rubber cylinders, 2 ft 6 in diameter. 3200 miles in 51 days.

ultihull to cross 3 oceans (Pacific, Indian and Atlantic): Honolulu–Futuna Is.–Bali–Surabaja–Cape Town–Tangier– 264 days at sea.

maran westwards across Atlantic: Sète, France–Casablanca–Porto Grande, St Vincent, Cape Verde Is.–Fort de France, que. 2100 miles in 20 days for crossing.

nsatlantic cat (S. Route) and first to set out on circumnavigation. Bordeaux–(Santa Cruz, Canary Is.–Fort de France, que in 31 days)–New York: 9000 miles in 90 days (voyage abandoned).

rt-crossing of Pacific by cat: Hawaii–Los Angeles (2250 miles in 15½ days). Returned to Hawaii as unofficial entrant Trans-Pacific Race.

uble crossing of Atlantic by same multihull crew: Las Palmas–Trinidad (41 days); New York–Conway, N. Wales s).

odern trimaran eastwards across Atlantic: Swansea, Mass.–Azores–Plymouth (3800 miles in 28 days).

lantic double crossing by multihull: Las Palmas–Trinidad (27 days); Bermuda–Fastnet (32 days).

nspacific multihull after *Kaimiloa*: Santa Barbara–Hawaii (15 days) with Bill Goodman, Lauren Williams, Fred Jukich; –Tahiti with Fred Jukich, Bob Coblentz; Tahiti–Rarotonga–Auckland, NZ, as shown.

multihull across two oceans after *Kaimiloa*: Wells, Norfolk, England–Auckland, NZ, via the Panama Canal Nimble class).

nglehanded transoceanic multihull: Ensenada, Mexico–Hawaii (Piver Nugget class).

nglehanded transatlantic catamaran: Plymouth–Newport, RI (38½ days) in 2nd OSTAR.

nglehanded transatlantic trimaran: Plymouth–Newport RI (35 days) in 2nd OSTAR (Piver Lodestar class).

smallest singlehanded transatlantic tri: Las Palmas–Barbados (20 days). Own design and build.

nglehanded multihull trans-Indian Ocean: Darwin–Singapore–Mauritius–Durban (95 days).

-ever transatlantic crossing by any yacht: Tenerife–Martinique, 10½ days, av. 253·8 mpd. Previous fastest in 1905: schooner *Atlantic* (1340 LWL): Sandy Hook–Lizard, 12¼ days, av. 246·5 mpd.

-ever transpacific crossing by any sailing vessel: Los Angeles–Honolulu, 8¹³⁄₂₄ days, av. 260·5 mpd. Previous fastest in Clipper *Swordfish* (1036 tons): San Francisco–Honolulu 8⅙ days, av. 259·2 mpd.

ver double crossing of Atlantic by singlehanded woman. Las Palmas–Barbados (33 days). Bermuda–Azores– ar (46 days). Also first solo woman transatlantic W–E. (Piver Lodestar class).

singlehanded transatlantic E–W crossing (N. Route): Plymouth–Newport, RI (20½ days) av. 145 mpd. Fastest- y same route in 1830: barque *Josephine* (86 ft LOA): Belfast–New York (16 days) av. 193·8 mpd.

24-hour run for singlehanded yacht – during 1st Azores And Back Singlehanded Race (AZAB): 328 miles. -ever by crewed yacht in 1905: 3-mast schooner *Atlantic* (134 ft LOA) – see above – 341 miles.

Jackson (1679 tons), Liverpool–New York in 15 days, averaging 207·1 mpd or 8·6 knots. The tiny barque *Josephine*, Cape Wrath, Scotland in 6¾ days, averaging 17·3 knots. This passage takes some believing, since the next fastest mpd.

MULTIHULL CIRCUMNAVIGATIONS

OWNER/CREW	NATION-ALITY	NAME OF MULTIHULL (TYPE & DESIGNER)	LOA	BEAM	DRGHT	HULLS	RIG	ROUTE	DATE
David Lewis Fiona (wife) Susie, Vicky (children) Priscilla Cairns	NZ SA NZ GB	*Rehu Moana* (cat – Mudie)	40′	17′	3′	Ply	Bermudan cutter	E–W (M)	1964
Heinz J. Wagner (crew various)	GER	*World Cat* (cat – C/S/K)	43′	16′ 6″	2′	Ply	Bermudan ketch	E–W (P)	1966
Nigel Tetley	SA	*Victress* (tri – Piver)	40′	22′	2′ 9″	Ply	Bermudan ketch	W–E (H)	1968
Michael Kane (crew various, total 38)	USA	*Carousin II* (tri – Piver)	40′	22′	2′ 9″	Ply (HB)	Bermudan ketch	E–W (P)	1967
Clark Barthol Meta (wife)	USA USA	*Cetacean* (tri – Piver)	36′	20′	2′ 6″	Ply (HB)	Bermudan ketch	E–W (P)	1967
Bernard Rhodes (crew various)	GB	*Klis* (tri – Rhodes)	22′	14′	1′ 9″	Ply (HB)	Bermudan sloop	E–W (P)	1967
Quentin Cultra (crew various)	USA	*Queequeg* (tri – Piver)	35′	20′	2′ 6″	Ply (HB)	Bermudan ketch	E–W (P)	1968
Charles M. Sturkey Mary (wife) (crew various)	USA USA	*Chamuru* (tri – Manners)	49′ 6″	23′	2′ 9″	Ply	Bermudan ketch	E–W (P)	1969
Mark Hassell Bonnie (wife) David (son)	USA USA USA	*Talofiafaoe* (tri – Brown)	37′ 4″	22′ 3″	3′	Ply (HB)	Bermudan sloop	E–W (P)	1970
Wolf Hausner	AUS	*Taboo* (cat – Manners)	32′	15′	3′	Ply (HB)	Bermudan sloop	E–W (P)	1966
Alain Colas	F	*Manureva* (tri – Allegre) ex-*Pen Duick IV*	70′	35′	9′	Alloy	Bermudan ketch	W–E (H)	1973

MULTIHULL CAPE HORNERS

OWNER/CREW	NATION-ALITY	NAME OF MULTIHULL (TYPE & DESIGNER)	LOA	BEAM	DRGHT	HULLS	RIG	ROUTE	DATE
Nigel Tetley	SA	*Victress* (tri – Piver)	40′	22′	2′ 9″	Ply	Bermudan ketch	W–E	Mar 1969
Colin Swale Rosie (wife) Eve, James (children)	GB GB GB	*Anneliese* (cat – O'Brien)	30′	14′ 10″	2′	Ply	Bermudan ketch	W–E	Feb. 1973
Alain Colas	F	*Manureva* (tri – Allegre) ex-*Pen Duick IV*	70′	35′	9′	Alloy	Bermudan ketch	W–E	Feb. 1974

Notes:
1. Hulls: HB = Home Built.
2. Route: (P) = via Panama Canal.
   (H) = via Cape Horn.
3. The five southernmost capes which must be rounded to ensure confirmation of a circumnavigation entirely in
   South-West Cape (Stewart Island, NZ), Cape Horn. Of the singlehanders, only Bill King (GB), Kris Baranov
   Good Hope, Leeuwin and Tasmania and Stewart Islands for a second time without stopping.

DETAILS

tihull to circumnavigate: 41,609 miles in 3 years 2 months. First multihull through Magellan Straits. (*Note*: ge began when Lewis raced across the Atlantic in the 2nd OSTAR – see Multihull Records. With a crew, she then Cape Verdi Is., and then to Salvador, Brazil. The first triple Atlantic crossing by a multihull.

os Angeles westabout via NZ, Australia, Cape of Good Hope, Trinidad, Panama Canal. Claimed 200 mpd peed crossing Indian Ocean.

glehanded, non-stop circumnavigation in multihull. First multihull to round Cape Horn. Abandoned near Azores g knot in 179 days.

aaran to return to home port after circumnavigating (but Tetley was first to tie knot by 37 days).

rt Hueneme, S. Calif., via Pacific Islands to Bali, Seychelles, Durban, Cape Town, Panama Canal, Galapagos, les. Dennis Fontany helped build, and crewed.

umnavigation by the smallest multihull to cross two oceans. From Barrow, England, to Russell, North Island, NZ this list because of size).

e River Mississippi, through the Panama Canal, across the Pacific to Australia, Bali, Madagascar, Durban, Cape id via stops to New York and Chicago.

sebo, Japan, westabout to Seattle – so did not tie knot. (*Note*: Erick Manners, British, is to date the only designer ooth a cat and a tri built from his plans complete a circumnavigation.)

os Angeles, via Hawaii to Micronesia, Solomons, New Zealand, Torres Strait, Cocos–Keeling, Seychelles, ique, Durban, Cape Town, St Helena, Trinidad, to Guatemala. Survived two hurricanes. Did not tie knot.

glehanded circumnavigation in catamaran. Sailed south of Cape Leeuwin, via Cape of Good Hope and Panama nd returned across Pacific to Australia.

ver singlehanded circumnavigation: St Malo–Sydney–St Malo, 167 days.
nglehanded monohull (in 1966–7): Chichester's 53 ft 1 in *Gypsy Moth IV*, Plymouth–Sydney–Plymouth, 226 days.
rewed monohull (in 1974): Chay Blyth's 70 ft *Great Britain II* (ex. 3 stopovers), 144 days.
lipper (in 1869): 1405-ton *Patriarch*, London–Sydney–London, 138 days.

DETAILS

r non-stop rounding of five southernmost capes by singlehanded multihull. First ply vessel to make a long solo avigation. From Otago, NZ to Horn: 44 days.

amaran to round Cape Horn. Sailed from Gilbraltar, 1971, via Panama Canal to Sydney, Australia, with many turned via Wellington, NZ–Cape Horn (47 days) to Plymouth, arriving in July 1973 so did not circumnavigate.

ver singlehanded crossing of Southern Ocean: Sydney–Horn in 37 days. Fastest solo monohull (in 1973): Kris ski, 45 ft 3 in *Polonez*: Hobart–Horn in 45 days. Fastest crewed yacht (in 1974): Chay Blyth + 9 crew, 72-ft *ain II*: Sydney–Horn 25 days. Fastest Clipper (in 1854): 2084-ton *Lightning*: Melbourne–Horn in 19 days.

Forties are, Eastabout: Cape of Good Hope, Cape Leeuwin (SW Australia), South-East Cape (Tasmania), nd Bernard Moitessier (F) have equalled this feat – the latter being the first to do so, and sailing on to round

Appendix VI Trimaran Selection Calculator

(refer to page 56 for graphs)

© Copyright Norman Cross

STEP

1   Number of persons aboard _____

2   Number of weeks at sea _____

3   From chart No. 1 determine the weight required for one person for the
    number of weeks at sea _____

4   Multiply step No. 1 × step No. 3 _____

5   Weight of equipment NOT normally carried on a BASIC SAIL BOAT:

        AUXILIARY MOTOR _____

        FUEL _____

        BATTERIES _____

        FUEL TANKS _____

        EXHAUST AND MUFFLER _____

        PROPELLER SHAFT AND STRUT _____

        GENERATOR _____

        RADIO AND NAVIGATION EQUIPMENT _____

        EXTRA ANCHOR AND CHAIN _____

        LIFE RAFT OR DINGHY _____

        TOOLS AND SPARE EQUIPMENT _____

        OTHER ITEMS OR EQUIPMENT _____

                TOTAL _____ _____

6   Add steps No. 4 and No. 5 _____

7   Multiply step No. 6 × 3 (not step No. 3) _____

8   Multiply step No. 7 × ·07 (7% of step No. 7) _____

9   Subtract step No. 8 from step No. 7   DISPLACEMENT: _____

10   Chart No. 2 can now be used to find the size trimaran YOU should need or consider.

NOTE: Normally a boat will not be fully loaded for average sailing, this is the reason for
      step No. 8.

The DISPLACEMENT shown on chart No. 2 will be the weight of the boat LOADED to FLOAT
ON ITS DESIGNED WATERLINE.

182

APPROXIMATE WEIGHTS TO USE AS A GUIDE

Auxiliary Engines

Horse-power	Outboards (lb)	Petrol (inbd) (lb)	Diesel (inbd) (lb)
5	41	200	280
10	60	230	320
15	75	255	360
20	90	280	390
25	105	310	420
30	120	330	460
35	135	355	500
40	155	395	535
45		420	570
50		450	600
60		500	670

Fuel

Petrol $6\frac{1}{4}$ lb per gal.   Diesel Oil $7\frac{1}{4}$ lb per gal.
Fuel tanks   approx. 2 lb per gal.   Water   10 lb per gal.
Propeller shaft and strut (inboard motor)   25 to 50 lb.
Exhaust and muffler (inboard motor)   25 to 50 lb.
Batteries   40 to 100 lb each.
Instrument panel and controls   30 to 60 lb.
Generators   20 to 50 lb.
Radio and navigation equipment   20 to 50 lb.
Extra anchors and line   30 to 70 lb each.
Dinghy   50 to 75 lb.

You should run through the chart several times with different requirements to find out the capability of the boat. Maybe some of the items you thought you needed are not really necessary. It takes about 200 lb of boat to carry 100 lb of equipment.

Courtesy of Norman A. Cross, Designer of CROSS TRIMARANS (see Appendix II)

Index